Heterophobia

Heterophobia

Sexual Harassment
and the Future of Feminism

❞ DAPHNE PATAI ❞

ROWMAN & LITTLEFIELD PUBLISHERS, INC.
Lanham • Boulder • New York • Oxford

ROWMAN & LITTLEFIELD PUBLISHERS, INC.
Published in the United States of America
by Rowman & Littlefield Publishers, Inc.
4720 Boston Way, Lanham, Maryland 20706

12 Hid's Copse Road
Cumnor Hill, Oxford OX2 9JJ, England

British Library Cataloguing in Publication Information Available

Library of Congress Cataloging-in-Publication Data

Patai, Daphne, 1943–
    Heterophobia : sexual harassment and the future of feminism /
Daphne Patai.
        p.   cm. — (American intellectual culture)
    Includes bibliographical references and index.
    ISBN 0-8476-8987-5 (cloth : alk. paper)
    1. Sexual harassment in universities and colleges.   2. Sexual
harassment in the workplace.   3. Misandry.   4. Men's studies.
5. Feminist theory.   I. Title.
II. Series.
LC212.86.P37   1998
305.42—DC21   98-27901
                                                          CIP

Printed in the United States of America

∞ ™ The paper used in this publication meets the minimum requirements of
American National Standard for Information Sciences—Permanence of Paper
for Printed Library Materials, ANSI Z39.48–1984.

To the men in my life (they know who they are),
all of them as much sinned against as sinning,
who made it impossible for me to abide
grotesque caricatures of manhood,
even when asserted by feminists

AND ESPECIALLY
to the memory of my father,
Raphael Patai (1910–1996),
who could not tolerate the abandonment of
his two little daughters and, in June 1950,
brought us to this country to live with him

NOT EVERYTHING IS NARRATIVE
D.P.

Who is she that looks forth as the dawn,
Fair as the moon,
Clear as the sun,
Terrible as an army with banners?

The Song of Songs 6:10

Contents

❧

Preface

❧

Like many women in our society, I have experienced what is now labeled "sexual harassment"—on the street, in school, and at work. In Paris, a man once grabbed my breast as he walked by me (I knew, as he approached me, that he was going to do something, but I didn't have the nerve to cross the street). In a crowded subway in Rio de Janeiro, a man behind me masturbated while pressing up against me. In New York, a man whispered as he passed me, "Boy, would I like to eat that!" Before graduate school, when I worked as a secretary, one of my bosses was constantly irritated with me because I refused to date him. I finally complained to his superior, who rebuked us both: my immediate boss for pestering me, and me for being flirtatious. In another job, a boss said to me, "You must be horrible in bed—you're so efficient!" This same man asked me to count the steps up the Eiffel Tower (for the guidebook he was writing) and to do it on my own time. I refused; no, he did not fire me.

As a graduate student, I was pursued for two years by a professor from whom I nonetheless learned a great deal. When I went for a job interview after completing my Ph.D., an elderly male faculty member said, while shaking my hand, "She's pretty. Hire her!" (This didn't unnerve me nearly as much as did a female professor who sat filing her nails while I gave a public lecture as part of my interview.) Especially in the early years of my career as a teacher, I had male students occasionally make rude and arguably sexist comments to me. One wrote on my lectern, "Dafney, you are a feminist bitch!" Another, on a teaching evaluation form, advised me which of my hairstyles was sexiest. In class, when I was an assistant professor, a boy disagreed with a fact I had cited by saying out loud, "You know what you can do with your facts!" Still another borrowed books from me and repeatedly tried to come to my house to return them. And (in a reversal of my graduate school experience) an undergraduate student of mine, a young woman, declared herself to me and pursued me (in person, by mail, and by phone) for two years.

These episodes were not pleasant, but neither were they devastating. Least of all were they typical of my interactions with other human beings. Unlike many present-day commentators on the subject, I would feel exceedingly foolish if I were to refer to myself as a "survivor," or even a "victim," of sexual harassment. None of these experiences did me any real harm. But even if they had—and even if I grant that other women might react differently or have more disturbing experiences—I would have to weigh and measure the benefits of being spared this sort of behavior against the costs of preventing it. Certainly I cannot join forces with those activists who want to see all such events—even the pettiest street harassment that is not (yet) actionable in most places— become illegal.

There is, moreover, another side of the coin, which must also be acknowledged. True, I have never groped a strange man's crotch, but when I was a student, I did indeed aggressively pursue professors who interested me. So did many of my female friends. I used to find excuses to go to their offices and lead the conversation to personal subjects. Sometimes my girlfriends and I would follow a "favored" professor around in a car. Once I even trailed a man on foot for a block or two because his aftershave left an enticing fragrance in the air. (Was this "stalking"?) I have written "unwanted" letters of invitation to a professor-and-boss I found attractive. Rejection depressed me and made me angry. But I got over it.

From these incidents I take a simple lesson: that the experience of sexual interest and sexual play (which can indeed be obnoxious at times) is an ordinary part of human life, manifest in different ways in different societies but predictably present in one way or another, as it must have been since the Garden of Eden. It seems to me that except for egregious offenses such as assault, bribery, or extortion (whether sexual or not)—for which legal remedies have existed for many years— the petty annoyance of occasional misplaced sexual attentions or sexist putdowns has to be tolerated. Why? Because the type of vigilance necessary to inhibit it would create a social climate so unpleasant, and ultimately so repressive, that the cure would be much worse than the disease.

Would we really want to live in a sanitized world in which each of us is fully protected from any offensive or otherwise unwanted word or gesture? In which every interaction must be scrutinized for possible sexual implications or slights based on gender? In which a kind of paranoia poisons the very idea of sexual expression between people in situations containing that supposedly fatal element, a "power imbalance"? I don't think so. Yet from the very beginning, the subject of sexual harassment has been marked by definitions rooted in feminist assumptions about the relations between men and women, assumptions that are long overdue for questioning.

Today those with sensitivities heightened by feminist rhetoric are rewarded by being handed legal weapons to wield against their colleagues and teachers. A psychology professor at one school filed a grievance because someone in her department had put up a sprig of mistletoe. Result: a campus regulation stipulating that mistletoe has to be removed if anyone complains. Ironically, as story after story in the mounting literature on sexual harassment reveals, teachers who are most devoted to their classroom work, who are most ready to chat with students and to demystify the boundaries between teacher and student (as recommended by feminist pedagogy), are most often the ones who find themselves caught in the web of sexual harassment charges.

Consider the case of Michael Bullock, a popular forty-nine-year-old high school math instructor known for his devotion to teaching. A female student poked playfully at Bullock, in front of the class, commenting on his corpulence by saying that his chest was big. He replied that hers was small. This response led to his suspension from teaching. While waiting to hear whether he was to be reprimanded or transferred to an administrative job, Bullock killed himself. Now his students say, "He cared too much. That's what got him."[1] In the emotional confusion that followed this event, a school spokeswoman defended the girl who had made the charge, expressing concern—and this is the most telling detail of the case—that the suicide would have the effect of discouraging other students from filing complaints.

At a California junior high school, in early 1998, all displays of affection were prohibited, including hugging, kissing, back-patting, and even "high fives." Some brave fourteen-year-old girls objected, insisting that they wanted to be able to hug their friends without fear of punishment. School officials replied that such rules have existed at many schools for years but have been enforced only recently because "hugging" seems to have become a fad.[2] When interviewed on CNN, the principal of the school said with a straight face that long hugs between

boys and girls were actually her target, but since she was unable to spec-
ify that, a blanket rule seemed the best alternative.[3] Evidently, fears of
heterosexual touching, and efforts to reform the behavior of unregen-
erate adolescent girls, are far from over. These days we must be grateful
for the occasional optimistic sign, such as the dropping of charges
against a nine-year-old boy who was alleged to have rubbed himself
against a girl of the same age in the lunch line.[4]

In the supposedly more adult universe of higher education, rational
people are devising their own measures for warding off trouble. I have
spoken to many colleagues who now say that they will not close their
doors after a student enters their office. They watch their words and
wonder whether it is wise to discuss "sensitive" issues in class, however
germane these may be to their subject. Up and down the academic
ranks, people are acutely aware of the dangers of doing something,
however innocuous, however inadvertent, that another person, especially a subordinate, might possibly consider offensive or inappropriate. Lawsuits about matters that would have seemed ludicrous just a
few years ago have now become commonplace. An offhand remark or
misperceived gesture can threaten an entire career. A professor's encouraging words or practical help can be retroactively interpreted as
"grooming" for sexual demands at a later time. On the other hand,
criticism of students' classwork or disagreement with their ideas can be
construed as contributing to an environment that impedes their full
participation in academic life. A metaphor that happens to strike some
student the wrong way can be claimed to have created a hostile environment in the classroom. A friendly hug may turn up months, or even
years, later in a lawsuit, transformed into a "demand for a hug." These
are not hypothetical situations. They are drawn from actual cases in
recent years.

Senior professors and junior colleagues find themselves caught in a
web of "power" and "hierarchy" that is viewed as precluding any kind
of personal relationship. Many universities now have "consensual relations policies" regulating, or simply prohibiting, sexual relationships
between people in "asymmetrical" positions. Yet despite the absence of
"power differentials," student-to-student complaints are rapidly multi-
plying. In a particularly notorious response to this situation, Antioch
College has adopted rules requiring students to seek explicit verbal
permission for every step of sexual intimacy.

While such a policy will strike many as the sort of "solution" that any
sane society would laugh out of existence, it is patently not enough to

satisfy the sex regulators, whose main objective—as I will show throughout this book—is the dismantling of heterosexuality altogether. Meanwhile, unable to openly attempt to ban sex and thereby totally alienate
their public, feminist reformers and their sympathizers have instead
tried to set up an obstacle course in the relations between men and
women.

This agenda is abetted by the frequent overreactions of college administrators fearful of lawsuits from alleged victims but not from alleged harassers. Thus it is that the former are given assistance,
counseling, and support while the latter are often suspended or otherwise punished at the mere threat of a sexual harassment charge and
well in advance of any investigation. No one can be sure when the atmosphere around him (or, less often, her) will turn sour and charges will
be made. Such an academic environment, I contend, is neither intellectually productive nor morally tolerable. That is why I now feel moved
to speak my mind on an issue on which twelve or fifteen years ago I
took the opposite position. Much has happened in the intervening
years, and it has made the university a very different place from what it
used to be.

This book will argue that the current judicial, quasi-judicial, extra-
legal, and administrative application of sexual harassment law, especially as manifested in the "hostile environment" doctrine and as
practiced in colleges and universities, represents an unwelcome and
dangerous shift in both law and custom. Hostile-environment actions
are now based upon the subjective experience of "unwanted" or "offensive" conduct (including speech), as perceived by the accuser and tested
by the "reasonable woman" standard, a concept I will discuss at length.
It is becoming increasingly clear that this development transfers the
burden of proof from the accuser to the accused, in violation of American due process. In addition, this shift has profound repercussions on
the conduct of daily life. And such a consequence is, as I will demonstrate, no accident. It is precisely what the proponents of sexual harassment regulations have in mind.

But university students are not children who need to be guarded
against predatory adults. Nor are they mental health patients requiring
tender care. Universities are, in fact, splendid places where mature and
young adults—all postpubescent, most of them with the right to vote,
to reproduce or not (through elective abortion), and to kill and be
killed in military service—congregate, teach and learn, get to know one
another, pursue intellectual and personal relationships (universities'

"latent function," as Robert K. Merton called it, is to provide opportunities for people to seek romantic partners),[5] behave sensibly and foolishly, and generally get on with their interesting lives. Universities are, moreover, a unique domain in American life where academic theories are codified into policy and their effects are played out for all to see.

How did this admirable setting, in a remarkably short period of time, come to be redefined as a danger zone where abuse lurks in every corner, where "difference" must be unmasked as "power," which—to those trained in the rhetoric of sexual harassment—is logically tantamount to "abuse of power"? How did it happen that the notion of sexual harassment has with such apparent ease pervaded institutional and private life in contemporary America? This book gives the long answer to these questions. At this point, a short answer will suffice, simple and, alas, obvious: The mere allegation of "sexual harassment" now provides women with an extraordinarily effective weapon (albeit an altogether traditional one) to wield against men. Even women who reject the view that women's victimization is at the very heart of a society that is unrelentingly patriarchal have accepted the instrument handed to them by sexual harassment legislation. But a feminism that has latched onto sexual harassment as a means of bringing men to heel is, I believe, a feminism that will ultimately discredit women, too.

I warn my readers that it is difficult to write about the current epidemic of sexual harassment charges without sometimes falling into a tone of incredulity or cynicism. This, of course, tends to trivialize the genuine sexual discrimination that does sometimes occur. The fault here, I believe, lies with what I call the "Sexual Harassment Industry"—a growth industry in the past few decades, with both material and ideological incentives to spread its tentacles far and wide. That our society should so willingly have acceded to the authority now commanded by a cadre of "specialists" in this burgeoning new field seems like a symptom of some generalized social lunacy. But as countless historical examples show, the pursuit of righteousness, when unaccompanied by common sense and goodwill, is a risky business.

Redefining the World

Redefining the World

❧

Ah love! could you and I with Fate conspire
To grasp this sorry Scheme of Things entire,
Would not we shatter it to bits—and then
Re-mould it nearer to the Heart's Desire!

THE RUBAIYAT OF OMAR KHAYYAM,
trans. Edward Fitzgerald, 2d version, 1868

The key question raised by the discourse on sexual harassment and the great lengths to which it has been pushed is this: What sort of world do we live in and what sort of world do we wish it to be? Feminism has always had grandiose ideas about improving the human lot. I myself expressed such ideas years ago: "Feminism, today, is the most utopian project around. That is, it demands the most radical and truly revolutionary transformation of society, and it is going on in an extraordinary variety of ways."[1] Full of hope, energized by the rapid growth of women's studies programs in the United States, I wrote these words in the early 1980s. They expressed the belief I then held that feminism's enormous intellectual and social reach made it the fulfillment of generations of utopian aspirations. Now I recall that line with dismay as I observe the kinds of transformations that have been brought about, or are attempted, in the name of feminism.

It may well seem that, in writing this book, I am making an argument out of an obvious truth. But perhaps it is necessary these days to start with the obvious. We are, after all, witnessing a restructuring of male–female relations to the point where "harassment" threatens to become the predominant word associated with "sexual." Perhaps this is an illusion bred by my own preoccupation with the peculiarities of academic and workplace cultures and the proliferating legislation governing these sites. Climbing down from the ivory tower, one does experience a shock. Go to the beach or the movies, and see heterosexual couples cavorting unself-consciously. Could it really be that all these people are unaware of the "power differentials" and "asymmetries" that supposedly distort their relationships? They appear not to have heard about them. This indifference goes some way, I believe, toward explaining the fervor with which workplace and academic reformers approach the task of regulating sex. No doubt they are discouraged by the persistence of rampant heterosex as a fact of life, feminist warnings and strictures notwithstanding.

I focus in this book on the activities of those reformers, which I label the "Sexual Harassment Industry" (sometimes abbreviated SHI), because I believe that from the point of view of feminist ideology it appears as the great success story of contemporary feminism. When women began in large numbers to enter professional and educational settings that until then had been primarily the privileged bailiwick of men, feminists wondered what sorts of changes, if any, would follow in the structure and ethos of organizational and workplace life. Now we know the answer. Not content with the new reality in which women and men, together, could work out accommodations according to their joint and separate needs, some feminist activists have moved to ensure that their vision alone would prevail.

What do women want? I doubt that feminists have a better handle on that age-old question than does anyone else. But some of them—whether motivated by the desire to consolidate their institutional power or driven by their ideological zeal—evidently feel entitled to impose on the world their own views, which are based on highly questionable analyses and beliefs. This, in turn, means that some of us can no longer celebrate victories claimed by feminists. Instead, we should deplore them as posing a threat to civil liberties, to personal autonomy, to the dignity of women and men, and to the legitimacy of feminism itself.

*   *   *

In late February 1998, I attended a conference on sexual harassment held at Yale University to celebrate the twentieth anniversary of the publication of Catharine MacKinnon's *Sexual Harassment of Working Women.* To me, what was most interesting about this event was what was not said at any of the sessions, by any of the participants. Sitting in the audience, not knowing whether I was the only person there with a dissenting opinion of the new dispensation brought to us by the Sexual Harassment Industry, I avidly took notes during the two days of the meeting.

Many SHI luminaries were there, including MacKinnon herself, fresh from her role supporting the suit brought by Joseph Oncale, a young man who was repeatedly sexually abused (both tormented and assaulted) by men with whom he worked on an offshore oil rig in the Gulf of Mexico. At that time, the case was before the Supreme Court, which finally, in March 1998, addressed the issue of whether same-sex harassment on the job constitutes discrimination as prohibited by Title VII of the Civil Rights Act of 1964 (it does, and Oncale's suit against his former employer, Sundowner Offshore Services, Inc., charging it with illegal sexual harassment in tolerating a hostile work environment, can now continue).[2] I heard much concern expressed that the Oncale case would incite homophobia. Several speakers voiced this fear. But at no time during those days did any of them acknowledge, much less address, a different prejudice that quite openly underlay the panel discussions of case after case of males harassing females. Not even a hint was given that the great success of sexual harassment law might be stimulating what I call "heterophobia," meaning fear of, and antagonism toward, the Other—in the present context men in general—and toward heterosexuality in particular. Not a word was uttered about false, frivolous, or opportunistic accusations.

The MacKinnonite orthodoxy was in full swing. Disagreements were minor and limited to opinions on what sort of approach would be most useful in curtailing sexual harassment: Was prevention the key? Isn't the conflict between equality and freedom overdrawn? What is "unwelcomeness"? Why not require men to prove that they knew their advances were welcome? Should personal liability be recognized, along with employer liability? Would this be a good way to address "street harassment"? Should sexual harassment liability be an insurable risk? Should certain words automatically be considered evidence of sexual harassment? Where do bisexuals fit in?

Other papers provided an international perspective: Do sexual harassment claims resting on a notion of affronts to women's "dignity" (as in India) reinforce traditional stereotypes about women? Would the Israeli Knesset adopt the draft law on sexual harassment prepared by Orit Kamir, present at the conference? (It did, making Israel's sexual harassment law the most far-reaching in the world; it even covers street harassment.)

Speaker after speaker appealed to tried and presumably true propositions: We must carry on the good fight, despite the difficulties. The law does work. Harassment victims are hesitant to speak out; we have to be sure not to victimize them a second time. Women's words are routinely ignored. Male power structures harm gay men. More stringent control of information is needed to protect victims, to keep them from becoming pariahs. The goal is to end women's subordination; that's what sexual harassment is all about. Sexual harassment law is women's form of collective bargaining regarding the conditions of their employment. Black women's experiences of sexual harassment reveal that it is a collective injury; what happens to one woman has an impact on all others. Sexual "liberals" are—insidiously, it was implied—trying to rehabilitate sexualization of the workplace. Sexual harassment arises from misogyny; it punishes women for transgressing the boundaries of their traditional roles. Unwelcome sex does a unique harm to psychic integrity.

At no time throughout these proceedings was any divergence of opinion expressed—much less discussed—about basic definitions and principles of the problem of harassment. The one notable exception was a paper by Professor Kingsley Browne, who argued that sexual harassment law restricts workplace speech and is a form of censorship aimed at reshaping conduct. Much praise was bestowed on MacKinnon for the role her work played in the Violence against Women Act, which takes sexual harassment law as a model and, like its prototype, sees crimes of violence as rooted in gender and hence requiring special sanctions. MacKinnonite terms were universally accepted as the key to social problems: Battery is "about" male power, control, and domination. So is rape. So is stalking. A tone of urgency was sounded by speaker after speaker, many of them seemingly alarmed that issues of "privacy" were resurfacing, as in the Monica Lewinsky matter, and were fueling a "backlash."

At the conference's opening session, Andrea Dworkin, the radical feminist, her voice heavy with emotion, informed an audience of several hundred people that the "backlash" began when white middle-class men saw that sexual harassment law was going to affect them. This reaction, Dworkin thoughtfully suggested, showed us that "millions of men wanted to have a young woman at work to suck their cock."[3] Did anyone rise to contest such outrageous slander directed at all or most men? On the contrary. As Dworkin made her way back to her seat, Judge Guido Calabresi, a courtly gentleman sixty-six years of age, stood up and warmly shook Dworkin's hand. Did Judge Calabresi feel that Dworkin had his number? Or did he believe himself to be one of the rare exceptions?[4]

It is hard to imagine any other group of people in the United States today who could be so crassly maligned in a public setting without arousing immediate protest. Somehow men seem to have been cowed into silence. None objected when MacKinnon, in her opening comments, declared, "Droit du seigneur is dead. Women are citizens."

Citizens, perhaps, but constantly traumatized, according to the Sexual Harassment Industry, which portrays a social scene where women who experience sexual harassment are "devastated," go through a process of "grieving," and if they are lucky, emerge as "survivors." For obvious reasons, SHI rhetoric maximizes the damage supposedly inflicted on them: Sympathy will be garnered, counseling provided, male wickedness confirmed, and women's victimhood—today a prized commodity for which women are in passionate competition with other victim groups—enshrined.

But those of us who are not entranced by this vision, who recognize it for the ideological construct it is, look at the world in very different terms. We see it as one in which men and women are not nearly as separated by their differences as they are united by their common humanity; in which expressions of sexual interest are ever present, sometimes inappropriately, most often not; in which sex is an enjoyable part of life, not a constant threat; and in which women are as likely as men to experience sexual interest and attraction, enjoy sexual banter, bring sexual alertness into the workplace and classroom, and are aware that the sexual dimension in human relations adds zest to life even when not acted on (as it usually is not).

*   *   *

Abuses cry out for correction. But before we can correct them, as reformers constantly argue we should, we need to be made aware that they are abuses. One instrument for heightening awareness of abuse is the imaginative device of reversing the situation. This is the technique utilized, for example, in sex-role reversal fiction, such as Annie Denton Cridge's 1870 work *Man's Rights, or How Would You Like It?* which makes a poignant plea for women's rights by describing a society in which women rule and men are confined to the domestic sphere. It seems to me, however, that one need not invoke a complete role reversal in order to present an estranged view of our own society, a view in which some of its invisible mechanisms are exposed. It is enough to look at what we already know from a slightly different angle. In such a spirit, I suggest the following scenario, merely in order to demonstrate how readily it, too, could appear as an entirely plausible version of reality.

In contemporary America, women and men, not having learned how to behave like human beings, still act out ancient social roles. From the point of view of the men, the society is a matriarchy: Women have physically less demanding jobs (with the sole exception of childbirth, by now a rare event in the average woman's life, and in any case soon to be abolished through reproductive technologies). They sustain far fewer injuries on the job, are not required to go to war, are trained to take better care of their health, and for these reasons and many others enjoy a lifespan significantly longer than that of men. In this society, men use their physical strength, when necessary, on women's behalf. Women claim to be equal partners when that suits them, and claim to be entitled to special consideration when that suits them.

They insist on autonomy in maintaining or aborting pregnancies, but at the same time they determine the fathers' duties—and rights, if any. Women claim child support. They can either demand or impede fathers' continuing involvement with their offspring, as the women see fit. The result is that women have advantages over men in child custody suits, having learned to use the legal system to readily get protection orders against men (on the flimsiest provocation) when that suits their purposes, just as they have learned to use charges of child sexual abuse and domestic violence.

Though dozens of studies show that women initiate violence against their domestic partners as often as (if not more often than) men, and cause as much injury, somehow the social mythologies of this country keep that fact from gaining public attention, let alone credence.

But worst of all, in terms of the interactions of daily life, are women's emotional demands on men. At home, men routinely sit through harangues that demonstrate women's greater verbal skills and emotional agility. Men try to figure out what is required of them in a given situation. Not by accident, verbal therapies in this society archetypally began with men listening and women speaking. Even as little boys, males learn to be in awe of girls' verbal fluency. The feeling of ineptness, of being no match for females at the verbal level, is the common inheritance of all but a few exceptional males.

The matriarchy here described, structured to protect women's interests as against men's (and, ironically, having conned men into defending precisely such interests), puts a premium on women's special social and emotional skills. Every-

where women engage men and one another in personal conversation, offering and receiving disclosures, demanding commiseration, giving advice, spreading censure. Men, trained to keep to their workhorse style, are uncomfortably cornered by women, in the workplace and at home, demanding that they speak from the heart. When asked "How are you?" women give a detailed and precise accounting. In offices, they spend valuable time discussing personal matters. Studies are done of the economic costs of smoking and poor health, but not of the costs of women's work habits.

In the private sphere, women endlessly complain that men are not on their wavelength. An observer of this society, coming into a shop toward the end of a conversation and hearing one woman say heatedly to another, ". . . stood there like a tree and said not a word!" knows that a man is being described. Or on the street, overhearing one woman say, in anger, to another, "It was like talking to a plot of grass!" knows that an unsatisfactory encounter with a man is being recounted. At home and on the job, men are reminded of their emotional inferiority and verbal inadequacy. Nowhere are they as quick as women in their emotional responses, their verbalization of those responses, or their acuity in gauging the dynamics of an interaction or situation. And constantly they are reminded of this disadvantage. Women berate them, browbeat them, even physically attack them out of frustration at these characteristics.

Somehow it is always men who are to blame. Even in the school yard, little boys suffer from puzzlement, pain, and ostracism as little girls make comments and express expectations they cannot quite grasp or respond to. Thus boys are trained into a lifelong awareness of inferiority. At home, mothers demand expression of their sons' and husbands' feelings and berate them when they are puzzled and tongue-tied. At work, women smile knowingly to one another when men "just don't get it."

Finally, some men organize around the issue of emotional harassment, the problem that hitherto has had no name. A sophisticated analysis of the matriarchal bases of this social practice springs up. Everyone denies that it has anything at all to do with biology, which allows women to be fully blamed for this domineering and demanding behavior, highlights women's shortcomings, and pushes them into corrective political action. A men's movement develops. Men who have been in "denial" for years hear the news, attend workshops, go to counselors, and learn to be on the alert for any sign of emotional harassment. Courts, overwhelmingly made up of individuals who feel condescension toward these male complaints, uphold new laws and interpretations that outlaw emotional harassment in school and workplace. The economic costs of the underutilization of men's emotional capacities begin to be gauged.

The constant pressure on men to tell personal stories and focus on analysis of their feelings is finally recognized for what it is: a gender gambit designed to maintain female superiority by reminding men of their place and of their vulnerability to women's more high-powered emotional and verbal style. Mass culture is rewritten, and all those "strong silent types" in film and fiction are now understood to be men damaged by matriarchal values. Cases flood the courts as men seek redress and financial relief for the emotional harassment imposed on them by a woman who said a wrong word or hinted at an emotional demand, creating a hostile environment for these men and making it impossible for them to participate fully in school or workplace.

Mystified women start watching their every word, guarding against any idle gesture or expression that might inadvertently express something that, to vulnerable men, translates into emotional harassment. A new day is celebrated, one in which a neutral, not to say mechanical, form of behavior will be demanded of everyone.

If this scenario seems far fetched (and I agree that it does seem so); if it leaves dozens of pertinent elements out of the picture; if readers want to protest that it doesn't convey an accurate image of reality, that it grossly oversimplifies relations between men and women, exaggerates differences, and vilifies behaviors that have quite different sources—let me say only: That's the point! It makes no more sense to focus in isolation on sexual interactions and heightened gender sensibilities, as the Sexual Harassment Industry does, than it would to insist on "emotional harassment" as a master key to understanding gender dynamics and as an instrument by which women routinely keep men in their place. The sterile world promoted by the Sexual Harassment Industry, in which both sexuality itself and the very fact of sexual difference are suspect, represents nothing so much as the ultimate triumph of ideology over humanity.

*   *   *

From its early days, feminism was divided into factions that were not generous toward or tolerant of one another, and even less so of people judged to be outside the fold of the good feminist fight. A great deal of holier-than-thouness was always present. This feminist intolerance and self-righteousness contributed to a situation in which heterosexual women are made to feel that they are not "real" feminists. Aware of being "compromised" by their attachments to men, such women have often acted apologetic toward their lesbian feminist colleagues and friends. This, in turn, has been a major contributing factor to the failure to challenge the extreme antimale rhetoric produced by some feminists. Certainly, without the complicity of a great many heterosexual women, the heterophobic discourse so prevalent in feminism could not have found so fruitful an expression in the contemporary Sexual Harassment Industry.

But nothing is merely what it seems; I do not doubt that buried within the SHI were some positive impulses to genuinely help women escape from discriminatory conditions. A social reform movement contaminated by hatred cannot, however, expect to remain sound and whole. What started, arguably, as a utopian impulse to improve women's lot has, it is now clear, come to entangle not only men but also women, and not only heterosexuals but also homosexuals, in the quixotic pursuit of a sanitized environment in which the beast of male sexuality will at long last have been vanquished.

"Sexual harassment," in my view, is a concept that has in a few short decades exceeded its usefulness. For a brief time it did identify something outrageous that needed to be stopped—what Lin Farley in her 1978 book called "sexual shakedown."[5] By now, however, sexual harassment has become so loosely defined as to be incapable of serving any constructive purpose. Even Anita Hill, of Clarence Thomas–Senate Judiciary Committee fame, recently deplored, in a *New York Times* opinion piece (on March 19, 1998), the unconscionable stretching of the term to the point of subverting a law whose intent was ostensibly not to inhibit sex but to ban discrimination. Why the dividing line between these two has never been clear will emerge in the course of this book.

At the present moment, "sexual harassment" seems often to be little more than a label for excoriating men. It has become the synecdoche for general male awfulness. Its real function at this moment, in addition to keeping feminist passions at fever pitch, is to serve as the conduit by which some extreme feminist tenets about the relations between the sexes enter everyday life with minimum challenge. No longer a well-intentioned effort to gain justice for women, it has been turned into a tool (powered by a legal apparatus and manipulated by a professional cadre of trainers and enforcers) for implementing, and indeed normalizing, what was once merely a marginal and bizarre feminist worldview. That worldview has many tentacles, but at its core is the effort blatantly named "couple busting" by the unapologetic tragicomic feminist Valerie Solanas in her *SCUM Manifesto* thirty years ago.[6]

Any criticism of feminism, however, is usually greeted in feminist circles with the riposte that there is no one feminism, that feminism has many faces and voices. This is true in the sense that feminism is the many things that women who call themselves feminists have done and are doing. In this book I criticize one important aspect of what is now being done in the name of feminism. I do not offer an archaeology of the Idea of feminism; any attempt to do so would quickly run aground on the problem of competing definitions and allegiances. Readers will no doubt note that I sometimes use "feminism" in a positive sense and sometimes in a negative. Let me therefore be clear that what I am mainly criticizing here is an important—and to me profoundly disturbing—aspect of feminism: its predilection for turning complex human relations into occasions for mobilizing the feminist troops against men.

There is within much feminist writing today (as there has been for the past few decades) a pretense that the charge of male-bashing is a slanderous mischaracterization motivated by political impulses that are conservative (and thus assumed to be reprehensible). But it is plain and irrefutable that much contemporary feminism is indeed marred by hostility toward men. The virulence of it varies from group to group. But the antagonism is pervasive, and through the attack on "sexual harassment" it has entered society at large.

True, feminist extremists do not yet enjoy substantial political power. But it is also true that their writings have contributed enormously to a climate in which individual autonomy is under attack and its sexual manifestations in particular are vilified. And the justification for this assault is that it will advance the greater good; such niceties as the democratic process and the protection of civil liberties may simply have to be sacrificed—a small price, many feminists tell us. Is it an irony of history that feminist efforts should come full circle and, through the agency of the Sexual Harassment Industry, be in a position to implement a skewed view of the world? Is this endeavor the fulfillment of the feminist agenda—by now savvier and more articulate than before, with its own lawyers, theorists, expert witnesses, consultants, trainers, and therapists, but indelibly marked by its origins in an unrestrained hostility toward men? I believe that it is.

*   *   *

In the chapters that follow, I concentrate on the academy. The university is in many respects a privileged setting in which social experiments are readily undertaken and can, for that reason, be most effectively studied and their consequences gauged. I will argue that the sexual harassment fervor now in evidence should be considered such an experiment, but an experiment that has failed. It has produced not greater justice, not the disappearance of discrimination against women, but a climate that is inhospitable to all human beings. My argument will in the first instance attack not the law but rather the way in which it is being implemented and the purposes and preconceptions that lie behind that implementation. In universities, people with limited understanding of the law, and perhaps little respect for it, are helping to write and enforce policy; others with inadequate legal knowledge are acting in a sub- and extra-legal capacity as investigators, trainers, and overseers.

The feminist literature on these matters assumes that sexual harassment can never be accidental or trivial. It is always seen as part of a concerted effort to keep women in their place as an inferior social group. It is, so many serious commentators on it insist, an essential part of patriarchy's ongoing plot against women.

In this book, I will attempt to address the matter of sexual harassment from the point of view of a still-avowed feminist who nonetheless does not subscribe to deeply rooted presuppositions concerning perpetual male aggression and female victimhood. In approaching my subject, I have asked myself some basic questions: Will the solutions proposed for ending what is now called sexual harassment lead to a better society? Better for whom? In what ways? At what cost and at whose expense? With what trade-offs and side effects? I thus move from an analysis and description of writings on sexual harassment to an interpretation of what lies behind them. I will impute the same lack of "innocence" to the writings and actions of reformers and enforcers as they attribute to those (mostly men) whose behavior they wish to transform through sexual harassment laws and the ensuing regulations.

Part I, "The Making of a Social Problem," reviews the development of sexual harassment regulations. It then uncovers the ideology, rhetorical strategies, and institutional structures deployed by the Sexual Harassment Industry to promote procedures within academe for identifying, tracking, punishing, and—supposedly—preventing cases of sexual harassment. Reading through the abundant literature generated by this industry without the presupposition that sexual harassment is ipso facto the devastating experience it is claimed to be, one discovers quite an arsenal of linguistic and ideological sleight of hand: coercive discourse, ever-expanding definitions, bias in investigation, systemic misandry, old-fashioned sexual imagery of male predatoriness and female passivity and helplessness, and—often flagrant—disregard of due process in the pursuit of a purifying agenda. Once institutionalized, these practices themselves become major factors contributing to both the vigilantism and the paranoia directed especially at men but sometimes also at women, and to the sense of real and potential victimization prevalent among women.

Part II, "Typifying Tales," takes a critical look at what the ideological framework described up to this point means in practice. First, I trace a number of stories of "devastating" experiences retailed by "survivors" featured in the SHI's current literature. Second, to these stories I counterpose several lesser-known tales of faculty members (both male and female) who have lost years of their lives, reputations, and sometimes livelihoods as a result of false or frivolous charges directed against them. Until now (and in contradiction to the reigning feminist theme of the "silencing" of women), we have heard primarily from the accusers, not the accused. Of special significance here is the utter lack of attention, in the vast literature on sexual harassment, to the issue of false or trivial accusations, and this despite the fact that the damage done to the accused is typically far more grievous than the distress suffered by the majority of "victims." Third, I analyze a characteristic feminist defense of women accused (by other women) of sexual harassment, as manifested in Jane Gallop's recent book, a defense that conspicuously excludes men.

Part III, "The Feminist Turn against Men," reveals what I have come to recognize as the underlying agenda of the Sexual Harassment Industry, namely, the restructuring of male–female relations to the point that men will be put perpetually on the defensive. I trace the pursuit of a "comfortable" environment for women—an important objective of sexual harassment activists—to heterophobia. This hostility toward men in general and toward heterosexuality in particular is not limited to the lunatic feminist fringe where it originated in the late 1960s. Indeed, it has by now deeply pervaded male and female interactions in the public sphere. It has succeeded in putting all men—and also some women—on notice that their every word and gesture will be watched. In part III I also explore the claims for women's "authority of experience," on which feminist rhetoric about sexual harassment often relies. Finally, I analyze the demand for rules and regulations that flows from these claims, showing its overlap with totalitarianisms, both real and imaginary.

PART I

The Making of a Social Problem

~X~

Chapter 1

Saving Womanhood

☙❧

We are going to reeducate you, boy.

WORDS SPOKEN BY A DEAN TO A MEMBER OF
HER FACULTY ACCUSED OF SEXUAL HARASSMENT

Setting the Stage

It has been nearly twenty-five years since the terminology of sexual harassment began to enter public discourse. In her groundbreaking book *Sexual Shakedown: The Sexual Harassment of Women on the Job* (1978), Lin Farley recounts how, while teaching a class on women and work at Cornell University in 1974, she came to realize that she and her women students had a crucial experience in common: All had left a job because they had been made "too uncomfortable" by the behavior of a man at work.[1]

At the same time, also at Cornell, a forty-four-year-old woman named Carmita Wood, having been promoted to the position of administrative assistant in one of the university's laboratories, found herself in constant contact with a Cornell official in a nearby office who subjected her to unrelenting sexual attentions. After repeated efforts to be transferred, Wood resigned. Denied unemployment compensation, she began to talk about her situation.[2] A group of women gathered to help her pursue her case, and in this context, the term "sexual harassment" was first used to designate a problem that until then had been nameless.[3]

A potentially effective legal mechanism already existed in the United States for dealing with this newly identified problem, but how forceful an apparatus this actually was became clear only as the result of a number of judicial and administrative events that unfolded between the 1970s and the early 1990s. Title VII of the Civil Rights Act of 1964 had made it unlawful for an employer to discriminate in hiring, firing, promotion, and terms and conditions of employment on the basis of sex, as well as race, color, religion, or national origin. (Ironically, the addition of sex discrimination took place during the House floor debate by opponents of the act attempting to sabotage it.) In 1972, the Equal Employment Opportunity Act enlarged the authority of the Equal Employment Opportunity Commission, which is charged with the enforcement of Title VII, over claims of discrimination. Because Title VII had excluded educational institutions, Title IX of the Education Amendments, also in 1972, outlawed any and all discrimination on the basis of sex in educational institutions receiving federal dollars. Title IX, furthermore, obligated these institutions to set up and publish formal grievance procedures for handling complaints that allege acts of sexual discrimination. Such acts are defined by the Office of Civil Rights of the U.S. Department of Education, which enforces this federal statute, as

> verbal or physical conduct of a sexual nature, imposed on the basis of sex, by an employee or agent of a recipient of federal funds that denies, limits, or provides different, or conditions the provisions of aid, benefits, services, or treatment protected under Title IX.

How Title IX came about makes for an interesting story. Its protagonist was Bernice R. Sandler, today one of the leading specialists in, and the doyenne of, the Sexual Harassment Industry. Initially, Sandler's role was a heroic one; her campaign to prohibit discrimination against women in higher education was obviously an important undertaking. Writing in the newsletter she has edited for the past seven years, *About Women on Campus,* Sandler retold her story, in a celebratory vein, on the twenty-fifth anniversary of the legislation that "made it possible for women and girls to achieve a greater measure of equity than ever before."[4]

In 1969, when Sandler was teaching part-time at the University of Maryland while completing her doctorate, a friend told her that she was not being considered for any of seven openings in her department because "[y]ou come on *too strong for a woman*" (italics in original). To Sandler's then-husband, this was nothing more nor less than "sex discrimination." Assuming it to be illegal, because so clearly immoral, she was surprised to learn that Title VII did not cover sex discrimination in education. Some research led her to note that an executive order already existed prohibiting federal contractors from discriminating in employment on the basis of race, color, religion, and national origin. She reports that she shrieked with excitement upon learning that President Johnson, in 1968, had amended that executive order to include discrimination based on sex. She instantly realized that most universities and colleges, having federal contracts, were therefore forbidden from discriminating in employment on the basis of sex. A legal route, in other words, did indeed exist for combating sex discrimination, little known though it was at the time.

Meanwhile, at the U.S. Department of Labor, the director of the Office of Federal Contract Compliance had been waiting for someone to use Johnson's executive order in relation to sex discrimination and was delighted when Sandler approached her. Together, they planned the first complaint against universities and colleges.[5] Sandler also collaborated with the Women's Equity Action League on a national campaign to end discrimination in education. On January 31, 1970, the league filed a historic class-action complaint against all universities and colleges in the country.[6] This was an administrative complaint, filed with a federal agency (the Department of Labor), not a lawsuit filed in court, and therefore it did not require an attorney.

Over a two-year period, Sandler herself launched complaints against 250 institutions; other individuals and organizations filed some 100 more. Sandler documented admission quotas, financial assistance, hiring practices, promotions, and salary differentials. She also organized a letter-writing campaign to alert congressional staff to sex discrimination occurring in education.[7] In 1970, the first contract compliance investigation involving sex discrimination was begun at Harvard University. The first congressional hearings on education and the employment of women were held in June and July of that same year. The hearings, the records of which were widely distributed, established sex discrimination in higher education as a legitimate issue, though initially most educators had denied its very existence.[8] In 1972 Title IX of the Education Amendments was enacted by Congress and signed into law by President Nixon.

Sandler optimistically anticipated rapid results. She tells us that she expected all inequities based on sex to disappear within a year or two. Slowly, however, she raised her estimate—to five years, then to ten, then twenty-five. By now, as she wrote in 1997, she has learned that "we were trying to change very strong patterns of behavior and belief, and that would take more than my lifetime to accomplish."[9]

Today Bernice Sandler is a widely published author who also consults and speaks about harassment issues. Hers is an inspiring story. But it does not end there. Opposition to sexual harassment has come to mean something very different from the early efforts of pioneers such as Sandler to defeat gender prejudice. So what went wrong? The achievements of the early 1970s were not allowed to rest on the laurels they deserved. With all the energy and pluck that Sandler and her colleagues devoted to the cause, what they seem to have lacked was the conviction that given equal opportunity, women would compete and flourish. And this lack, in turn, has left them apparently incapable of recognizing the real successes women have in fact achieved: the excellent academic records of women compared to men; the higher percentage of women (56.1 percent overall, from every ethnic and racial group) than of men who enrolled in undergraduate programs in 1995;[10] the higher rate of graduation among women (currently 55 percent, again reflecting every ethnic or racial group as compared with men from the same group);[11] the ever-increasing numbers of women in law, medical, and other professional schools, and in doctoral programs. Women received 37.9 percent of the doctorates awarded in 1996 (by 2006 they are expected to achieve parity with men in receiving doctorates).[12]

Searching for a lasting outlet for their dedication to activism, Sandler and her associates could find it only at ever more microlevels. Thus we hear of the "chilly climate" for women in coeducational colleges and universities (improbably, this climate is often claimed by feminist activists to be colder today than it was in the past). Sandler's latest "chilly climate" report suggests that the more subtle forms of discrimination still being uncovered by feminists are even more damaging to women than the overt discrimination of the past. What are these subtle forms? Professors supposedly make less eye contact with female students. They call on them less frequently and give them less encouragement when they speak than they give to male students.[13] In view of the open record of academic successes by women, allegations such as these suggest something of the desperation with which feminist activists regard the changed academic scene.

"Sexual harassment" must therefore be sought out with an ever more powerful magnifying glass. In a column written for her newsletter in 1994, for instance, Sandler compiled a list of tips headed "How men can tell if their behavior is sexual harassment." Two of the tips indicate the drift toward vigilantism: "If I ask someone for a date and the answer is 'no,' do I keep asking?" If you reply "yes," you may be guilty of harassment. "Do I tell jokes or make 'funny' remarks involving women and/or sexuality?" Again, an affirmative answer reveals a potential harasser. "Such jokes," Sandler explains, "may offend many people." Her column concludes that if a man answers "yes" to *any* of the questions, there is a good chance that he will be considered a sexual harasser: "Because such behavior is likely to be high risk, if you have to ask, it is probably better not to do it."[14] Evidently she is unconcerned about the other kind of "chilly climate" such advice is likely to promote. In addition, for some years now Sandler has predicted that "peer harassment," especially student-to-student harassment (about which she coauthored a report in 1988),[15] will be the next major problem requiring the attentions of the sexual harassment experts. Could this be because faculty harassment has turned out to be not quite as fruitful a field as the SHI had anticipated? In any case, such moves illustrate the unmistakable trend for sexual harassment activism to expand its reach both horizontally (to include all public settings) and vertically (embracing all age groups).

"Sexualizing Subordination"

Looking back at this sequence of events from the vantage point of the present—a time in which sexual harassment has become one of the hottest issues around—I find myself much intrigued by the process by which a problem without a name has been transformed into a name that is itself a problem. How did we get from clear examples of sexual discrimination in school and workplace to a preoccupation with "comfort" levels, dirty jokes, and passing innuendos? How did sexual discrimination, sexual harassment, and just plain sex get entangled to such an extent that today a bit of overheard banter or a clumsy sexual overture in the office or school is considered as unacceptable, and potentially as actionable, as the sort of relentless sexual aggression experienced by Carmita Wood at Cornell?

It took some years for the notion of "comfort" to be raised to the level of law by way of the concept of hostile-environment harassment, but in Lin Farley's *Sexual Shakedown,* a key document, this development is clearly foreshadowed. On the very first page of her book, Farley characterizes as "uncomfortable" the situation she and her women students encountered in their places of work. What disturbed them was not sexual extortion, not pressure to perform sexual acts as the condition of continued employment, but a variety of overt manifestations of male sexuality—all perceived as "male assertions of dominance"[16]—that pervaded the workplace.

If Farley's 1978 book was an early salvo in the campaign to create workplace environments fit for women, Catharine MacKinnon's *Sexual Harassment of Working Women,* appearing in 1979, moved events to the litigious stage by arguing that sexual harassment, because it is a problem primarily for women, is a form of discrimination and as such a violation of federal law.[17] It was at this point that sexual harassment charges began to become widespread. MacKinnon's hugely influential book presented itself as a wake-up call. "Intimate violation of women by men is sufficiently pervasive in American society," it began, "as to be nearly invisible . . . it has become institutionalized."[18] Why have the courts paid so little attention to a form of discrimination suffered by perhaps seven out of ten women at least once in their lives?[19] Because they have failed to grasp the nature of the offense. According to MacKinnon, acts of sexual harassment do not spring casually or incidentally from the interplay of biology, personality, and circumstance. They arise necessarily out of the very structure of American society in which women occupy an inferior and distinct place.[20] Harassment subjects women to adverse treatment because of their different sex and because of their social inequality. Therefore, harassment *is* discrimination within the sense of both Title VII of the 1964 Civil Rights Act and the Equal Protection Clause of the Fourteenth Amendment.[21]

Crucial to an understanding of the severity of such discrimination is the realization of women's subordinate status, socially and sexually, in our society. Only when legislators and courts have learned to give full weight to the connection between social condition and discrimination can women hope to achieve the relief due them. "Sexual harassment . . . eroticizes women's subordination," MacKinnon has famously written. "It acts out and deepens the powerlessness of women as a gender, *as women.*"[22] Building on her well-known argument that violence against women is merely a variation of men's normal interaction with women, she concluded:

> If sexual harassment expresses the pervasive reality of normal relations
> between the sexes, and if these relations express unequal social power,
> then the feelings and practices that emerge are not reasons that the prac-

tices should be allowed. They support and evidence the discrimination. Violations that would not be seen as criminal because they are anything but unusual may, in this context, be seen as discriminatory for precisely the same reason.[23]

Recent legislation, as well as the Constitution itself, MacKinnon argued, offered courts the legal handles to take hold of the issue of women's inequality at long last.

The first federal cases to recognize sexual harassment as a form of sex discrimination came in 1976 and 1980: *Williams v. Saxbe* and *Alexander v. Yale University*. Both found sexual harassment to be a violation of Title IX. Although the U.S. Supreme Court had not yet spoken on the matter, quid pro quo harassment—what Lin Farley, more simply, had called "sexual shakedown"—was coming to be recognized as an impermissible form of sex discrimination actionable under Title IX. In 1980, the Equal Employment Opportunity Commission's set of guidelines for actions to be brought under Title VII enlarged the field considerably, proving sexual harassment to be a highly elastic concept. Conduct is offensive, the EEOC stated, not only "when submission [to] or cooperation [with it is] an implicit or explicit condition of employment" but also when it has the "purpose *or* effect of unreasonably interfering with a person's work performance or creating an intimidating, hostile, or offensive work environment" (my italics). This expanded interpretation was accepted by the court in *Moire v. Temple University School of Medicine* in 1986 and, that same year, by the U.S. Supreme Court in *Meritor Savings Bank v. Vinson*, which established that a working environment may be hostile to women, and may violate Title VII of the Civil Rights Act, despite the absence of economic consequences.[24] Sexual harassment, the Supreme Court held, consists of

> unwelcome sexual advances, requests for sexual favors, and other verbal or physical conduct . . . when (1) submission to such conduct is made either explicitly or implicitly a term or condition of an individual's employment, (2) submission or rejection of such conduct by an individual is used as the basis for employment decisions affecting such individual, or (3) such conduct has the purpose or effect of unreasonably interfering with an individual's work performance or creating an intimidating, hostile, or offensive working environment.

Once again, the key phrase "purpose or effect" endorsed the purported victim's subjective perception regardless of the intent of the alleged harasser. "Plaintiff may establish a violation of Title VII," the Court concluded, "by proving that discrimination based on sex has created a hostile or abusive working environment." *Meritor* did not, however, clarify what standard was to be applied to determine whether behavior was sufficiently pervasive or severe to qualify as actionable.

Legislation and litigation in the years following *Meritor* showed a marked tendency for both the concept and the application of sexual harassment to broaden further. In 1992, the Campus Sexual Assault Victims' Bill of Rights, binding on all institutions receiving federal funds, obligated university authorities to treat reported offenses seriously and to protect the complainants against unwarranted allegations that they had invited the complained-of acts. EEOC guidelines declared institutions liable for their employees' acts. They also legitimized complaints by third parties—those who, although not the direct targets of alleged harassment, feel themselves to be affected by it.

At the same time, several developments, in effect, encouraged the filing of sexual harassment suits against institutions, which in turn made it lucrative to establish consulting firms specializing in how to avoid such suits.[25] Congress enacted the Civil Rights Act of 1991, providing for both compensatory and punitive damages for violations of Title VII. Other legislation allowed jury trials in discrimination cases. And in February 1992, the Supreme Court unanimously declared that Title VII plaintiffs could collect monetary damages.

For all these reasons, universities were forced to adopt procedures intended to inhibit "discriminatory" behavior (including "offensive" speech) and, when such behavior was said to occur, launch a thorough investigation of it. As critics have pointed out, because employers (including universities) are constantly under the threat of legal sanctions, the result of these developments was bound to be an imbalance in which the rights of alleged harassers are routinely sacrificed to those of the alleged victims. As Mane Hajdin has noted, criminal sanctions in the Western tradition are imposed "only for conduct that is engaged in intentionally, knowingly, or at a minimum, recklessly."[26] In addition, in criminal law, guilt must be proven beyond a reasonable doubt. Civil law, by contrast, imposes liability for negligence, and requires merely a preponderance of evidence. The reasoning behind this distinction assumes that losing a civil suit affects an individual's life far less gravely than being convicted of a crime. The latter may well ruin one's life; the former normally does not. But, Hajdin argues, being found guilty of sexual harassment is, in its consequences, far closer to being found guilty of a crime than to losing a civil suit. Admittedly, sexual harassers do not go to jail, but in all other respects, one's life can be just as ruined by being found guilty of sexual harassment as by a criminal conviction. Those found guilty of sexual harassment are typically treated as outcasts, just as criminals are. If one is accused of sexual harassment, one stands to lose one's job . . . and one's respectability in one's community.

Yet despite these severe consequences, those accused of sexual harassment do not enjoy anything close to the procedural protection given in our legal system to defendants in criminal trials. Procedures—often implemented by people without proper legal training—may be slipshod; guilt need not be proven beyond a reasonable doubt; and culpable actions need not be demonstrated as either intentional or reckless. As Hajdin concludes,

> The law about sexual harassment in employment thus affects people's lives in a manner that is normally reserved for criminal law without giving them the rights that criminal defendants normally have. The state has managed to accomplish this, without causing public uproar, by giving the law a two-level structure.

Hajdin refers to an "upper level," where the state, through its legal apparatus, imposes on employers the obligation to see to it that no sexual harassment occurs. Employers carry out this mandate by putting in place various internal rules at what Hajdin calls the "lower level." The resulting two-tiered system works to the detriment of those accused of sexual harassment:

> An employer that ends up erring in favor of the alleged harasser, even if only slightly, may easily find itself in court, while an employer that errs in favor of the alleged victim is unlikely to find itself in similar trouble, unless the error is extreme. Employers are thus given an incentive to structure lower-level proceedings in such a way that errors in favor of alleged victims are more likely than errors in favor of alleged harassers.[27]

Important decisions handed down in the early 1990s further eased the burden on women in proceeding against acts perceived as harassment. In *Harris v. Forklift Systems, Inc.* (1993), the Supreme Court held that Title VII is violated whenever "the environment would reasonably be perceived and is perceived as hostile or abusive."[28] In order to sue, plaintiffs need not show that the harassment caused them any psychological injury. In *Ellison v. Brady* (1991), the U.S. Court of Appeals for the Ninth Circuit had already declared that offensive conduct should be judged not merely from the point of view of a "reasonable person" but from that of "a reasonable person in the position of the plaintiff"—in short, a "reasonable *woman*." The Ninth Circuit conceded that the "reasonable person" perspective, as previously adopted by courts, may not do full justice to the particular ways in which women respond to harassing behavior directed against them. The court concluded that "a sex-blind reasonable person standard tends to be male-biased and tends to systematically ignore the experiences of women."[29] Thus, a woman's subjective judgment of men's actions, regardless of their intent, became the standard by which complaints could be judged. EEOC guidelines made this new criterion explicit. They also extended it to still other identity groups: A "reasonable person" standard that includes consideration of the perspective of the plaintiff's race, gender, and other personal characteristics allows for a multiplicity of heightened sensibilities to determine whether something is or is not harassment.

"Reasonableness" itself, however, leaves a very large number of questions to be answered on a case-by-case basis, as does the "unwelcomeness," "severity," or "pervasiveness" of alleged acts. Because the Supreme Court noted in *Harris* that it "need not answer . . . all the potential questions" raised by the case, wide discretion to interpret sexually harassing behavior and its consequences resides with lower courts and governmental bodies, not to mention academic authorities who, under the law, must have in place administrative procedures for handling complaints of harassing behavior on campus. A clear implication of the "reasonable woman" standard is that it is not so much the intent (the "purpose," in the language of the law) of the alleged offender that should count in interpreting the gravity of acts of sexual harassment as, rather, the way in which these acts are perceived by the complainant (the "effect"). Subjective factors thus operate at every level of the sexual harassment scene. They open a wide space for discretionary applications. This is no doubt responsible for most of the troubles bedeviling sexual harassment surveillance in academic and workplace settings. When a woman's personal experience of "discomfort" can be readily converted into evidence of a "hostile" and "offensive" environment, which in turn is taken as a sign of "discrimination on the basis of sex," the most trivial allegation made by a "victim" can be regarded as a grave matter. For the accused in such a case, due process is likely to be given short shrift.

Far from focusing on the enormous legal and social problems generated by this elevation of subjectivity, sexual harassment activists treat it as an opportunity. Case after case shows them happy to blur, if not altogether elide, the differences between discrimination and discomfort. Discrimination calls for the removal of impediments and the creation of equal opportunity; a wrong is to be righted. "Discomfort" demands a near total absence of unpleasantness, thus aiming, quixotically, at perfection. This distinction does not trouble the SHI. The legal framework now available to its functionaries, because it addresses both issues together, occludes the crucial practical question: Is a casual comment containing a sexual reference, or an unwanted invitation that is (perhaps less than sensitively) repeated, a true species of discrimination? To say "yes" to this question is to adopt without qualification Catharine MacKinnon's extreme formulation of male–female interactions. We see here the characteristic unwillingness to draw distinctions that has plagued feminist activism for some time.

Industrial Growth

One result of the legal developments discussed in the preceding section is the Sexual Harassment Industry itself. The complexities of the laws, especially as they apply to the "lower level" of colleges and universities, raise issues that most academic administrators have not been equipped to deal with. A cadre of specialists has therefore developed, both inside and outside the university, to take on the task of guiding academic officials through policy-making, training, and implementation procedures. Overlooked in the eagerness to comply with EEOC guidelines was an evident consequence: Academics are now placed in a situation in which their employers have committed themselves to an unprecedented program of policing the faculty—a radical innovation in academic life.

But more is at issue here than faculty discontent. The Sexual Harassment Industry has been waging a struggle on two fronts. The first, largely won, has succeeded in rewriting the law. The other, more far reaching, has as its aim nothing less than a restructuring of patterns of behavior, customs, and traditions—specifically, the transformation of relations between men and women. The two efforts work in tandem, legal action being the threat that lends force to the insistence on redrawing the boundaries of permissible conduct. It would be foolish, in the light of feminist proclamations, to view the latter as merely an unintended consequence of the former.[30]

As Michael S. Greve has argued, when trivial conduct is characterized as sexual harassment, this

> is not an excess of but central to the feminist project. After all, if "sexual harassment" captured only serious offenses, we might as well make do with torts and contracts. Feminism's aspiration is to capture the conduct that escapes the common law and to subject it to ideological critique— and to legal sanction. "The entire structure of domination," MacKinnon writes, "the tacit relations of deference and command, can be present in a passing glance"—not to mention repeated hugs and social kisses.[31]

If personal relations are a constantly negotiated game, what the Sexual Harassment Industry, inspired by feminist ideologues such as MacKinnon, is attempting to do is alter the terms of the negotiation so that women hold all the cards. Flirtatious behavior or a casual touch is recast as a potentially serious harm by the addition of the concept "unwanted" or "unwelcome," with its clear premise that only what a woman "wants" is permissible. Once this view becomes routinized, it will be difficult to challenge such a privileging of one sex's "wants" over the other's, for merely to raise a question about it invites the retort that one is promoting oppressive behavior toward women (or is selling out to the patriarchy).

In such a situation, it would be refreshingly honest if feminists were to say, "Tough! You men had a good run for your money; now we've got the winning hand." Instead, feminists dress up their game in utopian jargon about greater justice—although, as many critics have pointed out, were the extremist feminist cause to succeed, it would be just another instance of one abusive group being replaced by another. The basic dynamics of the game would remain unchanged.

Lin Farley's book made a strong case for the need for a concept such as "sexual shakedown." Recounting story after story of women who had appalling experiences in their jobs, Farley demonstrated that some recourse was indeed needed for women whose work lives were made intolerable by the sexual aggression of men. But there is a long distance between objecting to the intolerable and demanding the comfortable, and we have crossed that space in an astonishingly short period of time. The concept of sexual harassment has by now become so pervasive that it is hard to imagine a time when the awareness of it, and the terminology it deploys, did not exist. Yet it seems as though the establishment of sexual harassment as a major category of illegal behavior is taking us into a future in which sexuality itself—as innuendo, as allusion, as a vital part of life—will increasingly be viewed as corrupt and illegitimate. Jeffrey Rosen captured this aspect of what is happening in a recent article on the incoherence of sexual harassment law, in which he commented that MacKinnon has "nearly won the war to transform Title VII from a law that bans sex discrimination to a law that bans sexual expression."[32]

Farley's work, however, also suggested another side of the coin. Some of the cases she discussed, such as that of Elizabeth Ray, who was employed by Congressman Wilbur Hays for a job for which she was unqualified, testify to the ways in which women have always been able to use their sexuality as a means to upward mobility. Is closing this avenue down (assuming that this were even possible) what women necessarily want? All women? Obviously the answer depends on whether one is on the receiving end of such perks or is left out, an angry "third party."

The issues lurking behind sexual harassment, then, have to do not only with fairness and equality in the public sphere but also with our expectations of the kind of society we want to live in, and of who we are—bodies and souls—as we go about our daily activities. These are basic matters, arousing passion and resentment, for the truth is that women are no more united than are men in their pursuit of their individual ends and, like men, will use whatever means it takes to achieve them.

But it is the nature of feminism, as of all other social movements, to propose ever more expansive definitions of the problems over which it seeks to arouse public outrage. Rhetoric makes its own demands, and one does not draw public attention to an issue by declaring it to be only peripheral to most people's lives. This is borne out by the literature on sexual harassment. In their voluminous writings, the proliferating group of experts in this new field blur major and minor infractions, conflate gross offensiveness with a mere word or gesture that made someone—perhaps only a bystander—"uncomfortable," and even suggest that rape is implicit, if not inherent, in every unwanted touch or look. The connection is made explicit in a typical brochure, distributed at Southern Illinois University at Carbondale, which states, "Sexual harassment can be as subtle as a look or as blatant as rape."[33] And even lawyers specializing in sexual harassment write without embarrassment about the difficulty of defining the offense. Comparing it to the "I know it when I see it" view of pornography, attorneys William Petrocelli and Barbara Kate Repa, for example, advise women that the "gut-check is the best barometer in knowing whether you've been sexually harassed at work."[34]

Because the Sexual Harassment Industry defines its concerns as being above all with the wrongs that men do to women, there has been little feminist complaint about its excesses, about the tense environment it creates, or about the many ways in which it infringes on freedom of expression and association. But as is becoming increasingly clear, the charge of sexual harassment can be leveled against anyone. Women (both heterosexual and lesbian) are suddenly finding themselves on the defendant's end of legislation they thought could apply only to men. As we will see, some women consider this a corruption of sound policies and seek not a reconsideration of those policies but their restriction to agents of the "patriarchy," so that women may safely be kept out of their reach. To "feminists accused of sexual harassment" (to adopt Jane Gallop's catchy phrase), the landscape of sexual harassment law may look a bit different now. But to critics such as myself, women's ensnarement in the trap of sexual harassment allegations is simply a consequence of wrongheaded policies, wrong even when they target men, as was originally intended.

The power of the charge of sexual harassment is, at the present moment, enormous. It can unleash formidable institutional forces against an alleged harasser, often with a complete absence of due process. Institutions, which, as outlined above, are required by law to take allegations seriously, go into action as soon as the words "sexual harassment" are uttered. Southern Illinois's brochure, for example, contains not a single word of warning about filing false charges of this extremely subjective offense. To the contrary, it promotes vigilantism: "All members of the university community are encouraged to speak out when they see, hear of, or experience incidents of sexual harassment." For the accused, consequences can be so grave that the only way to justify them, it would seem, is for accusers and their advisers to magnify the harm supposedly inflicted on the person who claims to have been harassed. And this is what has been done, as "complainants" are rapidly transformed into "victims" and "victims" of sexual harassment gain the status of "survivors," tantamount to those who have suffered brutal assault, torture, or persecution.[35]

Not to be outdone, psychology has joined in the fray, as scholars refer to the "grieving" that women who have experienced sexual harassment must be "allowed" to do (preferably with the help of support groups and counseling services).[36] Even post-traumatic stress disorder is now routinely attributed to "victims" of sexual harassment, and therapists regularly testify to that effect.[37] It has been said, with a good deal of accuracy, that sexual harassment is the "whiplash injury of the nineties," as lawyers and opportunistic plaintiffs cash in on the available damages. But it is no laughing matter that a professor making this comment in class might well find himself branded a sexual harasser. Moreover, the advent of sexual harassment regulations is having an inhibiting effect on the free circulation of words and ideas on campus, as universities twist themselves out of shape writing policies that attempt, oxymoronically, to guarantee academic and expressive freedom while facilitating—as is required by law—charges of hostile-environment harassment.

It was probably only to be expected that sexual harassment vigilantism would be extended to the attempt to ban, or otherwise regulate, consensual relations between individuals who occupy "hierarchically" distinct positions relative to one another. This ban, increasingly put into effect in colleges and universities, can apply to administrators and their staff, to professors and students, to graduate teaching assistants or lab assistants and their students, and so on down the line—to anyone in a "hierarchically superior" position vis-à-vis any other person in the school or workplace. After all, according to MacKinnon, "economic power is to sexual harassment as physical force is to rape."[38] The banning of "asymmetrical" relations shows what can happen when such pronouncements are taken seriously and when a movement explicitly committed to erasing the boundaries between the private and the public spheres is allowed to influence policy-makers.

Chapter 2

The Sexual Harassment Industry

☙❧

[S]exual harassment constitutes one of academe's most persistent and serious violations of human rights.

BILLIE WRIGHT DZIECH AND LINDA WEINER,
The Lecherous Professor

No issue can make it into the limelight as a major social problem without the attention of the media and an intellectual support system in the academy. Television and print journalism, which for as long as anyone can remember have devoted rapt attention to tales of power, sex, fear, and money, seek legitimacy by shoring up their reports with the work of scholars and specialists. It is this work that takes tales of harassment out of the realm of the merely newsworthy and into the more substantial world of preeminent social issues of the day. No wonder, then, that scores of books about sexual harassment in the workplace and the academy have appeared in the past two decades.[1] Most offer practical instruction for administrators, resting their case on the sort of rhetorical claims exemplified by the epigraph I have selected for this chapter. They make very repetitious reading. Nonetheless, they are worth careful study for the inside view they yield of the Sexual Harassment Industry's sense of vocation, and of its mode of operation in the academic setting.

From this large body of literature, I propose to single out one typical example for detailed analysis here: *Sexual Harassment on Campus: A Guide for Administrators, Faculty, and Students.*[2] This volume, published in 1997, was edited by Bernice R. Sandler and Robert J. Shoop, a professor of educational law. Their book is much more than a mine of information. It is a fascinating cultural artifact. Were it to be placed in a time capsule, it would some day in the future acquaint readers with a major aspect of life in late-twentieth-century America: its obsession with sexual misdeeds and its bizarre propensity for reconceptualizing personal relationships largely in terms of power. As such, the volume merits wide-ranging exposure. But for my own purposes here, its chief interest lies in its stated goal: to serve as a complete and up-to-date how-to guide for functionaries of the Sexual Harassment Industry on university campuses.

A close reading of the Sandler and Shoop book leaves one with an acute sense of disorientation. What has become of feminism's early assertion of the dignity and drive of women? How have these admirable qualities come to be transformed into the frailty of perpetual victims, desperate to grasp the helping hand of the law so as to be shielded from the harshness of life, especially from the unrelenting brutality of men? What remains of feminist mistrust of authority and bureaucratic meddling?

These are rhetorical points. But they raise immediate questions with respect to the issue of sexual harassment, questions that should and can be answered. How much quid pro quo harassment actually exists? How often are serious offenses against women committed—offenses that ought to be, and indeed have long been, considered violations of law? The Sandler and Shoop book admits that there is, in fact, very little harassment of this sort. On the other hand, how much harassment occurs that is of the "soft" kind, the kind that lies largely in the eye of the beholder and depends for its disclosure upon the prior cultivation of a heightened state of sensitivity in those at the receiving end of it? A great deal, it appears, thanks to the tireless efforts of the Sexual Harassment Industry, which is happy to take credit for having brought it to light. By now sexual harassment is generally construed to include not only unwanted erotic attention but also any questionable behavior on the basis of gender. Thus the SHI has succeeded in creating a situation in which either merely expressing romantic interest or engaging in the second kind of "soft" behavior—for example, commenting on someone's appearance, or making a general remark about women— arguably constitutes an unwanted sexist intrusion, made worse by the implicit suspicion that an aggressive carnal interest must be at work. Even if "wanted," both kinds of "soft" behavior—until recently considered unobjectionable—are now being challenged, as we shall see in examining some recent feminist writing later in this book.

In so enlarging both the idea and the reach of sexual harassment, the real intent of the SHI seems to be to create not only a public setting altogether devoid of sexual expression but one in which not even a passing sign of personal interest is tolerated for fear that any overt revelation of it might well be found offensive by the recipient. If the SHI were to succeed in this objective, chiefly by enthroning hostile-environment harassment as an established category of perception and action, it would surely move us step by inexorable step toward an antiseptic world where human relations would be so ritually structured that the very possibility of sexually charged encounters in school and workplace will have been eliminated because, by definition, such encounters will be assumed to be damaging to women.

Why it is imagined that women might actually wish to live in such a world is another intriguing question. My own observations of students in women's studies classes have led me to believe that years of exposure to feminist-promoted scare statistics have succeeded in imbuing many young women with a foreboding sense of living under constant threat from predatory men. The offer of an escape from this threat is a strong inducement to conformity to feminist blandishments. This, at least, is the more generous interpretation of the vigilante atmosphere promoted in the name of feminism. A less benign explanation is also possible: No social group selflessly refrains from using whatever weapons its historical moment makes available in order to gain money, position, fame (of a sort), and retribution, all in the name of equity and righteousness.

In the preface to their volume, Sandler and Shoop remind us how new a campus issue sexual harassment really is. They note, however, that by the late 1990s, we are in the "second stage" of policy development. Awareness of sexual harassment as a social problem can now be taken for granted, and it is time to inaugurate more effective measures to deal with it. The purported aim of their book is to guide "institutions involved in that process." Note the wording: institutions, not individuals. The latter are, in the main, treated as mere subjects of the institutional policies being formulated with the help of the SHI.

Sexual Harassment on Campus is a large book. It contains nineteen chapters covering, with much reiteration, matters of law, policy articulation and implementation, the setting up of formal and informal procedures, newly identified problems such as peer and electronic sexual harassment, and consensual relations policies, as well as a number of personal stories of "those whose lives have been changed as a result of sexual harassment" (p. v). The two editors review some disagreements among experts in their field, but their account of these disagreements clearly presupposes that a basic consensus exists: The experts are of one mind that sexual harassment is invariably "a very serious issue" and a "devastating" experience for those to whom it happens.

Perhaps it is their unanimity on this presupposition that prevents the many contributors to the volume from even alluding to other "serious issues." None of them acknowledges that false allegations, for instance, can be a problem, as can trivial complaints and opportunistic charges. None raises the fundamental question of how desirable the sanitized environment they favor as the end product of their efforts really is.[3]

Claims-Makers and Their Techniques

In attempting to understand the Sexual Harassment Industry, I have found the work of the sociologist Joel Best a useful analytical model.[4] Best has studied the social construction of victimization in American life over the past few decades. His perspective allows us to focus on the *interests* of claims-makers in seeing certain issues come to the fore, and the *resources* that provide them with the means to this end. These resources must be assembled if those setting out to construct a social problem are to achieve success for their claims. Best points out that "ownership" of a problem can be said to have occurred when a particular construction of the problem has gained wide acceptance, when claims-makers have succeeded in becoming the authority on that problem, and when control of social policy respecting that problem effectively rests in their hands.[5]

In this light, Bernice Sandler is one of the major "owners" of the sexual harassment issue. She has written over a hundred reports and given over two thousand presentations on this and related subjects. She is a consultant on sexual harassment and regularly serves as an expert witness in legal cases. Her name is permanently associated with both sexual harassment and the "chilly climate" that females are said to suffer in education. She has been called the "godmother" of efforts to ensure fairness for women in education.[6] It is not merely chance that most of the other contributors to Sandler and Shoop's volume (whether writing as "victims," as a few do, or as legal and academic experts) are, like Sandler herself, in professions enmeshed with the SHI.

Joel Best's work also gives us a better understanding of the ideological fervor animating sexual harassment as a public concern. Using a variety of recent "victim" categories, Best demonstrates how society's perception of the existence and gravity of a problem is constructed by media coverage and by activists' rhetorical strategies. The Sexual Harassment Industry, and the spate of instructional books published for its officials and functionaries, confirms Best's detailed description of how "the rhetoric of claims-making" works and how it develops hand in hand with organizational arrangements that sustain it and in turn are sustained by it.

As a kind of thought experiment, I tried to read Sandler and Shoop's book with a distanced curiosity about the exotic landscape that its chapters, collectively, set before me. From such a vantage point, Best's theoretical framework proved to be enormously illuminating. All "victims" of sexual harassment (most contributors quickly move from "alleged victim" to "victim" while still discussing the complaint phase of a case) are depicted as possessing certain characteristics in common. Typically they are members of "oppressed" identity groups, often suffering from multiple forms of ill treatment at the hands of sexism and other assorted isms. "Harassers," in turn, are shown to share another set of characteristics. The most significant of these is their maleness and, thus, their possession of "power," the latter attribute automatically making them suspect. "Victims," by contrast, are always innocent and, by definition, weak. These are conditions sine qua non. It does not matter that they have little connection with the real world in late-twentieth-century North America. What matters is that they promote the Sexual Harassment Industry's rhetorical staging of the struggle it intends to wage. Female victims and male harassers act out their eternal "power imbalance" as a plot in which mere "misunderstanding" is obviated as an explanation of episodes leading to charges of sexual harassment. In the SHI-ratified view, such an explanation is worth no more than the comment that "boys will be boys." Both are simply excuses for patriarchal abuse of women.

The construction of a social problem on a national scale begins with a "dialogue over meaning," a colloquy in which the media and specific interest groups play a key role.[7] Primary claims-makers, as Best calls them, initially "define a social problem to their own satisfaction and then present their claims in a fashion likely to draw media attention." Thereafter, the media, by spotlighting the problem's most dramatic features, transform the primary claims into secondary claims. This process is always shaped by a debate over meaning—that is to say, over the cultural significance attributed to the emerging problem. As a result, the worthiest issues often do not make it in the "social problems marketplace," and while this debate is going on, one cannot actually gauge the importance of a problem by the public attention it receives.[8]

The business of advancing claims about a problem is rarely static, Best explains, for

> claims evolve over a problem's history. Initial claims-making must persuade people that a problem exists. Once these early claims gain acceptance and the problem becomes well established, with its own place on the social policy agenda, claimants may begin reconstructing the problem. Reconstructing a social problem requires revising the claims-makers' rhetoric. In particular, claims-makers are likely to offer a new definition, extending the problem's domain or boundaries, and find new examples to typify just what is at issue.[9]

Sandler and Shoop's (jointly written) opening chapter, "What Is Sexual Harassment?" exhibits these very traits. It contains the full complement of stock phrases from SHI rhetoric: Sexual harassment is "traumatic"; it leads to forms of behavior "typical of posttraumatic stress disorder" (p. 16)—by now a standard claim. "Like rape" (the comparison is intended to make us overlook the enormous substantive differences), sexual harassment is frequently trivialized and its consequences ignored (p. 15). "Often," professors involved in relationships with students are " 'serial' harassers" (p. 17)—a tag no doubt chosen for its ominous association.

Though in these opening pages we are also, now and then, reassured that "most men do not harass" (p. 14), this insight is rapidly forgotten in later chapters, virtually all of which project a social scene evidently derived from Farley's and MacKinnon's delineation of patriarchy's unrelenting oppression of women. In this projection, women are men's victims, ever demeaned, abused, browbeaten, overpowered. It is this assumption that is the engine driving the book and the entire SHI.[10]

The overt contradiction between fact and rhetoric appears in Sandler and Shoop's very first paragraph: "[M]any university campuses are rife with sexual harassment. Although most administrators, faculty members, and students do not harass, sexual harassment is a problem on every campus" (p. 1). In addition to the paradox, here also is a characteristic turn of phrase, found in many later chapters as well: the concessive "although," a grudging nod to the real world in which sexual harassment actually looms small. To neutralize the concession, there follows a sampling of recent campus incidents—said to be "numerous" and to happen "often," "regularly," or "routinely" (pp. 1–2). "On many campuses, dormitories are hotbeds of sexual harassment" (p. 2). Which is it, then: that most people do not harass, or that universities are "rife" with instances of sexual harassment?

The authors next contend that sexual harassment is "an organizational and managerial problem, not a people problem," from which they conclude that it is capable of being controlled by means of "a well-planned, active program of anticipation and prevention" (p. 3). One can, of course, turn any "people problem" into a bureaucratic opportunity. All it takes is to create a punitive climate where so much is put at risk that everyone will shape up. The authors are not above making the threat explicit. Would administrators, rather than being "proactive," prefer to learn of alleged sexual harassment on their campuses "when they receive court papers or a notice of an impending federal investigation" (p. 2)? Would they like escalating insurance costs, difficulties in obtaining liability coverage, and adverse publicity? If not, there is no alternative to the "active program of anticipation and prevention" (p. 3) proposed and supervised by the SHI.

If it genuinely sought to protect women from the proclaimed harm of sexual harassment, the SHI would first of all strive to separate serious from trivial offenses. It would not set out to frighten women into believing that all public-sphere environments are "hostile" to them. Nor would it wish to see precious resources squandered on investigating flimsy allegations. But the SHI appears unwilling to make such distinctions, or to give up its tendency to conflate all cases of "uncomfortable" reactions relating to sex and gender.[11] Shoop speaks of the "right to be free from sexual harassment" (p. 42), and this seems a laudable principle until one rewrites his phrase as "the right to be free from feeling uncomfortable." That this rewriting is in fact warranted, and that it represents Shoop's real intent, can be taken from the following statement: "Although conduct that is merely offensive, such as the mere utterance of an epithet which engenders offensive [sic] feelings in an employee, is not actionable sexual harassment, according to *Harris,* no one single factor must be present to find actionable abusive or hostile environment workplace sexual harassment" (p. 42). What is this but an assurance to the putative victim or her protectors that "although" not every single utterance may be actionable, the law is vague enough to allow many avenues of redress?

In keeping with its mission of finding ways to elevate the trivial into the actionable, the book typically strikes a regretful note whenever it touches on issues such as academic liberties, freedom of speech, and the due-process rights of the accused. Not a single cautionary account is given of how an accused person's life was "transformed" by made-up charges (I will provide such cases further on), and no words of warning are uttered against students who find in allegations of sexual harassment an effective weapon against their professors or against one another.

In the same vein, Sandler and Shoop, in their opening chapter, slip easily from serious and specific charges to vague and loose allegations, each buttressed by figures we are not meant to question:

> About two percent of undergraduate women experience the most severe type of sexual harassment—direct or indirect threats or bribes for unwanted sexual activity from faculty or staff. For graduate women, the incidence for sexual harassment increases; between 30% to 40% report they have experienced *some form* of sexual harassment from faculty or administrators. (P. 13, my italics)

Are readers meant to overlook the easy transition to "some form of," attached to the larger figures and repeated throughout the volume? It seems that they are. SHI statistics—which one scholar summarizes without embarrassment as "anywhere from 30 percent to over 90 percent of women surveyed have been sexually harassed"[12]—are usually unconvincing precisely because lists of harassing actions include "some form of" offensive behavior, or "one negative incident" reported,[13] or "one [unspecified] incident of sexual harassment during their time at the university" (p. 13). It is not difficult to see what such sleight of hand is meant to accomplish: It makes one embarrassing word or gesture, perhaps a single incident in four years of university attendance, count as much as a serious case of quid pro quo sexual extortion or actual assault. Each of these, without distinction, is "some form of sexual harassment."[14]

Women's "authority of experience" (a subject to which I will return in chapter 7 below) is relied on throughout the book. Sandler and Shoop tell us that "[w]omen seem less confused about sexual harassment, whether or not they use the term, than men. They know when they are uncomfortable" (p. 6). Here, again, the characteristic slippage of ideologically charged language occurs, from "sexual harassment" to "uncomfortable," the latter becoming the standard by which the former is measured. Women "know the difference between a witty comment and a sexual joke" (p. 6). Presumably, women who know this can never intentionally make false charges, which explains why no more than (estimating generously) two pages in the whole book are devoted to the subject of wrongful accusations.

There follows the by-now obligatory discussion of "power." "What makes sexual harassment different from ordinary flirting is that sexual harassment occurs in the context of a power imbalance" (p. 7). This insight, it must be recalled, is the central feminist contribution to the discussion of obnoxious behavior in the workplace. From its early appearance in the writings of Farley and MacKinnon, patriarchal "power" was a key element in the rhetoric developing around sexual harassment, and this theme has clearly not outlived its usefulness over the past few decades. "It is the power relationship that characterizes the insidious nature of sexual harassment," Sandler and Shoop write (p. 7). Dziech and Weiner, in their well-known 1984 book *The Lecherous Professor,* had depicted faculty members as particularly culpable on this score: "College faculty seldom admit one basic truth about their work: few professions guarantee so much potential for exerting control over so many other human beings."[15]

Of course, the one kind of power never mentioned at all is the lure of sexual attraction, a power women have always understood and used. The SHI, playing innocent for the purpose, pretends that women do not employ this traditional asset. Nothing a woman does, not the way she dresses or how she acts or what she says, bears in any way on the "sexual harassment" she may experience. The message is clear: Women are never at fault. They need not examine their own ways. They need only to learn when and how to file complaints, although, interestingly, even this recourse is never construed as a "power" in their possession. Only men have power, and it is men, not women, who need to change.

Domain Expansion

A well-established social problem, Joel Best has argued, serves claims-makers as a bountiful resource:

> Once the initial claims have been validated, they offer a foundation upon which additional claims can be constructed. These new claims can be linked to the established problem: claims-makers present the new, peripheral issues as "another form of," "essentially the same as," "the moral equivalent of," or "equally damaging as" the original, core problem. In turn, some of these claims are validated, offering an even broader foundation for further rounds of claims-making.[16]

Of all these forms of claims-making, Best continues, the most hege-
monic is the defining and naming of a problem. Definitions establish a
topic's "domain." Domain statements, whether calling a problem "new"
or of long standing but only recently "recognized" (as in the charge
that a "chilly climate" still cripples girls academically), attract interest
precisely because they claim to identify a phenomenon that can now be
recognized by all.[17]

Claims-makers' definitions, moreover, do much more than merely
give a problem a name. They also give it a slant. An example of this
practice is the frequent assertion, made throughout Sandler and
Shoop's book, that "misunderstanding" and "miscommunication" are
to be rejected as possible explanations of events now classified as sexual
harassment. Similarly, a not so subtle bias is evident in the repeated
reminders of how difficult it is for victims to come forward with accusations: They expect not to be believed; they suffer from great emotional
stress; they fear retaliation (which would be a violation of federal civil
rights law). Such claims are fairly transparently meant to translate into
that shibboleth of the SHI: "Women don't lie" about sexual harassment
or rape.

Along with the slant or spin of claims goes their steady enlargement.
In the case of the SHI, the most far-reaching example of such "domain
expansion" is the extension of sexual harassment from quid pro quo to
hostile-environment harassment, that nebulous and endlessly negotia-
ble category of unwelcome looks, comments, gestures, and even opinions (whether positive or negative), into which virtually all workplace
and academic interactions can be made to fit. The catalog of items cons-
tituting sexual harassment given in Sandler and Shoop's initial chapter,
"What Is Sexual Harassment?" perfectly illustrates the domain expansion that has already occurred. The list—typical of similar ones found
in virtually all the SHI literature—extends from "sexual innuendos,
comments, or bantering" and "humor or jokes about sex or females in
general" to "asking for sexual behavior," "touching a person," "giving a
neck or shoulder massage," "leering or ogling, such as 'elevator eyes,' "
calling women names like "hot stuff" or "cutie pie," "sexual graffiti,"
"sexual mail, notes, e-mail," or phone calls, and "laughing at or not
taking seriously someone who experiences sexual harassment" right up
to stalking, threats, and "attempted or actual sexual assault or abuse"
(pp. 6–7). It is the indiscriminate nature of this list (here only partially
quoted) that gives away the SHI's eagerness to extend its reach.

In a significant move toward this goal, Sandler, together with Jean

O'Gorman Hughes, in 1988 put out the first national report on the subject of "peer harassment."[18] Now, in *Sexual Harassment on Campus,* Sandler contributes a chapter on "Student-to-Student Sexual Harassment," which she declares to be the next major growth area requiring intervention by the SHI. "Peer harassment," she writes:

> can be a single serious incident or a series of incidents. Legally the behavior must be serious enough to interfere with a student's ability to learn, her or his living conditions, or any of the opportunities provided by the institution. However, institutions need to deal with all levels of peer harassment whether they rise to the legal definition or not. (P. 53)

Peer harassment, Sandler affirms, "sets the stage for campus rape" (p. 55). Once again, her emphasis on maximizing problems has succeeded in extending the limits of competence for the SHI. Incidentally, despite her inclusive title and a brief acknowledgment that all combinations of harasser and harassee are possible (p. 51), Sandler has nothing to say about women as aggressors.

Sandler also displays her gift for concept-stretching by declaring that rape is "the most extreme form of peer harassment" (p. 51). Could it not equally well be said that murder is the most extreme form of conflict resolution, and that it has the same effect? The point here seems to be to suggest, by means of semantic contamination, that a seamless continuum exists between passing comments, criticism in the classroom (which "silences" women students), and criminal sexual assault.

Many of the other essays in the volume also contain suggestions that sexual harassment is the precursor of rape (both acts being defined as essentially about "power," not sex). The frequent use of the honorific "survivor" to refer to those who have experienced "sexual harassment" at first hand invites the reader to elide distinctions, to treat all instances of sexual harassment as "equally damaging as" brutal sexual assault. Such claims violate empirical and conceptual boundaries, and they are intended to do so. They enable the SHI to greatly extend the need for its services, as increasing numbers of professionals are instructed in how to discover and identify proliferating instances of sexual offenses. Even more seriously, these claims inevitably lead to an erosion of the presumption of innocence in an atmosphere of hysteria generated by assertions about university campuses "rife" with sexual rapacity.

But it is important to understand why some feminists insist that there is a continuum of male sexual dominance of women, at the low end of which lie mere clumsy overtures and passes and at the high end (progressing through more unsavory grabbing and threats) of which loom rape, battery, and even murder. Their reason is evident. Once one agrees to this proposition, it is very hard to make light of the charges at the lower extreme, since even the most innocuous sexual overtures (easily rebuffed with no consequences) are contaminated by the shadow of the violent sexual attack at the other end of the spectrum.

When people disagree over how to think and talk about men and male sexuality, it is probable that they are at odds because they are looking at different parts of the continuum and drawing generalizations from their particular focus. It is true that some men rape and batter. It is also true that most do not. How can one do justice to both of these assertions? If one's concern is above all with protecting women from assault, it will matter little that injustices are done now and then to "nice guys" whose words or gestures were misunderstood. But when does such a miscarriage of justice begin to count? When will men, too, be viewed as fellow beings with lives, feelings, and fears that matter? Are we really making things better by threatening men with possible loss of job and reputation as punishment for a sexual overture or comment at the workplace or in the academy?

Those who would answer "yes" to this question are pretending two things: (1) that women are more deserving of concern and empathy than men; and (2) that by adopting such a course of action, we are succeeding in protecting women. Since the first position is immoral by any standard and the second is highly questionable, neither would seem to offer any ground for supporting measures designed to achieve small gains for women at great costs to men. Why, then, should so much of the SHI literature insist on both the range and the significance of sexual harassment?

One answer is obvious. A key element in the construction of a social problem is, of course, its size. The larger the problem, the greater the attention it can legitimately command.[19] In the pursuit of magnitude, elastic definitions go hand in hand with inflated statistics, each exaggeration reinforcing the other. In Sandler and Shoop's introductory chapter, for example, we are told that 20 to 30 percent of undergraduate women "have experienced some form of sexual harassment from faculty, administrators, or other staff" (p. 13). The lower figure, we hear, translates into 1.4 million students "experiencing sexual harassment." Again: From 20 to 50 percent of women faculty have reported "some form of sexual harassment from other faculty members" (p. 13).

Impressive numbers, these. But what if we were to rewrite those sentences as follows: "1.4 million students and 20 to 50 percent of women faculty claim to have experienced something that in light of current definitions might—if repeated often enough—be legally actionable as 'sexual harassment'"? Or: "claim to remember comments about their appearance that they took as compliments at the time but that later consciousness-raising made them understand should be viewed as demeaning and discriminatory"? Or: "remember expressions of sexual interest that, as it happened, they did not wish to reciprocate"? These are very different kinds of assertions, calling for very different responses. Plainly, the language in which the SHI presents its numerical evidence is meant to keep us from suspecting the possibility (probably the likelihood) that innocuous interactions are nowadays being retroactively interpreted as objectionable "sexual harassment."

Such rhetorical maneuvers ("range claims," Joel Best calls them) are intended to suggest that the problem at issue pervades the entire social structure. Range claims are useful because they allow activists to depict their problem as having reached, or being about to approach, "epidemic proportions." This, in turn, serves to create the impression that the solution to the newly identified problem must be recognized as a common cause, demanding the attention of all decent citizens. As the reach of sexual harassment claims is extended, charges of wrongful behavior move from employers and professors to peers and even to the school yard. Not long ago, the country was treated to the spectacle of a six-year-old North Carolina boy being suspended from his first-grade classroom for a day because he had kissed a female classmate on the cheek. We must now be grateful to the U.S. Department of Education for having reassured us officially, through its Office of Civil Rights 1997 *Guidance* that "[a] kiss on the cheek by a first grader does not constitute sexual harassment."[20] This particularly absurd case also provides a telling example of the antiheterosexual bias that has imbued the current SHI from its beginnings: Surely a six-year-old girl kissing another little girl would not have been the target of such vigilance.

In his chapter "The Legal Context of Sexual Harassment on Campus," Robert Shoop states that "[i]n the hope of achieving harmony, the majority of us voluntarily allow laws to regulate our behavior" and further, that "new laws are needed to respond to the emerging view of what is right and what is wrong" (p. 23). But is this an accurate representation of the public's view? Or does it merely express SHI dogma? Shoop's bland words conceal the reality of what is being attempted here, which is a modification of public behavior in accordance with the patronizing assumption that women always need protection from aggressive males. This agenda of social transformation is fundamental to all that the SHI undertakes to do. It explains why there has never (to my knowledge) been a workshop on, say, how to keep oneself from taking offense at trivial slights or innuendos, or how to respond to an unwanted sexual overture in a spirited way that ends the problem. Instead, the suggested (and, increasingly, mandatory) workshops and training sessions are designed to bring an ever greater range of behavior within the purview of sexual harassment regulations. They are meant to fill in the "gaps," as Brenda Seals explicitly states in her article in the Sandler and Shoop volume (p. 66), thus indicating the SHI's totalizing aspirations for social reform.[21]

"There are always people who continue to fight against a new value, even when it is passed into law," Shoop warns us, trying to inoculate readers against developing a critical view of the SHI. By implication, he stigmatizes critics of the SHI as reactionary opponents of social change: "While some people are fighting to gain equal treatment for women, others are resisting any change in the role and status of women" (p. 24). Rhetorically, he asks, "How much sexual harassment must a person endure before he or she has a case that will hold up in court?" (p. 39). But is "sexual harassment" as defined today really a kind of affliction that its victims must "endure" until it meets the standard of litigation—a standard that is, Shoop implies, unreasonably high? If the answer is "yes," then college women must depend for their peace of mind on the SHI's skill at detecting and publicizing cases of sexual harassment that do not rise to the legal definition.

At least Shoop's rhetorical question here encompasses "he or she." In his initial chapter with Sandler, by contrast, harassment in practice seems always to go in one direction only. Rarely is there any mention of cases of women students pursuing professors, harassing male students, or making the lives of other women unpleasant. The SHI's commitment to the idea of "power imbalances" inherent in "patriarchal" society compels it to ignore that these things ever happen, or at least that they have any significance. In such a perspective, an individual woman's "professional power" is always trumped by a male's (including a male student's) "social power." Several essayists in the volume assure us that this is so.

In this conviction, they can rely upon well-established precedents. More than fifteen years ago, Katherine A. Benson, in an essay in the influential feminist journal *Signs,* attempted to expand the domain of sexual harassment by coining some new terms that could still be accommodated within the prevailing feminist worldview.[22] "Peer harassment" is Benson's phrase (by now widely adopted) for harassment between equals. "Contrapower harassment" is how she labels male students' words and gestures toward female professors. Unlike in traditional "power harassment," in the "contrapower" type the harasser apparently has "less formal power" than the professor being harassed. Benson points out that such harassment may occur "at a time when the student does have some measure of power over the professor" (e.g., when filling out teaching evaluations). Thus, this type of harassment is made to fit within existing definitions that see the "abuser" as "always more powerful than the victim." As Benson puts it, "A man student has more potential earning power, he may be physically stronger, and he has the general prerogative of male dominance." Nor is the effect on the professor trivial: "Harassment contests a professor's stature and authority and may interfere with her work."[23] The antiheterosexual bias present in the entire SHI was clearly expressed in this early essay: "Hierarchy in a sexist society makes power harassment by heterosexual men invisible but brings contrapower harassment by heterosexual men into sharp relief."[24]

In a 1986 essay, Catharine MacKinnon reiterated the ultimate feminist line on sexual harassment that her own prior work had done so much to legitimize: "Basically, it is done by men to women regardless of relative position on the formal hierarchy."[25] One might think that such a contention cannot survive critical analysis. But it would be wrong not to appreciate its resonance. So tidy and predictable a version of reality has great intuitive appeal and is likely to be persuasive to many people seeking refuge from an indeterminate adult world in which individual responsibility must be acknowledged, and the complexity and unpredictability of human interactions are, for better or worse, engaged.

The "Good Policy"

How should universities cope with the problem of sexual harassment? Bernice Sandler's essay "Elements of a Good Policy," in her volume with Shoop, begins by declaring that an organized and tightly controlled effort is indispensable to institutions if they wish to protect themselves from liability. There must be "broad planning," and a comprehensive policy prohibiting all forms of sexual harassment; informal procedures alongside formal ones for the launching of complaints; ongoing education and prevention projects; and a "process to continually monitor all aspects of the program" (p. 104). Though she acknowledges that "technically, any policy dealing with discrimination would also cover sexual harassment" (p. 104), Sandler defends the "separate policy" approach to sexual harassment.

In this connection, the Office of Civil Rights is mentioned repeatedly in the SHI literature as the authority for the proposition that institutions bear the burden of responsibility in sexual harassment matters. It is interesting, therefore, to consider the new sexual harassment *Guidance,* released by this agency in March 1997. The document at least recognizes the rights of the accused and also is careful to be sex neutral in its language. But its main arguments reflect much the same ideological slant that governs Sandler and Shoop's work. And it contains some odd ambiguities of its own. In response to the frequently made claim that Title IX of the 1972 Education Amendments (which prohibits discrimination on the basis of sex in schools that receive federal money) "requires" schools to have a sexual harassment policy, the OCR document states, "[A] school does not have to have a policy and procedure specifically addressing sexual harassment, as long as its non-discrimination policy and procedures for handling discrimination complaints *are effective in eliminating all types of sex discrimination.*"[26]

The problem here is with the scale of expectations. Obviously, no policy can be guaranteed to "eliminate" all unwanted behavior. Since the standard of efficacy refers to *results,* not *intent,* mere endeavors at generic nondiscrimination can never be sufficient to address the particular wrongs of sexual offenses. Much work therefore remains to be done, and the SHI is best prepared to do it. It can draft "proactive" antiharassment policy, implement it, and run training sessions and workshops—none of which is actually "required" by Title IX; rather, all these efforts are legitimized by the impossibly high standard of zero tolerance for sex "discrimination." The OCR *Guidance* itself stresses that it is "incorrect" to conclude from its regulations that sexual harassment must always be dealt with "under an explicit sexual harassment policy rather than by use of a general disciplinary or behavior code." University officials may use "their own judgment regarding how best to handle the situation." On the other hand, sex discrimination must be "eliminated."[27] It is this state of ambiguity, in which "harassment" and "discrimination" come to be used interchangeably, that enables the

SHI to step in and guide the hands of uncertain and nervous administrators.

Of the many chapters in Sandler and Shoop's volume describing procedures for investigating and resolving sexual harassment complaints, the best that can be said is that they offer practical instruction likely to be useful to individuals interested in joining the SHI bureaucracy. They provide detailed advice for acting on the many legal and sublegal possibilities presented by the university's interface with harassment law, originally written for the workplace but awkwardly undergoing adaptation to the education scene. Like other titles in this still-expanding genre, the Sandler and Shoop book gives much concrete information about all this, but on page after page the intended readers—academic officers, it will be remembered—are urged to avail themselves of the specialized services of the SHI.

From my own perspective, one of the most telling features of the Sandler and Shoop volume is what it does *not* discuss. In its nineteen chapters, hardly a line is wasted on the rights of the accused. This is no exaggeration. The word "innocent" never appears in relation to any "alleged harasser," and presumption of innocence is entirely absent. The basic question is never raised whether it is really desirable to create an academic climate in which trivial complaints—as indeed, judging by the SHI literature itself, most accusations turn out to be—are encouraged.

By contrast, several of the chapters make much of the "problem" of "victims" who fail to complain. Reading for the dozenth or so time about the "reluctant complainant" and how institutions must do all they can to "encourage" the reporting of "sexual harassment activity" (p. 141)—this time in Elsa Kircher Cole's chapter "Formal Complaints"—my attention was caught by the assumptions underlying this "problem." Cole, who is general counsel for the University of Michigan and is identified in the book as a specialist in higher education law and sexual harassment, begins by stressing the benefits of filing formal complaints, for, she insists, "[t]he type of disciplinary punishment available under the informal complaint procedure may be too limited to satisfy the alleged victim" (p. 141). She appears to find nothing wrong with giving to the "alleged victim" the right to declare (as is routinely done in practice) what is to be a satisfactory punishment for the accused. One can only hope that the "victim" is more than "alleged" by the time said victim is handed the power to ruin someone's career. Though Cole acknowledges the need for fair treatment and "basic due process," her fundamental tenet is that complainants must always be protected from alleged harassers' presumed tendency toward "retaliation." She offers no discussion of the possibility that charges may be filed as a result of a complainant's own desire to "retaliate"—say, because of a poor grade, an ideological disagreement, an unrequited infatuation, or a personal conflict (some telling examples of which we will encounter in chapter 4 below). Reading Cole, one would think that only men and other offenders in positions of "power" engage in "retaliation." Students never do.

Cole is careful to write "his or her" and "alleged" in all the appropriate places. But her bias is obvious. Complaints are to be encouraged and their processing facilitated. Even where statutes of limitations have expired, she suggests ways of bypassing them if a complaint "appears" to be valid: "The untimeliness of a complaint [because, for example, a professor is on sabbatical or a student is in a foreign exchange program] does not mean an institution can do nothing about apparent inappropriate behavior" (p. 142). Note the usual verbal slippage: It is no longer "harassment" but simply "apparent inappropriate behavior" that warrants a stretching of the rules.

> The alleged harasser can still be confronted with his or her actions and warned not to continue them, and the harasser's unit can receive educational training about the institution's policies against sexual harassment. A sealed envelope can also be placed in the alleged harasser's file in the complaint administrator's office, not to be opened unless there are new allegations of sexual harassment against him or her. (P. 143)

Clearly, mere allegations are enough, as far as Cole is concerned, to warrant the "sealed envelope," the confrontation, the training session, and all the rest. Possible malevolence or opportunism on the alleger's part is never considered. Again, no words are wasted on rights of the accused.[28]

A major underpinning of the legitimacy of these procedures is the "devastation" said to be sustained by victims of sexual harassment. Without this claim, it would be all too easy to notice the bizarre disproportion between the pettiness of most offenses and the official apparatus set in motion by complaints about them.

This should make one think again about the theme of complainants' "powerlessness." What actually happens when a complaint is made? What are the immediate consequences of such a move? The picture that emerges from Cole's and other chapters is not promising. Before any formal investigation is even initiated, files are created; various campus administrators are informed; and an extensive "notification" process gets underway—all this without formally charging the supposed culprit, who, as we will see in part II, may in fact be kept in the dark for weeks or months that something is afoot against him (or, less frequently, her). The SHI literature wastes no comments on pointing out the prejudicial bent of this sequence of events; there is no awareness that the complaint process is itself a powerful weapon in the hands of—supposedly power-less—"complainants," regardless of the merits of their charges.

Nor do we hear of any warning that might be given to complainants concerning the consequences to them should their charges turn out to be worthless (or even patently false). And nowhere is it suggested that their accusations should be made under oath. Such cautions, it seems, are undesirable because they might be construed as "retaliation" and could tend to "discourage" complainants, something the SHI is explic-itly committed to preventing. (It may be noted here that it was not until early 1998 that one institution of higher learning, Simon Fraser University, in Canada, faced with a public relations disaster over its pursuit of a sexual harassment charge, revised its policy so as to include punishment for false or frivolous accusations.[29] It is clear that such a reform, though vitally necessary, works against the SHI's general en-deavor to promote complaints at every turn.)

And who will conduct the investigations? Cole thinks it advisable "to use a few trained individuals rather than committees" to inquire into charges (p. 144). These investigators should be male and female, work-ing together. "They should be skilled at asking the type of questions that extract needed information from reluctant individuals" (p. 144). In other words, a team of "experts" goes into action, armed with ex-traordinary, and entirely extralegal, powers, to launch a process that—it must be realized—can lead to censure and dismissal.

Cole believes that "[g]ood investigators know that they are neutral and represent the institution, not the alleged victim or the alleged ha-rasser. They do not come to any conclusion until the investigation is complete" (p. 144). But this declaration stands in blatant contradiction to what these functionaries routinely do. We will explore their investiga-tory procedures in part II. The cases discussed in chapter 4 below clearly show the consequences, for the accused, once the SHI begins to act on its assumption of guilt. Here it need only be noted, again, that nowhere in the Sandler and Shoop book is this assumption treated as a serious threat to a fair investigation, not to mention to the moral and social climate of the university.

In discussing standards of proof, Bernice Sandler is quick to remind us that unlike in criminal cases, the criterion of guilt in administrative procedures (as in civil suits) is not "beyond a reasonable doubt" but merely "a preponderance of evidence." It is enough that "a reasonable person would assume that the events did or did not occur given the preponderance of evidence" (p. 113). One wonders who this reasonable person might be. A critic like myself? Or Sandler and her coauthors? In view of the assumptions embraced by the SHI, "reasonable persons" can bring a lifelong career to an end in disgrace because (to use another metaphor endorsed by Sandler and Shoop's book) they decide that the scales "tip" a bit on one side rather than on another.

An investigation may lead to an inconclusive result. But this does not necessarily end matters for the "alleged" harasser, for records will be kept of all the charges made against him, and a dossier created for unspecified use in case of future "similar allegations" (p. 146). Repeatedly *Sexual Harassment on Campus* offers advice about the necessity of maintaining "central files" to which the accused often is not granted access (as in the case of the notorious "locked box" containing allegations, to which alleged harassers did not have access at Cornell University).[30] "Insufficient evidence" is a verdict the contributors to Sandler and Shoop's volume heartily dislike; some of them are surprisingly candid about suggesting ways and means of prolonging a case so that it may eventually end satisfactorily—from their point of view, of course. "Because an inconclusive result may seem to indicate a lack of commitment to eradicating sexual harassment"—and what an astonishing admission this is of the bias driving the entire process—"the administration may wish to schedule a workshop for the alleged harasser's unit" (p. 147). Thus the "alleged" offender's whole department undergoes sensitivity training not because of one member's confirmed misconduct but rather as the by-product of a failure to find that any misconduct occurred.

Can one defend oneself by establishing good character? Such an effort is made difficult: "Character evidence usually is not helpful in determining credibility. Of more use is expert testimony as to whether the complainant's behavior was consistent with that of a sexual harassment victim" (p. 151). This extraordinary statement is calmly made (by Cole) as if it were not, in itself, an inducement to violation of due process.

SHI spokespersons are ever ready to testify about how well the accused fits the established harasser's "profile." A hair-raising compendium of that "profile" is offered by Dziech and Weiner in their chapter "The Portrait of the Artist" in *The Lecherous Professor*. Their description of two types, the "public" and the "private" harasser, effectively covers the entire range of professorial styles and behaviors.[31] Meanwhile, as we will see in examining some actual allegations in chapter 4 below, the complainant might well be training herself in correct victim behavior by reading SHI-produced tracts made available for the purpose by the university's own sexual harassment officers. A script is being played out. All the characters have roles to perform. The dénouement is foreshadowed early on, as in a melodrama.

In a brief nod to due process, Cole concedes, "If there is not sufficient cause to believe sexual harassment occurred, the administration should take appropriate steps to restore the reputation of the alleged harasser"—for example, by informing all involved that "sufficient cause was not found." Even so, the ubiquitous "workshop" is recommended, "to educate the alleged harasser's unit about the subject, and to demonstrate commitment to ending sexual harassment on campus" (p. 147). One can think of few other areas in which even the failure to find any evidence of wrongdoing is always accompanied by protestations of total commitment to ferreting it out nonetheless.

Use and Abuse

Judging by the specialized literature, the world of sexual harassment is a perfectly transparent one—at least to the trained eye. Villains and victims are easily identified. Rarely does the evidence suggest ambiguity, nuance, or conflicting interpretations. Doubt is all but absent. In this crystalline world, Anne Truax (a sexual harassment officer at the University of Minnesota and the author of a brief chapter called "Informal Complaints") is an unusual presence, for she raises the possibility that someone may actually take advantage of a sexual harassment complaint for ulterior purposes—to be rid of an undesirable employee, for instance (p. 159). "Complainants and administrators, anxious to be free of an obstreperous person, often confuse sexual harassment with ordinary, nonsexual harassment," she writes, "which may be difficult to bear and irritating, but not illegal and not subject to the sexual harassment policy" (p. 159).

Truax also acknowledges that complainants themselves may sometimes be moved to action by unrelated pressures—a situation common enough, one suspects, but largely ignored by the SHI: "Is the complaint a means of postponing a threatened adverse personnel decision? Would she have filed if she didn't think she was losing her job? A complainant may accept or even participate in an office atmosphere that is offensive, but file a complaint if her probationary reviews are marginal" (p. 159). Truax here allows us an all too brief glimpse of the everyday reality of mixed motives, personal resentments on various sides, and unadmitted private agendas familiar in every setting, a scene that has little in common with the stereotypes of male villains and female victims that populate most of the SHI literature.

The possibility certainly exists for sexual harassment charges to be used strategically by administrators to get rid of people they don't much like.[32] The question is, Are charges of sexual harassment more vulnerable to this sort of misuse than other charges? I believe the answer is "yes." The controversy over President Clinton's alleged behavior provides a good illustration, as people condemn him or defend him not because of his alleged actions but because of a priori positions they hold in relation to his administration.

Many commentators have pointed out the initial feminist silence in response to Paula Jones's allegations against the president. That silence is usually attributed to unwillingness on the part of feminists to denounce their best political hope in Washington. Legal scholars such as Susan Estrich have even gone to great lengths to explain why Paula Jones's allegations should not be treated as a case of sexual harassment; Estrich rather unabashedly admits it's all politics.[33] More recently, Gloria Steinem wrote an op-ed piece in the *New York Times* arguing that men are entitled to one grope and defending the president because he recognizes that "no" means "no."[34] Steinem thereby confirmed the views of those denouncing the hypocrisy of feminists for abdicating their usual vigilance toward men's behavior when, opportunistically, it suited them to do so. Where was she until now, critics have asked, when charges of sexual harassment were running out of control? Presumably in the same support group as most feminists who were happy to see such charges play havoc with men's lives in the workplace and in schools—as long as their own allies weren't targeted.[35] Thus, the perception of feminist double standards appears valid.

If existing rhetoric already reveals the vulnerability of the entire sexual harassment arena to double and triple reinterpretations and guesses, it is perfectly reasonable to fear tactical use of this wonderfully vague weapon when and if someone wants to get a particular man—

whatever the motivation. This is what Michael Crichton's novel *Disclosure* was about—not sexual harassment in itself but sexual harassment charges as a weapon (in this case, the real issue was a corporate struggle for power and had nothing to do with sex, which was merely a tool in the hands of the villain-heroine). Similarly, in David Mamet's play *Oleanna*, sexual harassment charges are used as part of a more complex pattern by which a student works out (with the help of a feminist support group) her emotional problems and emerges "empowered." That is precisely the point: Accusations of sexual harassment are unusually well suited to serve as a weapon. A law that rests so comfortably on the victim's say-so and others' reactions to that say-so, a law that deals so cavalierly with evidence, is ideally situated for abuse. In fact, it could transpire that abuse is the normal use made of such a law and the regulations it has spawned.

Feminist Mythology

Like other members of the SHI, Sandler and Shoop no doubt think of their work as a contribution to social problem-solving. A better case can, however, be made for the suggestion that their book belongs to the vast literature of contemporary feminist myths. Indeed, mythology is alluded to in their volume, in a chapter by Susan J. Scollay and Carolyn S. Bratt, called "Untying the Gordian Knot of Academic Sexual Harassment." Although the title metaphor is inappropriate to their purpose, given the very unfeminist way in which Alexander the Great solved the problem of the Gordian knot, their essay takes us directly into the realm of mythology.

Seen through the prism of their mythical view, the university is a hotbed of prejudice, where the "systemic sexism of contemporary society" is replicated and where "[e]ntrenched and institutionalized sexism is intertwined with the threads of academic classism and the bifurcated decision-making structure of the academy" (p. 274). Tinkering with piecemeal reform is useless. Nothing but radical overhaul can alter "the prevailing sexist organizational culture and institutional climate" (p. 276), for "the academy remains an essentially single sex institution. It is male-dominated, and that domination exerts itself in both numbers and power" (p. 274).[36]

"[S]ystemic sexism," we learn from Scollay and Bratt, is displayed by professors who "often" create "highly sexualized classroom climates" and engage in sexually harassing behavior toward their students

(p. 264). Fruitless though it is to impugn a mythic image, I might state here, for what it is worth, that in all my years in academe (starting as an undergraduate in 1960), I never encountered a professor who "sexualized" the classroom. Once, in a graduate course in French literature, an attractive and interesting professor referred to "governmental organs." I smiled, and the professor said, "Not that sort of organ." Today his remark might well be considered harassment, but the fact remains that he read my expression correctly, for I had indeed made the association. At no time have I met a professor, male or female, who embraced ideas (much less students) in the name of an erotics of pedagogy as does Jane Gallop, whose confessions as a feminist accused of sexual harassment we will examine in chapter 5 below.

It is hard to know where and how to begin to respond to Scollay and Bratt's intimations, so fantastic is their characterization of contemporary academic life, and so stuck are they in some time warp that renders their observations utterly anachronistic.[37] Their depiction of academe as inimical to women does, however, serve an important function in the propagation of feminism, and it is this function that needs to be noted here.

Myths are simple but powerful explanations, providing an escape from historically complex situations. They allow us to grasp not so much what *is* true but what we *believe*, or would like to believe, to be true. But myths are not static. Old myths are replaced by new ones, lending themselves to new purposes, in the name of which they are accepted in the same spirit of utter certitude as the old ones. Sometimes old myths are merely inverted, so that the positive and negative poles of a particular dichotomy change places, as in black = good/white = evil, or female = superior/male = inferior. New myths are no more likely to be accurate accounts of reality than were the former. They merely reflect a new zeitgeist.

It is easy to see why the Sexual Harassment Industry must rest its case on myth, and why it has adopted the particular myth of "systemic sexism" and pervasive discrimination against women.[38] That myth implicitly denies the profound and sweeping social changes which have occurred in our time, changes that, among other things, make university women today fully the equals of their male counterparts.[39] It also pits males against females, each being represented as an ineluctable type, thus making "sexual harassment" not a contingent result of specific social interactions but a necessary consequence of deeply rooted patriarchal patterns.

Furthermore, the mythic figure of the predatory professor effectively disguises the power game actually being waged in the name of feminism. If "sexual harassment" were relabeled "female privilege" or "demolishing men," it would not command much support. If it were merely seen as a temporary wrong to be righted, and not as a dire peril stalking the lives of perennially beleaguered women, our whole social landscape would look different, hostility between men and women might well abate, and the SHI, finding small demand for its services, would wither away.

As a matter of fact, the canard of the academy as typically hostile to women is belied by a mass of data about women's excellent academic performance. Women's increasing entry into professional schools and their growing claims on high salaries provide further evidence contradicting the mythical (but passionately embraced) view of rampant discrimination. Why, in the face of the evidence, would some writers insist that "systemic sexism" pervades academe today?

To answer this question, one must consider another traditional function of myth. As Malinowski said long ago, myths function as charters for social action.[40] They authenticate particular views of reality and, by doing so, provide a powerful rationale for political engagement. When new institutions are created in the course of this engagement, they seek to demonstrate their indispensability by constantly magnifying the version of reality that they enshrine.

Scollay and Bratt's chapter provides a case in point. They concede, "It is true that the U.S. Constitution offers significant protection of free speech, and its higher education counterpart, academic freedom" (p. 266). But the predicament of young women caught in a relentlessly sexist system makes it a "false conflict" to set constitutional guarantees in opposition to harassment policies. Distinguishing "false" from "true" conflicts is "untying the Gordian knot," they say, an act that, in a stroke, frees harassment policy, and its executants, from misguided fidelity to academic and civil liberties. Gleefully they cite cases in which individuals "may not be" within the protections of the First Amendment or cannot be allowed to use academic freedom as a defense (pp. 266–67). While granting that "the robust exchange of ideas embraced by the concept of academic freedom" may be impaired by vague definitions of "hostile environment harassment" as creating an "intimidating, hostile, or offensive academic environment" for the student, they show no appreciation of the harms that curtailment of free speech in academe can actually unleash, or of the sort of intellectual climate it is likely to create (and has already created in some places). To them, what is at stake is simply "exploiting students for private advantage" (something with which, ironically, the SHI itself could well be charged) and the supposed creation of "a classroom environment so charged with sexual hostility or intimidation that the individual student's ability to learn is seriously jeopardized" (p. 267).

"Education," they say, must be the touchstone of what is permitted in the classroom, and what is not (p. 268). But the point is precisely that what one person considers "educational," another deems "offensive" and "harassing." Just ask young men who unsuspectingly take a women's studies class in order to fulfill general education requirements. Scollay and Bratt give no thought to the "chilling effect" their facile and imprecise distinctions between "education" and "irrelevance" would be bound to have on teaching. No wonder that the conflict between free speech and protecting women in class "may be more apparent than real" to them (p. 268).

At my own university, a recent example of feminist exploitation of the myth of "systemic sexism" occurred as part of what might well be described as an attempted feminist coup. In 1997, a plan called "Vision 2000" was proposed, designed to promote "equity for women" in New England's six land-grant universities.[41] This project rested on the usual unsubstantiated claims about the sorry state of women in academe. "Women face sexual violence and sexual harassment in the classroom and in the workplace," the document (written by women's groups from the six campuses) declared, "and are too often silenced by a system that protects the perpetrators of these crimes."[42]

To attempt to remedy this situation by the year 2000, the plan targeted virtually all aspects of university life, from salaries to course contents, from research to teaching styles and campus life. It sought nothing less, in other words, than a feminist makeover of the entire academic enterprise, necessitated—here the invocation of the foundational myth—by the assumed fact that "[w]omen's status within American higher education reflects an intellectual bias that is deeply rooted in the disciplinary methods and social assumptions of university communities."[43]

Proposed solutions included obligatory "training" in how to avoid harassing others; loss of "recognition and support" for (unidentified) "groups" shown to manifest violence against women at a higher rate than the campus average; "women's centers" for campus officials to "rely upon"; creation of a "women-friendly and culturally diverse" curriculum, to be accomplished "with guidance from an autonomous Women's Studies site"; "equitable recognition" for the "substance and methodologies" of work in women's studies; and holding department heads "accountable for improvement in achieving gender equity" and rewarding or penalizing them accordingly. By the year 2000, the document warned, faculty members "whose students identify their courses, teaching styles, and mentoring as failing to be inclusive [will] not receive teaching prizes, satisfactory teaching evaluations, or merit raises."[44]

Responding to faculty critics of this plan who expressed concern about what some of the plan's provisions meant for the academic freedom of individual faculty members, Professor Ann Ferguson, director of the women's studies program at the University of Massachusetts and cochair of the Status of Women Council that presented the plan to the Faculty Senate, said, "We can't lose track of the wider goal in order to defend some narrow definition of academic freedom."[45] In the event, this was too much even for colleagues sympathetic to feminist aspirations. Only the plan's general goals were endorsed, not its stated rationales and ideas for implementation.

But why did the Faculty Senate (disregarding several committee reports expressly rejecting the entire document) vote to adopt the nine general recommendations? No doubt because these goals were presented as a claim for "equity for women," which (surely against the better knowledge of most faculty) was said to be lacking at the university. Refusal to capitulate to this principle—which the proposal's defenders likened to "motherhood and apple pie"—would have meant challenging the underlying myth.

As nearly all the sexual harassment literature is written by active members of the SHI, general agreement with the foundation myth is only to be expected. So is the set of biases that goes with this adherence: unexamined notions of male "power" and predatoriness; a belief in women's perpetual "silencing"; the persistent denigration and delegitimization of male fears of false accusations; and the automatic assumptions about female honesty and goodwill. This is a tightly knit worldview, unperturbed by the actual complexity of a university scene where people interact both professionally and personally, play multiple and shifting roles, develop elective affinities, and form temporary associations and antagonisms. All this—the texture of real life—is abhorrent to sexual harassment specialists.

The Perils of Advocacy Research

Given the many flaws inherent in the policies routinely endorsed by the SHI, it must be asked: Is the concept of sexual harassment redeemable? Is sexual harassment a legitimate and clear danger in the workplace and the classroom? And if it is, what should be done about it?

I am not sure what one should reply to these questions. I do suspect, however, that the accumulated evidence—opportunistic lawsuits, jobs lost without due process, cultivation of hypersensitivity and grievance-collecting on the part of alleged victims, increasing breakdown of what one social scientist has termed "cross-gender trust"[46]—suggests that the SHI cannot show us the way to a better society.

It is striking that Sandler, Shoop, and their contributors never even speculate about these matters. They cannot do so because they are wedded to the concept of sexual harassment as a sort of original sin, an innate evil produced by "patriarchal society" without gradation or mitigation, surfacing and resurfacing in a paradigmatic postlapsarian garden of academe inhabited by two complementary archetypes: the lecherous male (usually a venal professor) and the innocent female (normally a student).

The primary source of this view is, of course, Catharine MacKinnon, whose works display a distinctly cavalier attitude toward the many problems with sexual harassment legislation. MacKinnon opens a 1986 essay, reviewing a decade of sexual harassment law, with a general discussion of her subject, in which, by the third paragraph, she has moved seamlessly from "sexual harassment" to "sexual abuse." She then bemoans the amount of energy she has had to spend getting the law to recognize injuries to women as true injuries, and wrongs done to women as genuine wrongs. "The legal claim for sexual harassment made the events of sexual harassment illegitimate socially," she writes, revealing her larger agenda, "as well as legally for the first time. Let me know if you figure out a better way to do that."[47]

In the same essay, and with the hyperbole for which she is famous, MacKinnon asserts that sexual harassment turns women into "pornography." And when they go to court to act against it, they are, she says, turned into "pornography" yet again. "The first time it happens, it is called freedom; the second time, it is called justice."[48] With their most prominent spokesperson striking such a note, it is no wonder that lesser SHI luminaries do not hesitate to chime in. "Due process" thus becomes one more characteristic of the American injustice system, and little effort is spent by the SHI in defending it.

But advocacy research is an inherently problematic endeavor. In an insightful paper analyzing studies of sexual harassment (the sort of piece that seems not to find its way into the official sexual harassment literature), Harsh K. Luthar, who examines human relations in the workplace, has written about the biases distorting research on sexual harassment. Such research is overwhelmingly undertaken by women, and studies have shown that in this area of scholarship the sex of the researcher closely correlates with the research results. This circumstance, Luthar argues, has led to the suppression of many interesting issues related to sexual harassment.[49]

One of these is sexual harassment of males by females in positions of power, the incidence of which, one can anticipate, is likely to rise as women's professional status rises. This expectation is already borne out by EEOC data showing a steady rise in complaints filed by men. In 1991 males filed 7.5 percent of the sexual harassment charges received by the EEOC and the fair employment practices agencies combined. By 1993 this figure had grown to 9.1 percent; by 1997, to 11.6 percent. During the same time, the total monetary benefits awarded to all complainants rose from $7.1 million to $49.5 million.[50]

Of course, to even raise the issue of "male victims" is to challenge the feminist dogma that sexual harassment is a patriarchal tool for keeping women in subjection, a notion that as we have seen, explicitly lies behind current sexual harassment law. The standard SHI view of this matter is that harassment of men by women is a minor problem, as is, presumably, same-sex harassment.[51] Sandler and Shoop assure us that instances of women as harassers are "relatively rare," a claim that no doubt explains why the majority of essays in their book entirely abandons pronominal equality. The volume's editors confidently assert that false accusations by students are "exceptionally rare, probably accounting for less than one percent of all charges" (p. 19). Given the biases that govern the SHI, on what evidence could this conclusion be based? Perhaps it was the kind of evidence that also shows that women "don't lie" about rape.[52]

Harsh Luthar points to the absence of serious research on the incidence of false or baseless accusations against men, as another result of the gender bias afflicting the field. He also (correctly) identifies this bias as resulting from the sexual harassment literature's reliance on feminist rhetoric, going back at least to Susan Brownmiller's 1975 book *Against Our Will: Men, Women, and Rape,* according to which all men are potential rapists. Women's sexual aggression toward men is simply not recognized by the feminist literature, nor is it acknowledged by the Sexual Harassment Industry.[53] I am not, however, suggesting that justice will be served by training men, too, to bring charges against sexual innuendos or personal "gender" comments directed at them. Rather, sanity needs to be restored to the entire discussion by rejecting the feminist distortions that the SHI promulgates.

Domain expansion increasingly coerces agreement, or apparent agreement, with the slanted feminist view. Dissident voices come to be stigmatized as cold and unfeeling, yet another sign of "backlash" (as in the attacks on Katie Roiphe for her criticisms of the feminist claims about date rape).[54] Simply asking how large-scale a problem sexual harassment actually is, how loose the definitions of it are, or how representative the reported "incidents" are, thus appears a heartless interposition, easily met by the rebuke "Are you saying: this or that (lower) number of cases is permissible?" This is why critics of sexual harassment policies and related issues generally feel constrained to preface their objections with an expression of outrage over harassment itself—a conciliatory stance from which they can then politely register their opposition.

From my perspective, however, it is the SHI that deserves to be made the target of outrage, for the damage it has done to academic civility, and for the injuries it has inflicted on individuals caught in its web. When people are reluctant to even offer criticisms without engaging in elaborate apologies, it is clear that we are in the presence of a powerful orthodoxy and that it is high time we stood back and considered what this orthodoxy has brought us.

We have now had twenty years of sexual harassment training and consciousness-raising. Is the SHI resting on its laurels and enjoying its successes? Or does it continue to sound the alarm? Bernice Sandler and Robert Shoop foresee no diminishing need for their services. On the contrary. They offer a fifteen-point list of predictions of future developments on campus, and almost every item begins with the word "increased": increased incidence of sexual harassment (yes, this is what they say), increased reporting, increased training, increased recognition of nonsexual but gender-related "hostile environments," increased charges by men against women, increased use of a systemic, comprehensive anti-sexual-harassment program (p. vii). This rather blatant display of their conviction that their services will remain indispensable is, in its way, embarrassing. They appear not to have considered why, if twenty years of SHI ministrations have not helped us, we should let them guide us in the future.

PART II

Typifying Tales

≈≈≈

Chapter 3

The Accusers

❧

In the last two decades, feminists have built a real political resistance to male sexual dominance, i.e., to male ownership of the whole wide world; and it is clear that we are not saying no because we mean yes. We mean no and we prosecute the pigs to prove it.

ANDREA DWORKIN, *Life and Death*

Critical readers of the SHI literature would be far less likely to turn against it if only they had some help from its authors in distinguishing between egregious cases of harassment and incidents arising from the complexities of ordinary human relations in the workplace and the academy. But such help they do not get. On the contrary, Sandler and Shoop—I am still using their book as an exemplary text—give long and indiscriminate lists of what counts as sexual harassment, lists that if taken seriously, would drive any "reasonable person" to think that a sexually neutralized environment is indeed the only safe one for us to aspire to. But they also include in their volume some particular cases, whose circumstances typify the problem they set out to expose. These cases deserve a closer look. After all, by accepting them as subjects of chapters in their book, Sandler and Shoop invite us to view them as clear and telling examples of the wrongs the SHI wishes to extirpate.[1]

"Typifying examples"—usually horror stories—Joel Best explains, play an important role in the creation of a social problem. The gasps of disapproval they arouse serve to suppress legitimate questions waiting to be asked in each instance: How characteristic is this event, and how serious is it? Sandler and Shoop's volume devotes three chapters to such stories, two of which are highly ambiguous.

Electronic Sexual Harassment

To gain a proper appreciation of the vigilante mentality and self-righteous cant fostered by the SHI, one can hardly do better than read Denise M. Dalaimo's chapter, "Electronic Sexual Harassment." Dalaimo's "devastating" experience is related in the first part of the chapter. The second part is a technical discussion of e-mail and the psychology and etiquette it promotes, and of MIT's Stopit program, which Dalaimo calls a "revolutionary" effort to address electronic harassment. This discussion is of no relevance to her case, despite her chapter's title, but its inclusion in Sandler and Shoop's volume sheds considerable light on the SHI's impulse to be all-encompassing. Angst, concept-stretching, domain expansion, simple desire for revenge, and anger at procedures that dared show a modicum of concern for being "fair" to "my harasser"—all are on display in this chapter.

Both the complainant (Dalaimo) and the accused (called "Dan") in her case were graduate students, so status differentials were not at issue (although, as we have seen, it is presupposed in SHI thinking that women always necessarily possess less "power" than men). To compensate for the absence of such overt differences, the author dwells at length on the emotional trauma she suffered ("I was a strong, independent, and educated woman, yet I was experiencing anxiety and shortness of breath caused by the stress of the incident"), as well as on her "nightmares, the daily vomiting, the crying spells, and the feeling of being stalked" (p. 90).

What in fact happened to this student that "changed [her] life forever" and made her feel so "violated"? The story is a simple one. A close-knit group of graduate students spent much time together in person and on e-mail. One day Dan, a man in this group whom Dalaimo had considered her "best friend," sent her a long e-mail letter in which he disclosed, in graphic detail, his own past as a victim of sexual abuse, affirmed his friendship and appreciation for her, and asked for her sympathy and active participation in helping him to overcome his sexual dysfunction. She replied that she was not interested and urged him to get professional help. He at once responded, still by e-mail, thanking her for listening and saying he hoped they could still be friends. Subsequently, she learned that following her rejection, he had sent similar letters to several other friends. This discovery exacerbated her feelings of betrayal and disgust and prompted a deep concern, she says, for the innocent students who would be exposed to Dan, a teaching assistant, during the following semester. She then sought action. That is the story. All of it.

Now, what is this but a tale of an ill-considered overture that was spurned, with no pressure on the "victim" and no harmful consequences for her beyond the ones she invokes by labeling what happened as an act of harassment? What sort of policy could possibly have prohibited Dan's approach? Despite the chapter title, it cannot really be the "electronic" component of the episode that is the problem. Dan could as easily have sent the offending letter by snail mail or delivered it personally. He could also have made this overture by speaking to Dalaimo at one of their meetings or on the phone. And, it should be noted, Dan immediately apologized and stopped his approach to her (p. 100), in response to her expressed lack of interest. Just what, then, is Dalaimo objecting to? Should he have asked prior permission to make a sexual overture? Could asking such permission, in the present climate, not itself be defined as "harassment"? Or was Dan's failing, rather, that having been turned down by Dalaimo, he approached other women?

As for Dan, he faced the choice of "voluntarily" giving up teaching for one semester (p. 93) or of having the case proceed through "channels." He was told that there was "compelling evidence" against him (Dalaimo had erased the letter from her e-mail account, but another woman still had a copy of it). Dalaimo sarcastically comments that after one semester, Dan was allowed back in the classroom, his " 'little indiscretions' " forgotten. Although she considers that he suffered only "a 'slap on the hand' for his offenses," Dalaimo has the satisfaction of believing that by her action she protected other potential "victims" who might have succumbed to Dan for "fear of reprisal" or perhaps dropped out of school altogether. In addition, she says, "[M]y complaint will be in his file; so if he harasses again, the consequences will be much more serious" (p. 93). Dalaimo tells us that Dan, rumor has it, continues to feel "ganged up on" and not to understand the "big deal" that was made of his behavior.

A "Consensual" Relationship

Leslie Irvine's account of "A 'Consensual' Relationship" is one of the most interesting chapters in Sandler and Shoop's book, for, as a first-person demonstration of the replacement of one social script by another, it sheds much light on the preoccupations of our particular historical moment. The author was a thirty-year-old returning student, in the sixth year of a marriage that was "at the beginning of the end." Reflecting ex post facto on her experience, she redefines her evident interest in her professor as "vulnerability" and casts him in the role of villainous manipulator and herself as his innocent victim. She "could not refuse," she tells us repeatedly—a job offer, a dinner invitation, a relationship that went on for two-and-a-half years, during which time she kept on enrolling in courses with him. Her reconstruction of this long association, which was (by her own account) exciting, gratifying, and affirming, seems intended as a living illustration of Catharine MacKinnon's dictum that women in our society cannot give informed consent. "I had been well socialized," she confesses postconversion, "to think of my professors as intellectually omnipotent. I wanted desperately to believe that I was smart" (p. 236). In other words, her story is no longer about a woman who, until things turned sour, sought and got something from her professor; it has become the tragedy of injured innocence and "an appalling example of exploitation" (p. 235).

The professor had a partner; she had a husband. But only the professor's behavior counts as betrayal, not her own. He involved her, she says, in some grave dishonesties (such as falsifying his teaching evaluations), but she—self-portrayed as a feeble victim lacking all autonomy— bears no responsibility for going along. They had sexual relations while she was supposedly working for him. This becomes: "He used my job illegally. . . . The university, in effect, paid me to have sex with him" (p. 238–39). They exchanged vows of love. "I would later realize that he had even set the terms of our love by defining the word for me" (p. 239). Professors "have the power to make us want to please them," and with wielders of power, consensual relationships can only be "consensual" (p. 246).

Irvine broke up with her lover only after discovering that he had had similar relationships with other students. Now the "extent of the manipulation" she had undergone became clear to her. Her disillusionment with academe was profound, but she "became willing to relive those feelings so that other women would not be exploited in the future" (p. 242). Hence she took action. Her account ends with the recommendation that pointless though it may be to officially ban professor–student relationships, universities should have policies to control them. Pretending that such relationships are not problematic, Irvine says, echoing official sexual harassment doctrine, "denies all women equal access to education" (p. 245). The lesson she draws is that it is a bad idea to "become intimate with people who have significantly greater social power than you" (p. 246).

What kind of a reflection does this story cast on the image of women as responsible adults? Despite being a thirty-year-old, married, returning student, Irvine openly flaunts her incapacity to behave autonomously. Her (and many others') characterizations of woman-as-victim and man-as-predator are astonishing recapitulations of traditional, prefeminist stereotypes about men and women, according to which women have been socialized into passivity and weakness. Women bear no blame for this condition, which, however, prevents them from giving meaningful consent, even at age thirty![2] In men, on the other hand, there is no lack of personal responsibility for the role of "predator" and "abuser" into which they have (presumably) been socialized as well, and which is fully condoned by their culture. If we were to take such representations seriously, we would have to affirm that men have freedom (and responsibility) but that women have none—nor have they independent judgment. Yet the SHI, surely, believes that women should have the right to vote, to testify before a hearing, and to propose resolutions and punishments (a standard feature of the complaint process in sexual harassment cases on campus). Where did their sudden autonomy and thoughtfulness come from? No longer in thrall to her professor, Irvine now expects us to accept her new version of what happened as authentic and true, the product of mature reflection.

In short, Irvine's passage from excited lover to exploited and helpless female is a very clear example of the mythical reconceptualization of a life story under the influence of a new paradigm. It offers a typical conversion tale and an exemplary feminist fable of reeducation. It is the kind of document that, in the future, will be seen as shedding much light on the peculiarities of the gender wars in late-twentieth-century America.

But it also serves to remind us of the fundamental ambiguity and complexity of human interactions. In this instance, the key questions are, Does a consensual relationship between student and professor necessarily exploit the student? Or is it in fact a privilege given to one but denied to another who is not so favored? In the latter case, is such a relationship wrong because it disadvantages other students or because it is apt to make them jealous? If so, a serious question arises as to whether such liaisons are damaging to the student "victim" or, quite the contrary, beneficial to her but damaging to those left out. In the Sandler and Shoop book, instead of an honest discussion of these and similar messy conundrums, we get only demands for purifying the academy of the demon sex. Were we to recognize that particular students have all sorts of advantages vis-à-vis their professors, whether because of their brains or because of their winning personalities, we might start to notice that "personal" advantages do, in fact, exist everywhere in a nonregimented society and are by no means limited to sexual attractiveness. One graduate student I know complains bitterly about the advantages enjoyed by students who join their professors' preferred cause-du-jour. This, not romantic relationships between professors and students, is the real problem, he insists.

Scollay and Bratt (whom we encountered in chapter 2 above) devote several pages to the "regulation of amorous faculty–student relationships." They explain, according to SHI orthodoxy, that there is in such relationships an "inherent asymmetry" due to the partners' differing statuses, which "asymmetry" the authors treat as axiomatic evidence that these relationships are not "formed consensually" (p. 270).[3] Even if consensual, faculty–student relationships would be improper because (1) they threaten the distance and objectivity the authors consider desirable in education (virtues, ironically, that "feminist pedagogy" is explicitly devoted to dismantling); and (2) they give the "appearance of potential favoritism and unfair advantage for the student" (p. 270). But Scollay and Bratt fail to point out that these two reasons are in contradiction. Is an affair with a professor a disadvantage to the student or only to other students?

Scollay and Bratt proceed to give a vigorous but brief explanation of the right of privacy, which protects us from government-sponsored interference in intimate decision-making (p. 270). But they also argue that this right of privacy is not absolute (p. 271) and might not preclude limitations on a person's right to choose a partner. They present their position on consensual relations as occupying the middle ground between those who would ban such relationships and those opposed to banning. Their idea of evenhandedness is to emphasize the power of professors while reminding us that not all women are the same and that for some, their personal histories and circumstances "make the issue of consent less troublesome" (p. 272). The bias in their presentation is evident when one considers that the real issue should be that although some relationships may be potentially exploitive, we can prohibit those only by prohibiting *all*, without regard to individual circumstances or desires, and to do so would be to create a worse situation than we have now. Interestingly, they contrast the "savvy, returning female student" with the "sheltered" young high school graduate. Perhaps they should have read Irvine's chapter, for she denies their distinction. This shows how unwise it would be to prohibit relationships because some of them may be problematic. No one will agree on which are and which are not to be so judged.

Scollay and Bratt's aim, repeated in many "consensual relations" policies being promulgated in universities throughout the country, is to remove students involved in a relationship from the professor's grading or supervisory power. Their means are careful, narrowly tailored policies that would strongly advise the avoidance of all such relationships and oblige professors to "disclose" their liaisons to an administrator. Such a requirement is, of course, a grievous infringement on the autonomy of adults. And it fails to consider that it would compel gay people and adulterers to "out" themselves to potentially unsympathetic administrators. At least Scollay and Bratt say that no hard-and-fast rule is likely to work in such complex matters (p. 273). This has not, however, dissuaded many universities throughout the country from going beyond "disclosure" requirements and adopting full-blown banning policies.

The SHI as Career Option

Not content with freeing women from discrimination in their professional and academic lives, the SHI has, in addition, opened a new avenue for advancement as alleged victims find themselves rewarded with both monetary and professional gains. This is a rather different kind of typifying tale to come out of the current preoccupation with sexual harassment, but it is a significant one.

Consider the case of Susan Hippensteele, who won a sexual harassment suit against the University of Hawaii at Manoa. While she was a graduate student, her major professor, she charged, having repeatedly harassed her with sexual suggestions, once grabbed her and planted a kiss on her forehead. Such an experience, she later affirmed, "is life changing" (p. 299). This is true enough in her own instance, for after winning her suit and receiving her Ph.D. in psychology, she found employment on the same campus as a "student advocate."

In the Sandler and Shoop volume, Susan Hippensteele contributes a chapter entitled "Advocacy and Student Victims of Sexual Harassment." Her essay is of interest because of what it does and does not assume. Sexual harassment, as always, is a devastating experience. "Untold numbers of students who experience sexual harassment at school quit" (p. 296). Jokes, comments, and rape are all part of it; all are treated as equally damaging. "Complexity," in Hippensteele's world-view, is strictly a matter of multiple and interlocking isms (sexism, racism, heterosexism, ageism, classism, etc.) and identities (such as the ethnic or sexual "minority status" of the players). Never is it an element in the analysis of the players' actions. "Multiple forms of discrimination" evidently make for a fertile soil in which the SHI can take root.

Here is an example of the sort of "complex" awareness of discrimination Hippensteele argues for: "Strategies that deal with sexual harassment as a unidimensional phenomenon and deny the experiences of victims who are subject to multiple forms of oppression . . . cannot be effective for those persons" (p. 301). Hippensteele looks forward to "[t]he inevitable expansion of the common definition of sexual harassment," which "should ultimately improve the effectiveness of the definitions as tools for intervention and prevention" (p. 303). Her chapter ends with an affirmation of the value of a position that "validates" students' experiences of sexual harassment and "confirms their unique experience of the harm" (p. 313).

Such support is explicitly independent of any investigation of alleged misconduct. In her capacity as advocate for students, Hippensteele helped a student named Michelle Gretzinger to escalate and elaborate a series of charges against Ramdas Lamb, a professor of religion at the University of Hawaii at Manoa. These charges were found groundless by an arbitrator, but this did not prevent Gretzinger from pursuing the case before a federal court. By this time, the allegations (which are described in greater detail in chapter 4) had transmogrified, in the rhetoric utilized by the plaintiff's attorney, into "mentor rape," a label that was passed off in court as if it were an authoritative concept in the sexual harassment literature. Lamb was alleged to have raped Gretzinger sixteen times, earning him the additional epithet "serial rapist" from the plaintiff's attorney, as well as death threats from anonymous letter-writers.

It took a jury of four women and four men just a few hours to see the vacuousness of Gretzinger's charges and grant Lamb's counterclaim. Gretzinger was ordered to pay Lamb over $132,000, with the jury specifying that this was not merely compensation for defamation but included $80,000 in punitive damages. The campus SHI, however, which included faculty from the women's studies program, interpreted this judgment, according to newspaper reports, as a defeat for all women, another illustration of the sexist climate in which we all live.

As for Hippensteele, by the time she contributed to Sandler and Shoop's volume, she had moved from "student advocate" to a more broadly defined position as "sexual harassment counselor/victim's advocate for students, faculty, and staff" (p. xi). The Lamb case was ongoing at the time, and she alludes to but does not name it. In her account of it, as of every other case she mentions, the assumption is that allegations are invariably true and that the professor must be guilty as charged. What she does not tell is her own extensive role in the case, by now well documented.

A labor arbitrator's decision, a year and a half into the case, found that Hippensteele's procedures were "inconsistent with University policy, incompatible with the nature of an educational setting, and incorrect as a matter of law." The arbitrator went on to cite "a wealth of objective, reliable evidence to demonstrate that Dr. Hippensteele regularly used her status as a student advocate to advance her personal philosophies regarding the issue of sexual harassment."[4] Many witnesses, both faculty and students, who had heard her presentations testified to her approach, in which accusation equals guilt; to her assertions that "intent does not matter" and that a person could be found guilty of harassment without having been given the opportunity to confront his accuser (statements Hippensteele denied under oath); and to her boasting of her own lack of "objectivity." Under oath, Hippensteele affirmed that it was "absolutely not" her job to attempt to screen out valid from invalid complaints; all required her "support and assistance."[5]

Hippensteele's own account in Sandler and Shoop's volume confirms her self-definition as an avenging angel. Most frightening, perhaps, is that her handling of the case apparently did not discredit her. Her work appears in the volume as that of an authority. Despite the unfavorable outcome of the case, she, at last report, had been given a tenured faculty slot in the women's studies program, where she cultivates her specialization in sexual harassment.

Hippensteele, in other words, is not an extreme embodiment of the SHI but rather its logical fulfillment. The question her role in the Lamb case raises in the minds of people not involved in the SHI is, of course, whether offices whose occupants have so clear a *parti pris,* and that function in an extralegal capacity in advance of any investigation, should even exist in a university setting. How far Hippensteele is from being an exception can be gauged by considering a "training" session offered at another university, thousands of miles from Hawaii, in early 1998.

A professor at a state university described to me the harassment training initiated by his institution's office of harassment compliance. He had signed on as a volunteer for a one-day session early in 1998. This is what happened: When he entered the room, one of the senior staff members introduced herself to him by saying that she should have been a scientist but that in high school her science teacher molested her, as a result of which she is now in the sexual harassment field. Another staff member began her presentation by relating her college experiences of coarse male behavior. She then told the group about a student she had counseled who merely wanted to discuss a certain incident and get advice and guidance. Proudly, the speaker reported that she had spent three hours with this student, finally convincing her to disclose the name of the male "partner" to the incident, so that a formal complaint could be filed. Next came a review of the basic rules of the university's policies; then a group of students acted out sexual harassment scenes (which my informant considered highly unrealistic and biased) for the benefit of the newly trained sexual harassment advisers.

In response to my question "What did you learn that was of positive value from this session?" this professor replied:

> I came to the subject with absolutely no political preconception. I just wanted to help create a more harmonious working environment. Personally, I was pretty upset about the entire experience. I did not perceive any positive value in it except that I became very familiar with the tremendous sensitivities associated with the subject of sexual harassment. I felt that the most vocal and most extreme of the feminists suffer from an underlying psychological pathology. There was a totally irrational perception of a "grave danger and a real threat" posed by men in general and by harassers in particular. I had the sense that the entire topic was way overstated, and that normal, human heterosexuality was seen as an evil force rather than a pleasurable activity that benefits both men and women. I felt that the perception of the female as the eternal "victim" of predatory men was very much on the mind of the most vocal feminists. Now I believe that obvious cases of true harassment are relatively rare and that most of the movement feeds off minor incidents and consensual relationships that have somehow gone sour. I also learned the tremendous negative reaction towards anyone who does not accept the standard doctrine of the "weak female" and the "impossibility of consent in relationships that have a power imbalance."[6]

Early in the Ramdas Lamb case, the arbitrator noted that the university's flawed procedures for dealing with sexual harassment were likely to have "an adverse effect on academic freedom at this University."[7] That was in 1994. But Hippensteele, far from taking this admonition to heart, reveals in her 1997 contribution to the Sandler and Shoop volume the dangerous potentiality of SHI fanaticism. She writes about "ethnically identified victims" of sexual harassment and ends by aligning herself with critical race theorists. Such concepts as "merit, rigor, standards, and excellence" are viewed as code words to promote "discriminatory self-interest" on the part of the powerful (p. 311). "Academic freedom" is a slogan touted by "white male faculty" but, she gleefully affirms, one now increasingly challenged by "nonacademic" folk. "To many," Hippensteele writes, "academic freedom is currently being used as a license to speak and behave irresponsibly" (p. 311).

This conclusion gives the show away, revealing that the SHI, as represented by zealots such as Hippensteele, is not about safeguarding victims, and certainly not about protecting (for students and teachers) that fragile thing known as academic freedom, which has for decades allowed unpopular ideas to gain a hearing in academe. Rather, it is about waging a political struggle to impose an agenda of social reform as deemed necessary by a particular feminist-inspired worldview. Sexual harassment charges, rooted in the myth of pervasive sexism in the academy, are a powerful weapon in this struggle. But the indiscriminate use of this weapon can only damage the legitimate interests of real victims of discrimination, whose cases, lumped together with frivolous and fraudulent claims, are used by the SHI to pursue its own attack on the liberal tradition in universities.

At the University of Massachusetts at Amherst, where I teach, the trivial nature of sexual harassment complaints in academe was emerging as early as 1987. In a summary of actions taken under an interim sexual harassment policy, I came across an account of a female undergraduate who charged that a male faculty member had "touched and complimented complainant's hair." The investigating board initially found that the professor had not violated the university's sexual harassment policy. The complainant, however, appealed to the provost, with the result that the earlier decision was reversed and a letter of reprimand was sent to the professor.[8] The summary of other cases in the same document suggests much about the kind of climate that was spreading throughout the academy. Of the nine cases described, almost all resulted in a finding that sexual overtures qualified as violations of the policy.

By 1995, moreover, the concept of "grooming" had been added to the standard vocabulary of the Sexual Harassment Industry, with the result that professors' words of praise or offers of help, even months before any alleged overture took place, could retroactively be construed as unacceptable behavior. The term "grooming" allows properly indoctrinated women to find male behavior potentially dangerous long before any untoward advances are actually made. Thus no student need feel left out of the Sexual Harassment Industry's ministrations, even if (or particularly if) all her interactions with a professor have been positive. Billie Wright Dziech and Linda Weiner, in their much cited book *The Lecherous Professor,* after ominously admitting that "[t]here are no infallible predictors for recognizing sexual harassment," offer readers a nonexhaustive list of "warning signs" that includes *"[e]xcessive flattery and praise of the student,"* which is explained thus: "This behavior, exhibited with others present, is especially seductive to students with low self-esteem *or* high aspirations. By convincing a student that she is intellectually and/or physically exceptional, the lecherous professor gains psychological access to her"[9] (italics in the original). Since this definition, careful readers will have noticed, covers just about all students who have ever received encouragement or help from professors (something one would have thought professors should provide unstintingly), problems will obviously arise once a student reconsiders her own past in the light of "lecherous professor" scripts. It is no surprise, then, to learn that early in the Ramdas Lamb case, the principal accuser, Michelle Gretzinger, had been provided by the student advocate, Susan Hippensteele, with suggestions for reading, including *The Lecherous Professor.*

When giving her deposition in February 1995, Hippensteele was asked by the examining attorney how one determined whether a professor's comment that an A-student was "doing a good job" should be construed as part of a "grooming process." Hippensteele responded that it depends on the context. One would need to know "[w]hether or not there were regular opportunities for this professor to communicate one on one with all the students in the class, whether or not . . . this professor made a habit of complimenting students, whether or not this professor made comments equally to a number of students or to all of his students . . . who performed well." Thus, she went on to say, one would want to investigate the "specific situation in which the statement occurred, where they [the student and the professor] were, at what time, under what circumstances."[10]

This approach, it should be obvious, creates a situation in which professors, for their own protection, must cultivate near-paranoid attention to all their words and deeds. They cannot interact with students in a "natural" way, speaking spontaneously, offering criticisms and praise, without keeping in mind that every word they utter might, at some point, become part of an official complaint. And that, precisely, seems to be the intent.

As it happened, Hippensteele later had the opportunity to experience such surveillance herself, which she complained of in her deposition with no awareness that she had participated in creating precisely such an atmosphere for faculty members. She described her own reaction to realizing that (because of her handling of the Ramdas Lamb case) her training workshops in sexual harassment were coming under scrutiny and that she might herself be the object of a lawsuit initiated by the faculty union. This is what she said:

> [S]ince I've been learning of the allegations about . . . how I conduct training, what I say, I quite honestly have been afraid to conduct training. I have conducted training where there have been people who have attended training, who appear to be there to watch and take notes, people who I know to be hostile to my training efforts. I feel that my concern about every word that I say has impeded my ability to effectively communicate information, because I end up providing so many examples and so much qualification and so much detail and making sure that everybody understands exactly what I'm saying, that I end up getting through a quarter of the material that I need to cover in order to do an effective training session. So I'm essentially feeling harassed.[11]

The irony of this complaint seems to have been entirely lost on Hippensteele.

Chapter 4

The Fruits of Injustice

As long as the focus remains upon sex (and gender) rather than upon what it
is about a given sort of behavior that makes it wrong, the invitation to extremism in implementing the [sexual harassment] regulations will remain. From
unjust roots the fruits of injustice will always grow.

FERREL M. CHRISTENSEN, " 'Sexual Harassment' Must Be Eliminated"

Stories of predatory professors and boorish employers are staples of
the SHI literature, in which anecdotal evidence abounds. But when it
comes to false charges, frivolous accusations, and an abandonment of
due process, the SHI grows silent. And no wonder. Countertales—
alternative narratives that do not conform to SHI stereotypes of heroes
and villains—would destabilize the industry's presumptive authority.
For the dispassionate consideration of such countercases flushes sexual
harassment from the dark corners of despicable outrages and exposes
it to the light of observation, in which conflicts between human beings
turn out to be common and the truth about these conflicts is always
complex, usually ambiguous, and rarely easy to judge.

In the discourse of sexual harassment, I have argued, training in
victimhood plays a distinctive role. I can think of no other areas in life
in which putative sufferers require so much help in order to recognize
the damage supposedly inflicted on them and have come to depend on
such careful instruction in how to script the accounts of their victimhood. Article after article produced by SHI writers insists—and this in
itself should arouse our suspicion—that people need to learn how to
identify the injuries they suffer. A recent example was provided by a

professor from California State University at Chico, who sent the following query to the Women's Studies E-Mail List:

> The sexual harassment committee at my university has decided to survey
> faculty, staff and students about their experiences of sexual harassment.
> We need a survey that will allow us to identify problematic behaviors,
> even if the respondent does not recognize the behavior as a form of sex-
> ual harassment. We are in the process of compiling surveys used by other
> colleges and universities to provide us with ideas. Where might I find
> surveys? If you have a sample of one used at your institution, we would
> most appreciate having a copy.[1]

Clearly, most of us cannot be counted on to understand that every tacky
little episode of sexual (or gender) innuendo may really be a grave example of victimization.

A more moderate vocabulary, in which "victims" did not swiftly pass
into "survivors," might suggest that too much is being made of tactless
remarks, tasteless jokes, and witless insinuations. But even to speak of
tact, taste, or wit is to evoke the pre-SHI consciousness in which women
had not yet been turned into perpetual victims. And it is precisely the
function of the SHI to oversee this process of transformation.

But what about the other "victims," those against whom charges are
brought falsely, motivated perhaps by personal resentment, anger,
envy, or frustrated infatuation? The SHI pretends that wrongful accusations happen so infrequently as not to matter. In fact, national figures
concerning counterfeit charges are hard to come by because, while sexual harassment accusations receive much attention in local and national
newspapers when they are first made, exoneration, when it occurs, is
likely to be noted only briefly and obscurely. Furthermore, universities
tend to prefer the least expensive path to resolution of sexual harassment cases, and this often means settling out of court, usually by paying
off the complainant, regardless of the merits of the charges. Such settle-
ments are frequently shrouded in secrecy; all the outside world knows
about them is that charges were withdrawn in exchange for undisclosed
sums of money. The alleged harasser's name is never explicitly cleared.

Except for the work of a very few critics, in the vast literature about
sexual harassment little has been written from the point of view of those
"alleged harassers" whose lives have been brought to virtual standstills
by false or merely trivial accusations. This is an omission crying out for
redress. In the present chapter, I will focus on several cases that provide
vivid glimpses of personal misadventures in the sort of environment

the SHI has helped create on university campuses. The costs—it should become clear—are not only personal. They are also social and educational.

"Women Don't Lie"

There is a suspicious circularity to the shape of some sexual harassment cases. They begin and end with the worldview promoted by the Sexual Harassment Industry. Once one is caught in this vicious circle, escape is difficult. Professor Ramdas Lamb's experience of escalating charges of sexual harassment is a frightening example of this pattern.

Born in 1945 to an Italian-German family living in California, Lamb spent eight years in India (1969–77), becoming a Hindu monk and adopting the first name "Ramdas." Upon returning to this country, he married and attended graduate school, receiving his Ph.D. in religious studies from the University of California at Santa Barbara. In the fall of 1991, he took a position as an assistant professor of religion at the University of Hawaii at Manoa. One of his tasks there was to serve as undergraduate adviser for religion majors. In this job he was remarkably successful, doubling the number of majors in just two years. His students (many of whom later testified for him) described him as an immensely popular, enthusiastic, and unusually accessible teacher, one who kept his office door open and allowed his students to come and go virtually as they pleased. He had a following—a group of students who often hung out at his office, discussing issues raised in class, and generally drawing on his wide experience and genial personality.

Trouble began in his second year of full-time teaching when he offered a new course, one he realized would, by its very subject, be controversial. Entitled "Religion, Politics, and Society," it focused on contemporary social issues such as homelessness, gay marriage, animal rights, abortion, and AIDS. In February 1993, Lamb asked his class to read several articles on rape and sexual harassment from the textbook he had chosen for the course. One of these articles sparked a discussion among the students (two-thirds of whom were women) about false allegations of rape. One student said she could see both sides of the issue. She had herself been raped but had also seen her brother falsely accused when he broke off his engagement. Another young woman in the class, Tania Mortensen, who worked as a peer educator for a group called CORE (Creating Options for a Rape-Free Environment), vehemently denied that women ever lie about rape. Women must be believed, she insisted. She stated that data showed that a mere 3 percent of rape charges are false.[2] Two other students, Michelle Gretzinger and Bonita Rai, supported this view. Gretzinger, who the previous semester had told various friends and professors that she had herself been raped in 1989, was evidently upset by challenges offered by other students to Mortensen's views and spent much of the class close to tears.

Professor Lamb knew Gretzinger well. She was a straight-A student who had decided to major in religion after meeting him. He had urged her to become an honors student, had written letters of recommendation for her, had lent her books, and had allowed her, along with others, to use his computer. As tension rose in his class, Lamb tried to mediate according to the ground rules that—so several of his students later testified—he had laid down at the beginning of the semester: Everyone was to be allowed to have his or her say; everyone's views were to be treated with respect; if a discussion was one-sided, Lamb would play the devil's advocate and introduce contrary points of view. As Wanda Dicks later testified, Lamb tried to get his students to understand the other person's point of view; he did not try to convert them.[3] Another student who, as a Christian Fundamentalist, did not share Professor Lamb's beliefs, also testified to Lamb's open-mindedness.[4]

However, for the first time in his teaching experience, Ramdas Lamb found the class getting out of his control that day. Tania Mortensen dominated the class, did most of the talking, adamantly denied that more than one view of women's truthfulness about rape was possible, and generally seemed to intimidate the other students.

Out of that day's conflict issued an extraordinary drama. First, Ramdas Lamb found himself accused of sexual harassment by the three distraught students (Mortensen, Gretzinger, and Rai) who had argued that "women don't lie." They claimed that Lamb had created a "hostile environment" by challenging their position and characterizing them as "man haters."

It is fascinating to see intellectual controversy about a social problem itself become grounds for sexual harassment charges. As famous a figure as Alan M. Dershowitz came close to facing charges over precisely the same issue. Dershowitz considers the notion of hostile-environment sexual harassment a threat to both freedom of speech and equal protection (since it sets offenses to women apart from all other offenses). He recounts how a group of feminists in his criminal-law class at Harvard, objecting to his discussion of false allegations of rape, threatened to file hostile-environment charges against him. "Despite the fact that the vast majority of students wanted to hear all sides of the important issues surrounding the law of rape," Dershowitz states, "a small minority tried to use the law of sexual harassment as a tool of censorship." The significance of this does not escape him: "[T]he fact that it is even thinkable at a major university that controversial teaching techniques might constitute hostile-environment sexual harassment demonstrates the dangers of this expandable concept."[5] Still, in Dershowitz's case the feminist students eventually decided against bringing charges.

Ramdas Lamb wasn't so lucky. When the original accusations began to crumble, Michelle Gretzinger, who by all accounts had until then shown a special, and apparently personal, interest in Professor Lamb, escalated her charges—initially merely hinting at some sexual relationship between herself and Lamb; later, when pressed, accusing him of repeated rape. The offense was "serial rape" and "mentor rape," as her lawyer was to call it in court.

Reading through the two thousand or so pages of legal transcripts generated by this case, I noticed a distinct pattern emerging of how Gretzinger proceeded in her accusations against Lamb. First she tried to keep the charges vague, so that initially it was not even clear what precisely was being alleged—perhaps merely some suspicion of sexual misconduct to complement the hostile-environment charges she and her two classmates were pursuing. She repeatedly testified that there had been no specific mention of any rapes in the first few months of the investigation because, she said, she had assumed that the charges the three students had already filed would be "enough."

When the initial charges proved flimsy, Gretzinger began to allege that Lamb had sexually assaulted her during the preceding semester, identifying to different acquaintances different locations for the assaults, of which she had given no sign at the time. She variously claimed they had occurred in Lamb's office, in his home, and in her apartment. When forced to come up with specifics (months after her initial charges, even though university regulations expressly required that complaints when first filed were to be accompanied by precise details), Gretzinger asserted that Lamb had raped her between ten and sixteen times in her own apartment after driving her home from his once-a-week class. These rapes, she claimed, had taken place between early September and early October 1992.

Unfortunately for Gretzinger's case, when pushed to come up with concrete dates, she named some that proved to be impossible. In the time frame she mentioned, there were not enough class days, Lamb's lawyer demonstrated in court, to accommodate her charges.

Professor Lamb, for his part, categorically denied having had sexual relations of any sort with her and testified that he had never set foot in her apartment. Furthermore, Gretzinger's own actions throughout the period in which the rapes were supposed to have occurred made the story of rape unconvincing. She had failed to indicate to her husband or to anyone else that repeated assaults were taking place; she had continued to demonstrate enthusiasm for Lamb, his courses, and the extracurricular activities in which he was involved; she had signed up for an elective course with Lamb the following semester—all of which was attested to by many other students. This pattern of behavior was part of the challenge faced by the sexual harassment specialists when they came to Gretzinger's aid.

Confronted by irrefutable testimony of Lamb's innocence— testimony that left the plaintiff's case a shambles—Gretzinger's attorney fell back upon the very claims with which the entire drama had gotten underway: What motive could the plaintiff possibly have for making up such a tale? Why would she expose herself to the humiliation and pain of admitting to being the victim of rape? In short: Women do not lie. The lawyer's closing examination of Gretzinger before the jury in no way addressed the many problems with Gretzinger's testimony. Instead, he merely had Gretzinger confirm one last time (without citing specifics) that she had indeed been raped. Stressing the "painful, humiliating experience" Gretzinger was willing to relive by going to court, and the damage this indignity inflicted on her reputation, he claimed that his client's motivation was nothing more than to prevent other women from coming to the same harm to which she had been subjected.[6] Winding up, he asserted, "There is no motive to lie."[7]

However, this effort failed to persuade the jury to overlook the abundant evidence that Gretzinger had fabricated the charges. Plausible as it is to hold that in some past periods or in other countries the very charge of rape has been so self-vilifying that few women would willingly make it unless it was in fact true, hardly the situation in America in the 1990s, Gretzinger's lawyer's invocation of a prefeminist image of women's disadvantage in legal battles over rape thus proved unconvincing.

The Ramdas Lamb case is a particularly interesting one because of what it reveals about the inner workings of the Sexual Harassment Industry. Here is a professor of religion so profeminist that in class he referred to God as "she," a teacher whom many students described as always treating women with respect and encouraging their work in every way. None of these traits, however, carried any weight once the SHI involved itself in the case. What should have been dismissed at once as an instance of a few angry and vindictive students whose feminist beliefs had been challenged by a professor exercising his right of free speech quickly spun out of control. As Lamb points out, Gretzinger, while constantly alleging her powerlessness, managed, on the basis of mere accusations with no evidence at all, to turn his life upside down very easily—a good illustration of the increasing lag between rhetoric and reality: Victimhood is claimed while the very opposite is demonstrated.

Gretzinger's depositions reveal how thoroughly she knew the typical sexual harassment script. She stressed her vulnerability and "indebtedness" to Lamb, and for this latter case to be made she had to interpret his typical professorial gestures of kindness and helpfulness as instances of "grooming" (or, as some texts call it, "priming") her.[8] Fortunately for Lamb, many of his other students had witnessed Gretzinger's behavior—that she had phoned him, had sought him out, was always hanging around his office, and so on, all of which she denied under oath. Instead, she turned it all around, sounding well versed in the "how to make a case" literature, whose script she followed in every particular, above all in her psychological portrait of herself as a victim of an unscrupulous professor, whose path toward sexual assault she outlined with care.

All the charges made about Ramdas Lamb's behavior in class were refuted by other students, but to Susan Hippensteele, the university's "student advocate," and to Mie Watanabe, its EEO/affirmative action officer, whose handling of the matter also violated university procedures, they were self-evidently true.[9] Hippensteele suggested reading materials to teach the plaintiffs about sexual harassment injuries and how to be on the lookout for them. In that duplication of functions that often characterizes the SHI's involvement with local cases, she also served as adviser to a student group called SHarP (Sexual Harassment Prevention), in which Michelle Gretzinger participated after making her allegations.[10]

Testifying on behalf of the "victim" was Michele Paludi, the same sexual harassment expert whose *Ivory Power: Sexual Harassment on Campus* was one of the books suggested to the complainant by Hippensteele. What did Paludi know about the case? She had read only the supposed victim's account, not the masses of other testimony produced. But she could affirm that the charges were entirely plausible, her judgment being based on her general familiarity with student victims and predatory professors.

Professor Ramdas Lamb's three-and-a-half-year battle to prove his innocence—which is precisely what he had to do—is thus a scary example of the kind of reality the Sexual Harassment Industry has brought upon us.[11] That his case was an administrative outrage was plain as early as 1994—before claims and counterclaims were filed in federal court—when a labor arbitrator brought in by the faculty union examined the evidence and, in deciding in Lamb's favor, meticulously dissected the many abuses of due process that had characterized the university's handling of the case from the beginning. These abuses, the arbitrator made clear, resulted from the zealotry of the university's feminist sexual harassment officers. Nonetheless, the university settled with Gretzinger in 1995 for $175,000, citing inordinate delays in dealing with her case, but offered Lamb no recompense for suffering not only the same delays but also mistreatment by university officials. As we saw in chapter 3, Gretzinger lost her federal suit against Lamb.

But legal vindication is hardly enough to compensate the real victim in this case. In early 1998, this is what Lamb wrote about the repercussions of his experience:

> I still avoid interacting with women I don't know and trust. I rarely feel good about going to school. I still avoid meeting female students in my office, unless I know someone else will be there. I definitely treat my female students differently now than I do my male students.
>
> The case has had clear ramifications within the university, too. A lot of professors are being very careful with what they say. Several have told me they now avoid becoming advisors for female grad students. There have been policy changes, but that really doesn't mean a thing. In my case, nearly every administrator who dealt with me simply ignored the policy, from Hippensteele to the dean of the law school.[12]

In June 1998, Lamb was awarded tenure. But he failed in his attempt to save colleagues from an ordeal similar to his. In May 1998, the U.S. Court of Appeals for the 9th Circuit rejected his appeal of a district court's ruling that granted qualified immunity to the individual University of Hawaii officials who participated in the flawed sexual harassment investigation against him. These officials, the court declared, were entitled to qualified immunity; they were, in fact, obligated to investigate the sexual harassment charge. What the Court of Appeals declined to define were the "precise contours of the protection the First Amendment provides the classroom speech of college professors." The same Court of Appeals, however, upheld the federal jury's verdict against Gretzinger.

Finally, Lamb can put this entire episode behind him. But its effects linger: "I don't think I will ever feel the way I did prior to these accusations," he has said. "There are those at the university who still treat me as guilty even though every investigation has found me innocent."[13]

More recently still, Lamb has written: "I used to love to teach. Not any more. I used to love to interact with students and stimulate them to think critically. Not any more. I used to believe that university campuses promoted free speech and the truth. Not any more. I used to believe students when they would tell me things. Not any more."[14]

Academic Freedom Bites the Dust

If Ramdas Lamb's experience has disturbing implications for the state of academic freedom, another recent case raises even greater alarm in its demonstration of how charges of "sexual harassment" can serve academic inquisitors as an all-purpose warrant for intervention.[15] Ferrel Christensen has warned that the notion of "sexual harassment" has become "the greatest violation of freedom of speech to emerge in decades."[16] How true this is can readily be seen by the following example.

Eddie Vega was an instructor of writing at the SUNY Maritime College in 1993–94.[17] A Cuban by background (his father was imprisoned by Castro), Vega, a poet and novelist who has an M.F.A. in writing from Columbia University, was, according to colleagues, a very courteous and decorous man who worked hard to help his students develop the ability to express themselves in writing. His first year at Maritime had been a great success. His contract had been renewed for a second year, and he was looking forward not only to continued teaching but also to a position he had been offered as assistant dean of freshmen.

In July 1994, Vega was giving a summer course in writing. On July 21, he conducted a "clustering" exercise with his students, in order to stimulate their ideas and vocabularies. A woman in the class suggested "sex" as a topic for the session, which Vega expanded to "sex/relationships." Once the process of free association got underway, he wrote on the board the words and concepts the students came up with. Some of these were four-letter words, and Vega, out of discretion but still wanting to leave the students free to brainstorm, abbreviated them on the board.

Several weeks later, Vega was called into the president's office and shown a student's notebook that contained the X-rated words. He agreed that these words had been generated in his class. With this admission, he was accused of sexual harassment and fired on the spot. Of special significance here is the fact that Vega was not even asked what had occasioned these words, whether he had encouraged the students to use them in their compositions (he had not), and whether he had advised them about appropriate language (he had). His teaching career at Maritime was over; the promised administrative job disappeared. One of Vega's departmental colleagues, a specialist in Lawrence Durrell, wondered whether it was possible even to teach literature in such a climate.

What concerns me in the context of this book is that Vega was not charged with being an incompetent teacher, or with any other dereliction that, because he was an untenured faculty member, an "at-will" employee, might have led to his firing. Instead, Vega was accused of "sexual harassment," the catchall label that, in the minds of many administrators, would appear to obviate the need for due process, not to mention fairness. Vega is now representing himself in a federal suit against his former employer. In response to my asking him why other academics should care about his case, he wrote:

> Your thoughtful question, it seemed to me, sought a principled response, not one grounded in legal theory or case law. Your question, differently worded, was in fact the first and only question Judge Cote put to me during our teleconference in November of last year, "Mr. Vega, what is your case about?"
>
> I was surprised by the question, by its simplicity. I had a yellow pad by the phone with all kinds of legal citations and cleverly worded phrases that I had scribbled in preparation for the conference. I had anticipated questions and arguments. I was going to respond with the measured and commanding tone of an appellate court judge or a Yale law professor. . . .
>
> But she asked instead: "Mr. Vega, what is your case about?"
>
> In a flash the four or five theories of recovery that I had outlined in my complaint, the academic freedom, the free speech, the defamation, all of it vanished in a moment of telephonic silence. I stopped thinking and began talking: "Your honor, I was fired from my humanities teaching job because I was accused of violating the college's sexual harassment

policy. This was done without ever affording me a hearing, although I tried many times to get that hearing. I was fired because I allowed students to discuss sex in the classroom during a writing exercise. This was in violation of my free speech and due process rights guaranteed by the First and Fourteenth Amendments to the Constitution. And that's what this case is about."

It all comes down to that. Everything else is legal fluff. Had I spent five hours thinking about what the case is ultimately about rather than the 5 seconds I had, I would still not have given a more honest or to the point answer.

It answers your question, too. The sexual harassment policy was there because it was required by federal law. College administrators are using the weight of this federal law, Title IX, to deny even tenured faculty due process rights. If I can show in Federal Court that even an at-will teacher has due process rights under the U.S. Constitution, if not directly under Title IX, when accused of violating a federally mandated sexual harassment policy, it will restate the primacy of due process rights of the accused, the tenured and non-tenured, at public and private colleges. What happens in the Southern District of New York is carefully monitored by other districts.[18]

Vega's suit in state court, by contrast, is a straightforward defamation case, he says, and of limited interest to him. But federal court is a very different matter: "There we are talking about the most fundamental rights we have as classroom teachers and as citizens in a free and open democracy."

And what effect did this experience have on Professor Vega's teaching? In his new job in Florida, he still uses the same writing exercise, but now he allows only preselected topics and endures students' predictable complaints about their dullness. But even with a safe subject such as "The Right to a Public Education," Professor Vega reports, sex can somehow intrude itself.

For example, one student, in the nursing program, pointed out the need for adequate sex education and the distribution of condoms at the high school level. Some other students, sensing that the topic had gotten interesting, joined in with similar thoughts. I stopped them there; and here I think I violated their academic freedom and violated the integrity of the exercise (that thoughts should roam freely as one brainstorms the topic). I told them I thought we'd gathered enough material as a class and that we would continue the exercise working in small groups. They followed

my instructions without ever realizing that I had deprived them and myself of free speech.[19]

An interesting comparison might be made between Professor Vega's
experience and that of Joanne Marrow, who "showed slides of female
genitalia and discussed female masturbation in her psychology class" at
California State University at Sacramento. A male student filed a sexual
harassment complaint against Marrow, but the school ruled that
though the material may have been unwelcome or offensive to the student, it was not sufficiently pervasive or severe to create "an intimidating, hostile or offensive learning environment."[20] As Heinz-Joachim
Klatt observes, "It is unimaginable that complainants today would be
taken seriously who feel sexually harassed by the ways, for example,
feminist instructors lecture in Women's Studies courses."[21]

At my own university, an instructive case occurred in May 1998. John
Palmer, a sixty-five-year-old professor about to retire from the biology
department at UMass-Amherst, had, for some years, taught a large lecture course called "Biology and Social Issues," a course that, as the catalog description made clear, was designed to be provocative. On April
30, 1998, during a discussion of abortion, a student objected from the
floor to Palmer's assertion that from the point of view of biology, life
begins at conception. Another student, who worked at the Everywoman's Center, complained to the center's director, Carol Wallace, "on
behalf of a group of women" enrolled in the class. She alleged that
Professor Palmer had used inappropriate language and had drawn demeaning sketches of female anatomy to illustrate his lectures. Wallace
made no attempt to corroborate the truth of these allegations or their
meaning. Rather, she at once wrote to Professor Palmer's dean,
"Clearly such behavior constitutes sexual harassment, defined as 'conduct having the purpose or effect of unreasonably interfering with an
individual's work performance or creating an intimidating, hostile or
offensive working or academic environment.' "[22]

What had Professor Palmer actually said? As he had done for the
preceding six years, he had explained that from a biological perspective, the zygote is the first stage of human life. And he had pointed out
that various methods exist for killing that life by preventing the embryo
from becoming embedded in the uterine wall, where it could develop
into a fetus. Such methods, he noted, include IUDs and morning-after
pills (RU 486), which are designed to induce an abortion.[23] He stressed
that science had no answer to the moral questions raised by this issue

but that religions had developed a variety of positions on the subject. These statements were enough, Professor Palmer later wrote, to "set off one woman in the class."

> [She] jumped up and asked something about why I did not mention the role of women. She was so worked up that she had great trouble speaking and made little sense. Attempting to calm her I suggested she come to my office sometime where we could discuss her concerns. She paid no attention, feeling her agenda—whatever it was—was more important than class material. That is when the class turned on her and loudly told her to leave. She did stomp out, but first turned to the class and called them "a bunch of idiots."[24]

The case then went to the Ombuds Office, whose head, philosophy professor Robert Ackermann, wrote to Palmer that he was going to meet with nine complaining students, who clearly expected some sanctions to be imposed on Professor Palmer. The students had already gone to the Equal Opportunity and Diversity Office but had not yet filed a formal complaint there. The ombudsman was attempting to avoid including anyone from EO & D at his meeting, since if any such staff member were present and the "magic words" were uttered, a formal complaint of sexual harassment would have to be made and the university would be forced to respond.

By the time the students met with the ombudsman on May 8, 1998, they had learned of Professor Palmer's impending retirement, and this seemed to dampen the prospects for a formal complaint. Instead, the ombudsman wrote a lengthy letter to the chair of the biology department, outlining the charges. This letter is notable for the easy assumptions it makes about the direct consequences of any such charges. Professor Palmer's class, the ombudsman stated, had produced "an absolutely unprecedented negative response in this office"—a rather startling claim if one considers that only 9 students out of a class of 660 had complained and that some 2000 others had heard the same lecture over the preceding half dozen years. To Professor Ackermann, however, this "unprecedented" response required immediate action. His list of the students' complaints covered just about everything in the course—from Professor Palmer's lecturing style to his presentation of information and his syllabus—all of this based upon what the 9 students had reported in their meeting with the ombudsman, and all of it unsubstantiated. Nonetheless, the ombudsman did not hesitate to suggest to the chair that he might in the future wish to take "steps" in appointing faculty to teach this course, and might urge them to take special care to distinguish "fact" from "opinion" when lecturing.[25]

As another colleague commented, upon hearing of this case, it seems to show that the "reasonable person" criterion doesn't hold sway. By jumping to the conclusion that Professor Palmer's class had created a "hostile environment" for nine students, the Everywoman's Center must have assumed that the vast majority of students in the class (including four women who wrote warm letters of support for Professor Palmer) were "unreasonable."[26] As it turned out, Palmer was not given the opportunity to face his accusers. He does not even know the names of six of them.

One can only guess at Professor Palmer's feelings upon receiving such a parting gift from his university at the end of his teaching career. Perhaps it was counterbalanced by the standing ovation his six-hundred-odd students gave him at the last class of the semester, a day after the campus newspaper did a front-page story on the allegations. But what if he had not been on the point of retirement? Perhaps he would then have found himself in a position similar to that of Leroy Young, a tenured professor at Plymouth State College in New Hampshire.

Why Bother Investigating?

Since his appointment as head of graphic design in the art department in 1988, Leroy Young, a man now in his midfifties who describes himself as looking like Sean Connery's shorter, ugly brother, had built up a highly successful program. He had received much commendation for his efforts, and he thought he was doing good work in a good place. But all this changed abruptly at the beginning of the 1993–94 academic year when he was ordered to appear in the office of his dean. There, he was presented with a handwritten paper accusing him of sexually harassing one of his senior students, Jennifer Otten.

"You must be one of those touching, southern men," an administrator who was present said to him. Otten's charges were that Young had complimented her on her new blazer, had taken her to lunch "against her will," had made sexual innuendos to her at a party, had asked her for a kiss, had hugged her and put his hand on her shoulder, and had (at her request) provided a critique of Madonna's book *Sex*. But of these allegations Young was informed only in general terms. None of the specifics—about which he was to learn only later—were cited, and he was given no opportunity to tell his version of events. Instead, Young says, he had the sense that the real purpose of the meeting was to make him see the error of his ways. Times had changed, he was told, as a result of the Thomas–Hill hearings. "We're going to reeducate you, boy," his dean said to him.

Young denied having committed any impropriety. His initial reaction to the charges was that they must be based on misunderstanding, lack of communication, and misinterpretation. "I have no problem with an apology for misinterpretations, but I will not accept 'guilt' as a consequence of this situation," he wrote early on. If that concession did not suffice—and clearly it did not—he was prepared to fight.

Meanwhile, however, another student of Young's had come forward with more accusations of sexual impropriety. Before she could withdraw her charges (which she did a month later), at a formal hearing Young was found to be in violation of the college's sexual harassment policy and was placed on administrative leave. Though his salary continued, he could not teach and was barred from appearing on campus. He immediately appealed, and the college Sexual Harassment Appeals Board, concluding that there was no evidence to support the charges, eventually ruled, in February 1994, that Young should be reinstated.

By then, a third student who had graduated, Tracy Schneider, had come forward to allege acts of sexual impropriety that were said to have occurred three years earlier. She was not in fact eligible to file complaints against an institution in which she was no longer enrolled. At this point, the case took a different turn. The three young women, having engaged a legal firm that advertised its expertise in prosecuting sexual misconduct ("an emotional burden that can last a lifetime," the firm's ads proclaimed) by offering free seminars for prospective clients, proceeded to sue Young for five hundred thousand dollars in damages. They threatened to sue the college as well. In light of these new developments, Young's "administrative leave" was not rescinded, despite the recommendation of the Appeals Board. No formal charges had ever been filed; no proper investigation of the charges had taken place; indeed, Young was given to understand that the college administrators saw no need for such an investigation.

As often happens in such cases, Young's accusers had formerly been his admirers. Young says, "[From all three of them] I have received inscribed books, photos, invitations to lunch, art work, etc. I was even invited to lunch once and then it was canceled when I said my wife would attend also."[27] The complainants' lawyer asked college officials to meet with the third accusing student, Tracy Schneider, at his office, where they heard her describe various incidents of Young "groping," exposing himself, and trying to take off her blouse. Young responded with the results of a polygraph test (taken at the suggestion of his lawyer), which showed him to be truthful in his denial of each of Schneider's charges. But the college president, Donald Wharton, no doubt frightened by the threat of a sexual harassment suit against the college, declared that Schneider was to be believed and Young was not. Thus, in March 1994, Young was summarily fired for "deliberate and flagrant neglect of duty and moral delinquency of a grave order." The dismissal was effective immediately. As issued to the press, this notice of dismissal was accompanied by a specification of Schneider's accusations, which the president declared he had, on the basis of his own assessment, judged to be "well-founded."[28]

A local newspaper immediately understood the significance of this step and printed an editorial asking "Is Due Process Dead at PSC?" This is how the paper described the sequence of events: "[A]t the moment of his vindication on one set of similar allegations brought earlier, Young was summarily fired on the basis of the college president's own 'investigation' of separate charges brought by Tracy Schneider, a former student."[29] The prevalent attitude among the college's administrations seems to have been, "Why would she say these things if they weren't true?"

No formal hearing on Schneider's charges had been held; no investigation had taken place, President Wharton having acted entirely on his own authority. Young had not been shown any evidence against him. He had not been allowed to call witnesses. It took more than a year longer before Young was finally granted a hearing at which he was able to face his accuser and her "witnesses" (they witnessed only the accusations, Young explains).[30] Two years after his dismissal, a faculty panel found that the president of the college had acted inappropriately in unilaterally firing Young. But at the same time, the panel split over the merits of the charges against Young, finding, three to two, that cause for dismissal existed. Thus, without further procedures, he was fired again, immediately after having been reinstated.[31]

The moral Leroy Young draws from his experience is discouraging:

> If I ever teach again, I . . . would censor everything I say or do. To listen to all of the discussion [on this e-mail list] about philosophy of relationships, etc., is interesting, but I cannot let myself participate. I will tell no one of any opinions about sexuality, opinions about pornography,

or relate any personal experiences that I have ever had. Any of this could be used as ammunition against me. So I have been effectively censored.[32]

Ramdas Lamb faced far more serious charges and met with less dire consequences. Perhaps because the charges against Young weren't as implausible as "serial rape," his innocence was harder to prove—despite the polygraph test supporting him.

Having discovered that Young had no money, the three women dropped their suit against him. Tracy Schneider then sued the college in state court for negligence in not firing Young sooner. Because the college had not investigated her allegations, it lacked evidence with which to dispute her claims of negligence. As a result, Schneider was awarded $115,000. In a final touch of irony, the college's counsel asked Professor Young if he would be willing to appear as a witness for the college in its appeal of the award to Schneider.

Young's own suit against the college is pending, but as he comments, "[N]o one will win." He has already turned down the college's offer of $80,000, and still hopes for complete vindication. Meanwhile, he cannot find another teaching position. His wife and chief supporter, Tatum Young (a former member of the National Organization for Women), left her job as a special education teacher when they both decided to move back to North Carolina. They live on a small income while awaiting trial in their suit against the college.[33]

Recently, Leroy Young described his state of mind:

> In today's paper I saw an advertisement from a local college for adjunct positions in art. My excitement lasted but a few seconds. If I applied it would be just a matter of time before someone at the school [comes across] last year's libelous article in the *Chronicle of Higher Education*,[34] or remembers something someone had told them, or refers to an article in the local papers about the "accused Professor Young." Even if this doesn't happen, there is always, "have you ever been dismissed from a position and if so why?" How much longer will it be before the accusers must bear responsibility? My accusers dropped [their suit], but nothing happened to them. Why don't you sue them? I am told. With what? Lawyers must be paid. So I will continue to go into my studio and try and work and try not to spend the entire day playing solitaire so I don't have to think.
>
> Does anyone out there still believe that this is all coincidence? Does anyone still believe that all of this hysteria is not being fueled? A friend of mine, a retired professor from a prestigious university, told me recently, as I recounted my experience, that if he had not himself been

accused of harassment he would have only listened to me with a grain of salt. Somehow, some way, what is happening all across the country must be communicated to all involved.[35]

Woman against Woman

What happens when women accuse other women of sexual harassment? Does homophobia play a part in the way such allegations are handled? Some lesbians think so. In 1991, Valerie Jenness was hired as an assistant professor in the sociology department at Washington State University in Pullman. Only months before she was to come up for tenure, Jenness's contract was not renewed. The circumstances of this decision were murky, but allegations of sexual harassment played their part.

In the fall of 1995, Jenness assisted in writing five paragraphs of a paper for a graduate student with whom she had been sexually involved. She quickly realized that the help she had provided was improper and voluntarily disclosed the episode to the chair of her department. While her superiors considered the episode as no more than a lapse, requiring no action, when the student learned about the disclosure, she threatened to file sexual harassment charges against Jenness, but never actually did so. Nevertheless, the mere mention of sexual harassment triggered intervention. It caused the dean of the graduate school, whom the student had approached, to report the incident.

At this point, an earlier occurrence involving another female student resurfaced. In 1992, a graduate student had been turned down by Jenness when she expressed interest in a romantic relationship. Jenness had explained to the student that she could not become involved with her because they were in the same department. She had even spoken about this to her chair. Now, in January 1996, as the investigation of harassment charges got underway, the former student was contacted and asked to provide a statement. Like other universities, Washington State University was under pressure to "stem a tide of sexual harassment claims"—and was threatened with loss of federal funds unless it did so. But this does not explain why it was Jenness's case, and not other current ones, that was pursued.[36]

Not until several months later did Jenness learn she was being investigated. In April 1996, she was called to the dean's office to hear the results of the investigation. Jenness thereupon hired a lawyer. At a second meeting, the former student's allegations of sexual harassment were dropped, but the matter that Jenness herself had brought to her chair's attention—of having given inappropriate help to a graduate student—became the focus of attention. Based on this incident, the department chair, in consultation with other university officials, decided not to reappoint her. Jenness was informed of this decision on May 15, 1996.[37] In newspaper reports of this case, much was made of the sexual harassment issue. The former student is reported to have said she felt sexually harassed when Jenness gave her a book of photographs of lesbians.[38]

In 1997, Jenness filed a one-million-dollar lawsuit against the university, claiming that she was discriminated against because of her gender. She charged the university with having used the paper-writing episode as a pretext, its real reason for not renewing her contract being the belief that she had sexually harassed other women. Male faculty members accused of sexual harassment, by contrast, whether heterosexual or homosexual, were accorded quite different treatment, she claimed. Against them, no formal action was taken.[39]

Most instructive about this episode is that Professor Jenness (who is now employed at the University of California at Irvine) chose to defend herself not by challenging the entire atmosphere surrounding sexual harassment charges but by taking an approach typical of complainants of sexual harassment themselves; she argued that she had been discriminated against because of her sex. When Jenness filed her claim with the state of Washington, she began with the sentence "I am female and therefore a member of a protected class."[40] Like women making charges of sexual harassment, Jenness made use of the law as she found it. Just as the law facilitates sexual harassment complaints at this time, so does it allow a female professor such as Jenness (and not comparably treated male professors) to use the language of gender groupings to press her case.

Peggy Chevalier, chair of the Faculty Status Committee to which Jenness turned for a review of her treatment by the university, has commented that Jenness's case "got to be a witch hunt," with university guidelines flouted.[41] Jenness herself felt obliged to profess to the faculty of her department, "I have never preyed upon or exploited any student at WSU."[42] And surely this is the most deplorable aspect of the situation: that professors should be put in a position to make such statements, which serve as clear indications that a climate exists in which it is the supposition that professors *do* "prey upon" students!

Other instances of women being accused of sexual harassment by women have met with a variety of outcomes. One young woman I know (who declines to be identified) told me that both she and a male graduate-student friend of hers were falsely accused of sexual harassment by an opportunistic female student. The male alleged harasser was penalized, while she herself, she said, was not—because she is a lesbian and her university, she believes, was afraid of being considered homophobic.

In another case, Emory University and Elizabeth Fox-Genovese were the targets of a lawsuit by a former graduate student, an older woman married to a prominent local physician. After completing her doctorate with Fox-Genovese, the student had turned against her professor with charges of such offenses as demanding hugs and forcing the student to give parties in her stately home for visiting luminaries such as Rosalynn Carter. In this much-publicized case, Emory University settled for an undisclosed sum just before the case was to go to trial.

In still another case I know of, the defendant, a tenured professor falsely charged by another woman with whom she worked in the women's studies program, felt particularly vulnerable to accusations of sexual advances because, like Jenness, she is a lesbian. One lawyer she consulted was very interested in the case until it emerged that she was a lesbian, at which point the lawyer changed tunes instantly. This particular case, too, was settled by the university, with a six-figure sum going to the alleged victim in exchange for her dropping the charges. The accused professor fought long and hard against any settlement, and particularly against the demand that its terms and details be sealed—feeling that she needed to vindicate her honor. In the end, she was prevailed upon to go along with the terms of the settlement. Meanwhile, the complainant, having created a high-pressure atmosphere around her academic position, was awarded tenure by peer evaluators who, perhaps intimidated by the allegations, suspended the normal evaluation process. The defendant, on the other hand, who has described her experience as having induced a certain paranoia in her, now feels reluctant to apply for other positions since the record of the charges may follow her everywhere.

Valerie Jenness has endorsed the view that sexual harassment, which originated as a feminist-inspired term designed to combat discrimination, is increasingly being "appropriated" as a weapon in "less than feminist battles."[43] But as will be argued in chapter 5 below, such a defense rests not on a principled rejection of the Sexual Harassment Industry's ideology but rather on the much narrower ground that charges are inappropriate when directed at members of a "protected class," namely women.[44] Today, Jenness says, two main errors are occurring in relation to sexual harassment charges. On the one hand, some people get away with predatory behavior. On the other, innocent people are "nailed" for trivial things, which creates a climate in which it seems that policing sexuality is the main objective. Jenness sees these errors as two extremes that mirror one another, a situation made possible by the vagaries of sexual harassment law. She believes that sexual harassment law must be refocused so that preventing discrimination based on sex, not policing sexuality, becomes the goal.[45]

Precisely such a proposal has been made by Vicki Schultz in an article in the *Yale Law Journal*. While this may sound like an improvement, Jeffrey Rosen has recently argued that such a reorientation would in fact expand the reach of harassment law and turn it into a weapon for achieving strict proportional representation of males and females on the job (and, presumably, in academic programs).[46] Like MacKinnon, Rosen argues, Schultz is attempting to use harassment law "as an engine for the wholesale restructuring of the American workplace."[47]

Exporting Vigilance

Feminist-inspired vigilance is by no means a problem confined to the United States. Rather, it seems that the entire English-speaking world is in thrall to feminist ideology.[48] A look at one more "typifying tale," this one from Australia, should demonstrate this.

The case has been made the subject of a detailed study, *The First Stone* (1995), by Helen Garner, an Australian writer. Halfway through her book, Garner wonders how it is that institutions can inspire in men such deep feelings that they, as she writes in italicized wonder and admitted distaste, "fall in love with an institution *for life*." Such loyalty, she notes, "might unsettle [one's] broader ethical judgments."[49] Yet Garner herself had experienced a comparable falling in love, which, though never stated explicitly, is implicit throughout her book in her deep sorrow at the loss of her faith in feminism's capacity to make the world a better place.

Perhaps it is this tone of loss, setting a dark counterpoint to the "quiet, thoughtful" book Garner had hoped to write, that led reviewer Janet Malcolm, with her keen ear for the scathing put-down, to characterize Garner's text as the "ravings of a rejected lover."[50] But Malcolm is wrong on both counts. There are no ravings in Garner's account of the Sexual Harassment Industry in her own country, only sadness and bewilderment, and now and then a spark of deep anger. Nor is Garner the "rejected lover" in her tale. Rather, hers is the voice of an older-and-wiser feminist who discovered rather abruptly that she could not tolerate denials of fairness, justice, and common sense even when perpetrated in the name of feminism. And like men's passion for institutions, commitment to feminism, she now sees, can warp one's judgment of individual cases.

The course of events leading to Garner's critique is told in a highly personal account of what happened in Melbourne beginning in October of 1991. Her case in point is the dismissal of the master of Ormond College, a residential college at the University of Melbourne, after he was accused of groping two women students at a college celebration. It is a rather typical conflict between men and women, a conflict more and more often classified these days by the label "sexual harassment." Such a struggle, fought stereotypically over the terrain of the female body, extends itself (as we saw also in the Ramdas Lamb case) far beyond corporeal geography and rapidly invades the alleged harasser's livelihood, reputation, and family life. It is not surprising, then, that such cases increasingly take on the dramatic form of a morality play.

Garner pursues two main questions. First, why did two women students decide to go to the police to press charges of indecent assault against the master of Ormond College rather than attempting to settle the matter in less adversarial ways? She never quite reaches an answer, though it seems clear that what happened had much to do with both feminist rhetoric and the instant support given to the students by other women in the college, who resisted more informal solutions. It is this sequence of events—"He touched her breast and she went to the *cops?*"—that shook Garner's commitment to feminism to the point of her sending a letter of sympathy to the accused, expressing dismay at the "ghastly punitiveness" and "warfare" directed against him.[51] This letter, in turn, once it circulated, seems to have made Garner the target of general antipathy by feminist forces both within and without the college, which explains the two complainants' persistent refusal to discuss the case with her when she tried to interview them.

The second main question Garner addresses is this: Why did the master—who repeatedly denied the allegations—lose his position even though on appeal he was found not guilty of indecent assault? While Garner sees this latter question primarily in terms of the particular personalities, history, traditions, and ethos of the college, I suspect that the force of feminist ideology played an important role, just as it did in the other cases reviewed here.

But Garner's book is not a simple tale of feminist justice gone awry. As a long-term feminist herself, one who had her own experiences with unwanted and offensive sexual overtures, she is sensitive to the students' allegations and reflects interestingly on women's odd passivity, which keeps them from handling such situations on their own. She is also aware of the real violence to which women are sometimes subjected, and episodes of it intrude into her narrative. In April 1993, for example, while working on her book, Garner heard about a fourteen-year-old girl who, on her way to school, was raped at knifepoint in a public toilet: "I thought, contemplating [the news item], that our helpless rage and grief at this eternally unpreventable violence against women and girls—our inability to protect our children from the sickness of the world—must get bottled up and then let loose on poor blunderers who get drunk at parties and make clumsy passes."[52]

It is a very revealing passage. First, many feminist activists would denounce Garner's "sickness of the world" as a weak euphemism for "the aggressions of men," a condition demanding strong corrective measures. Second, the pronouns in the quoted sentence hint at something else: Garner does not see herself as one of the potentially raped, as one of the victims.

In contrast, many feminists who insist most vociferously on the need to take drastic measures against sexual harassers do, in fact, identify with the offended parties, do see themselves as sufferers, indeed see all women as men's victims. Considering that much feminist discourse has been devoted to eliding the distinctions between types of offenses and degrees of suffering, this identification should come as no surprise. Sexual harassment specialists intentionally blur the lines. When Garner concludes, therefore, that "the ability to discriminate [between outright attacks and clumsy overtures] *must be maintained*" and that "otherwise all we [do] is increas[e] the injustice of the world,"[53] she is not only saying something that has never won general agreement in feminist circles. She is asserting a proposition expressly denied and actively contested by some of the most vocal feminist writers. For my part, I agree with Garner. Distinctions are always important. Unfortunately, we live in a climate (and evidently so does Garner) in which many women are doing their best to prevent nuanced thinking from dissolving their caricature of the male menace.

Garner rejects the view that sees an exaggerated male power at work in all heterosexual exchanges. She worries that "Eros, 'the spark that ignites and connects,' "[54] will be extinguished by the new dispensation with its ferocious insistence on conflating "harassment" and "violence."[55] But even Garner occasionally genuflects to feminist discourse, as when she categorically describes sexual harassment as "bullying,"[56] forgetting her own suggestions, elsewhere, that a provocative word or gesture may be the positive expression of desire, even awe, when encountering female beauty and vitality. Why, she asks more reasonably, should flirting have to be harmful? Why must it *mean* something beyond itself? "It's play. It's the little god Eros, flickering and flashing through the plod of our ordinary working lives." She concludes, "Feminism is meant to free us, not to take the joy out of everything."[57]

But that is precisely the problem. What Garner is calling "joy" and "play" has been effectively reconceptualized by many feminist theorists as the patriarchy oppressing women through the very "institution" of heterosexuality. Thus, unless a great many women step from the sidelines to support Garner's call for reasonableness, and to declare that they would rather live in a world in which the inconvenience of an occasional unwanted sexual overture is a small price to pay for freedom of expression and association, it is a good bet that the theoretical battle will continue to be won by those who talk the most and the loudest.

Once her book appeared, Garner's dismay was compounded, as is made clear in an afterword to the North American edition, in which she reflects on the reactions to the book itself and to her personally. Like other women who have written critically of feminism, Garner found herself instantly vilified, her words and attitudes distorted, her motives assumed to be mercenary.[58]

This is still happening. Janet Malcolm, for example, contemptuously dismisses Garner's suggestions for "less destructive responses" to harassment (such as letting one instance of groping pass with a warning). "This isn't good enough," Malcolm admonishes. "This is closing ranks with the abuser. . . . Sexual harassment isn't sexual abuse—exactly. It lies on the border between a crime and a mistake."[59] Yet Malcolm ignores Garner's call for responses suitable to borderline situations, that is to say, for measured reactions to highly diverse episodes, all of which are today viewed strictly through the distorting prism of "power," so beloved by practitioners of feminist discourse.

Two fundamentally opposing worldviews are currently in collision. One of them sees sex (especially male sexuality) as a perpetual danger. The other sees sex as primarily a source of pleasure for both women and men. Not surprisingly, Garner's view is at once an irritant and a threat to the regulators of sexual behavior who would leave nothing to chance, risk no unpleasantness, opt always for safety and certainty over improvisation and the hazards of chance. This is a major battle, turning on divergent views of what is to be permitted in a society in which women are now everywhere in the public sphere, thereby exacerbating the pervasive sexual awareness that is characteristic of our species.

But cultural pressures, as we all know, alter our behavior. Garner suspects that much of the conflict she is experiencing between herself and the younger women who supported the complainants may be due to differing generational perceptions. In light of what I myself have seen of sexual harassment cases in academe, I would dispute that this is so. Older women who have absorbed and sustained what Garner aptly labels the "punitive feminist" line on sexual harassment are likely to be as ferocious as the students to whom they teach that line.

What is most significant about Garner's book is its commentary on the implications—for women and for feminism, as well as for men—of the new behavioral demands that pit women against male sexuality. She does not rave, though sometimes she bristles (is only feminist-inspired rage at supposed male privilege legitimate anger?). Mostly, she deplores the atmosphere newly created as a result of the wide acceptance of a punitive feminism with its insistence on women as victims.

One of the most poignant and most illuminating lines I have ever encountered about sexual harassment charges comes from the Ormond master's wife, the subject of a sympathetic chapter in Garner's book. This woman incisively appraises the devastation to her family life caused by the charges of indecent assault. "Deep down," she says, "under this extraordinary pain I feel, there's a sense of the *triviality* of this destruction."[60]

Chapter 5

Galloping Contradictions

༄༅

When the crimes become ideological, and the net is cast wide, many innocent victims are ensnared.

KLAUS DE ALBUQUERQUE, in Sexuality and Culture (1997)

The stories told in chapter 4, of faculty members guilty of no wrongdoing but nonetheless ensnared by the SHI, exemplify the havoc that can be, and has been, wrought in academe by the pursuit of women's comfort. Unsurprisingly, these professors have become outspoken critics of sexual harassment policies. But there are some women faculty members, also falsely or frivolously accused, who do not attribute their troubles to wrongheaded ideas. Some of these, lesbian as well as heterosexual, identify the problem as sexual harassment policies set adrift, cut loose from their feminist moorings. This purportedly feminist critique of sexual harassment charges leveled at women needs to be carefully appraised.

What does one make of a professor who dedicates a scholarly book thus: "To my Students: The bright, hot, hip (young) women who fire my thoughts, my loins, my prose. I write this to move, to please, to shake you"? Should we conclude that the writer of these lines is unconventional, rash, provocative, exceeding the bounds of good taste, not to mention wisdom? How would we react to such a dedication if we knew it to be by a man?

In fact, it was written by Jane Gallop in a book she published several years ago, *Around 1981: Academic Feminist Literary Theory*.[1] The flamboyance of her words is vintage Gallop, and it therefore causes little surprise to learn that at just about the time she was finishing this book,

Gallop found herself accused of sexual harassment by two female graduate students who evidently did not appreciate her style.

In *Feminist Accused of Sexual Harassment,* her recent response to this accusation, Gallop both critiques and endorses the Sexual Harassment Industry.[2] Her posture is that of an inspired teacher who also plays the jester, the narcissist, the performance artist. Her self-defense, as offered in *Feminist Accused,* invites close scrutiny, for it allows us to discern important aspects of the sexual zeitgeist and of the contradictory forces that feminist activists have set in motion. Though Gallop attempts to unravel the connections among sex, sexism, and sexual harassment (condemning the last two as inextricably linked to discrimination while attempting to salvage the first from any contamination), she manages in the end only to confirm and reinforce the double standards that currently reign in feminist discourse and in the new legal scene they have brought into existence.

Judging by a review that she wrote of Billie Wright Dziech and Linda Weiner's *Lecherous Professor,* Gallop would reply to the above comments by dubbing them "heterosexist," for she defends sexual freedom by the odd strategy of tainting SHI activists such as Dziech and Weiner with the label of homophobes.[3] What Gallop fails to see is that they are not homophobic but heterophobic, that they make very little of same-sex harassment, while aiming their attack at the paradigmatic case of a male professor and a female student. As a result, Gallop's criticisms of *The Lecherous Professor* seem to be oddly tangential, as if she feared being accused of defending men's rights to express heterosexual interest. So she takes the tack of demolishing the book for its purported homophobia. This is an altogether bizarre proceeding, which reveals that sexual correctness is going on even among those who try to defend sexual liberation, as Gallop certainly does.

By denouncing the supposed homophobia of the authors of *The Lecherous Professor,* Gallop goes them one better. In doing so, she returns to the mother lode of MacKinnonite reasoning. In her book about her own ordeal as an alleged same-sex harasser, she openly declares that *only* male-against-female aggression can count as harassment.

Gallop begins *Feminist Accused of Sexual Harassment* by calling attention to its "tabloid" title, the "newsworthy anomaly" (rather like "Man bites dog") of a feminist finding herself accused of sexual harassment.[4] This is, alas, no longer as unusual an event as she imagines. As noted in chapter 4 above, there have been a number of such cases—some very well publicized (such as that of Elizabeth Fox-Genovese, former director of women's studies at Emory University); others less so (such as the charges against the director of the women's studies program at the University of Alabama by her ex-lover, a forty-year-old woman who thereafter became a man); still others having thus far attracted hardly any attention nationally. All have in common that the women so accused not only were feminists but were actively involved in women's studies and that their accusers were other women also involved in these programs.

Most notable in Gallop's tale is her failure ever to connect her experiences with those of the dozens of men who have faced similar accusations from women in colleges and universities. That some of these men may be as innocent as Gallop feels herself to be seems never to have crossed her mind. Instead, her criticism focuses on the current penchant of universities for prohibiting consensual relations between professors and students. In an earlier comment on her ordeal, she accurately noted, "[M]ost people take an accusation for a finding of guilt. Simply to be accused of a sexual crime is to be forever stigmatized."[5] But nowhere in *Feminist Accused* does she acknowledge that it is above all the inflated concept of "hostile-environment harassment" that has swept men, in particular, into a vortex of accusations, stigmatization, disrepute, and—in some cases—broken careers. Instead, she worries only that such accusations will put feminism under suspicion of being "antisex," a charge from which she wants to save it.

Gallop's defense rests on her own experience, back in 1971, of feminism as a simultaneous discovery of both sexual and intellectual desire. As she puts it, in italicized exclamation, *"Feminism turned me on."*[6] Knowledge and sex "bubble together," for Gallop, not as an occasional heady brew but as the alchemy of the best sort of teaching, with an honorable pedigree going back to Plato. There is, indeed, in Gallop's prose a good deal of bubbling, plus repeated descriptions of herself and other people as hot, hip, clever, sassy, bold, daring, smart, original, sexy, and, of course, fucked, screwed, laid, and generally turned on by transgressive possibility. Her heavy-breathing rhetoric undergoes no change at all as she records the passing decades from her initial feminist transformation in 1971 to her response to her students twenty-some years later.

One wonders, then, why Gallop was shocked to discover that her playful exploration of erotic-plus-intellectual energy was viewed as something quite different by two female graduate students who got to experience it first hand. Evidently tired of the game she was playing, they accused her of extorting sexual favors from them and then retaliating after they turned her down—classic quid pro quo harassment. One of the students pointed to an event Gallop could not deny but certainly would subject to her own ludic interpretation: a very public French kiss at a 1991 gathering, the First Annual Graduate Student Gay and Lesbian Conference.

This conference was itself an exhilarating experience for Gallop. It reminded her of her youth: "Once again I was surrounded by bold young women, exploring the possibilities of a new mix of political, intellectual, and sexual liberation." Compared with those presented at other professional meetings, the papers were "smarter, more original, and more daring."[7] "Everyone seemed so clever and sassy," Gallop confesses, "[that] I wanted to rise to the occasion."[8] Hence Gallop's announcement at one of the conference sessions that "graduate students are my sexual preference,"[9] followed that evening by the long kiss. Not until a year and a half later did that remark, together with the public kiss, come to be reinterpreted as part of a pattern of quid pro quo harassment. Gallop suspects that this delay gave the students (aided by their university's affirmative action office) much time to contemplate just how harassing her behavior had been.

The university, to its credit, eventually dismissed the quid pro quo charges. But the kiss—the public spectacle of which Gallop was so proud—was sufficient evidence that she had violated a university policy prohibiting "consensual amorous relations" between professors and students.

The most interesting aspect of this saga, at least for the purposes of this book, is Gallop's disingenuous self-defense against the charge of sexual harassment. "Female sexual harasser seems like a contradiction in terms," she writes. After all, "feminism invented sexual harassment."[10] Sexual harassment, Gallop explains in an earlier article dealing with her case, "is a way men obstruct women from doing work. University policies against sexual harassment aim to insure that women have as much chance as men to pursue knowledge."[11] In saying this, Gallop is merely following the line laid down by feminists in the 1970s. Not sex but sexism is the issue in sexual harassment. It is, Gallop writes hyperbolically in her book, "criminal not because it is sex but because it is discrimination."[12]

On such an account, feminists by definition cannot be sexist. It follows that they cannot commit sexual harassment. But if "sexism" is discrimination or "disadvantaging" on the basis of sex, why can't women's negative treatment of other women, if it occurs "on the basis of sex" (because they are women), be "sexism"? Only the false tautology that to be feminist is never to be sexist (at least not against women) can defend Gallop's claim. But as everyone who lives in the real world knows, the notion that women never discriminate against other women is a pious fiction.

Even the egalitarian demand for "sisterhood" can take a very negative turn. Ti-Grace Atkinson discovered this when The Feminists (a group she had founded in 1969) passed a resolution criticizing her "for allowing the media to define her as the group's leader." As Alice Echols, in her history of radical feminism, recounts, the group, insisting on its commitment to being "leaderless," "contended that Atkinson's growing stature in the media made a mockery of The Feminists' much-vaunted egalitarianism."[13] They meant business, too: They threatened to expel anyone who disobeyed their ruling that the group would collectively determine contact with the media, by drawing lots. Atkinson withdrew from the group.

Atkinson's experience is, evidently, one of "sexism without sex," a clear example of an impediment placed in the way of a particular woman's advancement by a group of women. Her sin (not yet a crime) was excessive individualism. The twin targets—males and individualism— very much present in the early radical feminist movement, have left their mark on subsequent feminist thought.

The Erotics of Pedagogy

For Jane Gallop, to be charged, rather than celebrated, for having engaged in "consensual amorous relations" with a student is an assault on the very core of her pedagogy. Her defense is two tiered. First, she articulates her disapproval of the consensual relations policies increasingly adopted by universities all over the country. These, she argues, mistake sex for sexism, and erotics for discrimination. No doubt she is right about this confusion, though her analysis does not go nearly far enough.

Unable to resist the urge to be shocking, she can't leave it at that, but has to defend her erotic pedagogy as the pinnacle of good teaching. This is her second tier of defense. I, too, have had "passionate" engagements with students, but these did not, as Gallop insists, necessarily involve sexual energy, unless one simplistically converts *all* energy into sexual drive. As a student, moreover, I learned much from professors I found not at all attractive, and I was sexually "turned on" by professors from whom I learned little. Gallop's formulation of an iron law of pedagogical erotics, or erotic pedagogy, strikes me as arbitrary, unconvincing, and self-serving, and by no means the secret truth that she alone has the guts to admit.

For a feminist to be accused of sexual harassment is, to Gallop, the mark of "an issue drifting from its feminist frame." Why did this happen to her? She is in no doubt as to the reason: "[B]ecause I sexualize the atmosphere in which I work." "When sexual harassment is defined as the introduction of sex into professional relations," Gallop notes, "it becomes quite possible to be both a feminist and a sexual harasser."[14] Most instances of what is called "sexual harassment" in academe today do involve sex in its erotic sense, not merely sex as gender. To Gallop, however, this is a "misunderstanding" of sexual harassment and its meaning:

> In the 1990s, sexual harassment has replaced pornography as the high-profile feminist issue. Like pornography, harassment allows feminists to reach a broad audience. Like pornography, the focus on harassment runs the risk of being widely misunderstood as an objection to sexuality rather than sexism. And like pornography, the issue of harassment seems to produce a protectionist feminism that objects to intellectual inquiry.[15]

But the SHI itself, Gallop's articles of faith notwithstanding, makes it quite clear that its antisex animus is no misunderstanding, no accidental "drift" from a proper feminist perspective. It is, instead, a conscious and deliberate attack on sex, sexual awareness, and sexual expression. And since the vast majority of people are heterosexual, how can this attack be seen as anything other than an assault on heterosexuality? Susan Hippensteele, for example, who presents herself as an expert on harassment, in her deposition in the Ramdas Lamb case (discussed in chapters 3 and 4 above) defined sexual harassment as "the inappropriate sexualization of an otherwise nonsexual relationship."[16]

Would Gallop necessarily disagree with her? It is difficult to say with certainty whether she would or not. Despite her self-representation as a sexual brinkswoman, Gallop is careful to defend everyone *except* heterosexual men. The main strategy she uses to discredit the charges brought against her is to garb her "sexualizing" behavior in the mantle of feminism: "It is because of the sort of feminist I am that I do not respect the line between the intellectual and the sexual."[17] In describing her 1971 "bacchanalian frenzy," when she was intoxicated by "our young feminism" and by the bare breasts of a beautiful young woman, Gallop writes, "Our breasts were political."[18] But what if a shy woman in the room had decided that this display of breasts made her uncomfortable and impeded her education (after all, this was at a campus feminist event)? Would this make the others vulnerable to a charge of sexual harassment? In today's world, it well might.

Gallop notes that the "chill winds of the current climate threaten to extinguish what feminism lit for me."[19] The problem is that, contra Gallop, it is *not* because these chill winds might damage feminism that they should be resisted but rather because they are unrealistic, abusive, and unfair—to men and women alike, to heterosexuals and homosexuals—and a threat to both freedom of association and academic freedom. But that is not the argument Gallop makes.

Defending her sexually provocative teaching style, Gallop is entirely accurate in her characterization of feminist pedagogy as an attempt to efface hierarchical boundaries between professors and students: "This commitment to a freer, less rigid knowledge meant exploring new kinds of pedagogical relations."[20] Today, she complains, "rather than playing with our pedagogical roles, we seem to be trapped in them."[21] The nostalgia for an irretrievable *temps perdu* lends a pathetic quality to Gallop's account: "Twenty-five years ago, I thought women's studies was hot."[22] Today, it has cooled down, no longer able to distinguish between "sexism" and "sex."

Longing for the heroic phase of feminism, Gallop evidently tries to enact it in her classes, a task that surely becomes increasingly difficult as time and age leave their marks on her. Still, she says, there are moments when she can recreate the "electricity, the buzz of live knowledge, the excitement of women thinking freely together. I always try to get us to that place where learning begins to dance. When we get there, my students love me and I'm crazy for them."[23] This is one aspect (not the only one) of her "sexualization" of the classroom, and Gallop does not disguise her narcissism as she details her gratified responses to those students who seek her out, adore her, want to be just like her. Evidently she either sees no problem with this strategy or is unaware of what her evocation of it might convey to readers of her book. She has already announced her love of "spectacle" (and of making a spectacle of herself), and it is too late now to withdraw into discreet silence.

Power: Who's Got It? Who Wants It?

Gallop notes, accurately, it seems to me, that "sexualizing is not necessarily to women's disadvantage."[24] But she does not then go on to comment on the problem arising from the current expectation that women alone should decide when "sexualizing" is appropriate and when it is not and that men are to be held legally liable if they make a wrong guess about this. Here we have a double standard whose consequences are being played out on a daily basis.

Far from speaking to these issues, however, Gallop makes explicit her objections to "a gender-neutral notion of power," which she considers to be "a serious departure from feminism."[25] Once again we see how deeply rooted her rhetorical commitment to feminism remains; "feminism" is her by-now familiar defense against the charge of abuse of power. Only men are capable of abusing power; hence, only men are capable of harassing. If a woman harasses a man, such an assault lacks weight because, Gallop explains, "social expectations," accompanied by economic power, psychological intimidation, and social coercion, are absent. She quickly clarifies that she exempts male homosexuality and female sexuality in general from potential abuses of power because both "tend to signify weakness and vulnerability." Only "male heterosexuality in our culture connotes power."[26]

Objecting to arguments that reduce power to "mere institutional position,"[27] Gallop nonetheless attempts to reduce it to gender and sexual orientation. In this she is evidently in complete agreement with the National Organization for Women, which, on its Web site, presents some interesting information regarding sexual harassment. The very first words reveal that the feminist line articulated twenty-some years ago has undergone no refinement: "Sexual harassment is a form of violence against women, used to keep women 'in their place.' "[28] How, then, one might well ask with Gallop, could a woman ever be guilty of it? Gallop urges us to remember "the feminist insight that the most destructive abuses of power occur because of widespread, deeply rooted social and psychological reinforcement"—elements she feels women invariably lack.[29] Her double standard becomes quite explicit here; she is attempting to defend her own *particular* behavior by hiding behind men's social and institutional power, which must make any behavior of hers necessarily innocent, lacking in power (in a negative sense), and unactionable. This is a patently dishonest and illogical analysis. What it reveals is how far Gallop goes to retain her own autonomy while still being politically correct.

Yet in describing her successful eventual seduction of two of her professors while in graduate school, Gallop makes it quite clear that exercising her own power was what that particular effort was about. She wanted to get her professors into bed, she says, "in order to make them more human, more vulnerable."[30] She wished to change the balance of power, "wanted to see them naked, to see them as like other men."[31] "Screwing these guys," Gallop explains in her usual elegant prose, "definitely did not keep me from taking myself seriously as a student."[32] On the contrary, it was a leveling technique intended to aid her self-confidence.

Janet Malcolm, in a review, calls Gallop's comments on students seducing professors a "novel view of professor/student sex as a transaction that *reduces* rather than increases the power of the putative 'greater man.' "[33] Actually, the use of sexual prowess to overcome the coveted and despised "higher" traits symbolized by the superior is far from novel; it is entirely traditional. Women have always used sexuality as a source of personal power and reinforcement (and often also as a path to upward mobility, as is evident now in many charges of sexual harassment against institutions and organizations with "deep pockets," which can substantially enlarge women's financial resources).

There is nothing either new or radical in the perception that a teacher's power and authority can be drastically undermined by sexual vulnerability. That is the whole point of Heinrich Mann's celebrated novel *Professor Unrat*, memorably made into the movie *The Blue Angel*, where a tyrannical professor is utterly undone by a seductive and vulgar cabaret singer. If Malcolm finds Gallop's embrace of this technique "novel," perhaps this is because she has bought into the SHI's version of academic sexual harassment in which a "lecherous professor" uses his vast power to sexually exploit an innocent student. Listen to professors talk about the manipulative behavior of their students and a very different picture emerges of student–teacher relations, far from the stereotype of female passivity and victimhood.

Gallop, too, notes that in all the relationships she describes (whether as student or teacher), it was always the student who made the first move.[34] That seems plausible to me. Does this mean it is always wrong of professors to take the initiative? Gallop seems to try to have it all ways. "Although I no longer actually have sex with students, I still embrace such relations in principle," and "I am still convinced that desire is good and that when mutual desire makes itself felt, it is a very fine thing indeed."[35] But by her own account, she only toys with her students; she does not "actually" act on either their desire or her own. This may not make her a sexual predator (the preferred designation of *The Lecherous Professor* and other stereotyped representations of male professors vis-à-vis female students), though it certainly suggests that students caught in her intricate web might feel both confused and abused. She tries to defend sex as not bad, nasty, or debased but belonging "more to the world of conversation and friendship."[36] Perhaps her problem is that although she is now a heterosexual partner and mother, she still needs to hang onto the "transgressive" behavior of her younger years and uses her students for that purpose.

In other words, Gallop is a tease. Perhaps it was that realization, and not her students' fear that she really was expecting them to sleep with her, that led them to rebel against her. Here was a teacher who held enormous intellectual interest for them and who used it to play erotic games in which they, at least, were unlikely to find satisfaction. Perhaps her students felt toyed with. Were they not merely playing walk-on parts in a drama of which she was author, director, and star? Some such resentment is certainly suggested by a curious detail of Gallop's case. The complainants, taking advantage of the extraordinary practice of permitting the "victim" to stipulate at the outset what would satisfy her as a resolution to her charges, specified that Gallop was not to be allowed to use the episode as the subject of intellectual inquiry and that doing so would constitute "retaliation," always specifically prohibited in sexual harassment cases. Gallop comments that her accusers were asking the university to censor her scholarly writing and control her thinking,[37] which, to its credit, it declined to do.

Once broken loose from its feminist moorings, Gallop argues, the attempt to control sexual harassment can become not "just independent of feminism, but actually hostile to feminism."[38] This is the trap she feels caught in. And her response is clear: She wants sexual harassment law and regulations to exist *only* within a framework that provides her and other feminists with license, while restraining the behavior of men. And this she presents in all seriousness as a right and just demand.

While Gallop continues to enjoy her position as Distinguished Professor at the University of Wisconsin at Milwaukee, she might ponder the fate of a young male academic who took it upon himself to practice the very same feminist pedagogical principles she advocates. Adam Weisberger, a sociologist at Colby College, also breached the boundaries between professor and student. He did not do it by so daring a gesture as Gallop's public French kiss. Weisberger's female students merely charged him with having delved into their private lives, acting more like a psychotherapist than a teacher. Some complained that his style made them "uncomfortable." Others accused him of being a "crude voyeur." Eventually he was charged with creating a "sexually threatening environment in his classroom."[39] Having been turned down for tenure, he has brought charges against Colby for defamation and infliction of emotional distress. He plans to file suit in federal court as well.

Weisberger's claim is that the school discriminated against him because he is a man. He argues that the students would not have complained about his actions had they been those of a woman. This, indeed, is not a far-fetched assertion, for feminism has defended and thoroughly "theorized" the intentional undermining of the teacher as a remote (i.e., masculine) authority. It is, above all, feminist pedagogical writings that denounce the "distanced" and "objective" teaching style, excoriate it as masculine and authoritarian, and seek to replace it with a passionate and engaged classroom dynamic in which the teacher essentially abdicates authority—an attitude that has been known to turn classes into virtual group-therapy sessions.[40]

For years, Barry Dank, professor of sociology and founder of the Academic Sexual Correctness E-Mail List, as well as of the journal *Sexuality and Culture,* has been pointing out that feminist pedagogical practice displays a deep contradiction. Because it fully supports the lecherous-professor-versus-innocent-student model, it seeks to raise boundaries between (male) professors and (female) students. At the same time, feminist pedagogy undermines these barriers in both the theory and the practice of the feminist classroom, which is based precisely on erasing boundaries, encouraging disclosure and intimacy, and doing away with hierarchical separation. The coexistence of these apparently antipodal positions can be made sense of by noting that it is logical to insist on boundaries and careful surveillance in the classroom when heterosexual male professors are seen as a threat to their women students. The woman-to-woman intimacy of feminist teaching, on the other hand, exempts feminist teachers from any such insistence on proper professional boundaries.

Gallop, ever subtle, affirms precisely this view when she writes, "Personal pedagogy by feminists fosters women's learning, but when sexist pigs get personal they curtail women's opportunities for education."[41] This statement is a telling one because it clearly reveals her defense for what it is, a personal apologia, not a brief for all those who are opportunistically accused of sexual harassment.

The eroticization of pedagogy is hardly an invention of Gallop. She herself mentions Plato's academy as a kind of precursor. Most commonly, in the erotically charged classroom, young female students develop a mad crush or "pash" on their female teachers, as in Muriel Spark's *Prime of Miss Jean Brodie* or in Christa A. Winsloe's play *Yesterday and Today* made into the 1931 film *Mädchen in Uniform*. But teachers such as Miss Brodie and Winsloe's Fräulein von Bernburg, though they are able to give both students and studies a sense of life, probably do little deliberately to sexualize their classroom atmosphere. At the opposite pole is Heinrich Mann's Professor Unrat, whose dry pedantry squeezes whatever life there is out of the subject he teaches. These are two extremes, well known to anyone with interest and experience in teaching. They are hardly pedagogical models. Gallop, however, defends the erotic alternative, bringing to it the post-1960s penchant for outrageous behavior and obvious, even obnoxious sexualization. And she tries to do this while maintaining her credentials as a feminist naturally opposed to real "sexual harassment."

Gallop does not recognize that the issue of consensual relations in academe is merely an extension of an antiheterosexual mood at this moment in time. Hence, she does not note the need for a questioning of the very category of sexual harassment and of the legal and institutional apparatus that has grown around it. She fails to challenge the feminist double standard that merely reverses the old ways, replacing male prerogatives with female privilege. Women surely are not claiming that they alone should initiate sexual advances, while men have no such rights. Nor does it make sense to think that most women want to live and work in a sex-free atmosphere, once again treated like shy maidens terrified of male sexuality. Yet such a view of the sexes lies at the root of contemporary laws and regulations regarding sexual harassment. It is this fact that makes implausible the distinction between sexuality and sexism. No wonder, then, that sexuality has come under attack in the fight against sexism. The two cannot, in practice, be separated, much as Gallop tries.

An example of this kind of assault on sexuality is a recent article, "Recognizing Sexual Harassment," included in the Sandler and Shoop volume analyzed in chapter 2 above. Its author, Linda Vaden Gratch, having stated that "unwanted" is the "litmus test," moves her discussion smoothly from "touching" to "touching in *power* situations" to "unwanted sexual touching"—different actions entirely, but here conflated into the single category of "sexual harassment," which Gratch evidently wants us to learn how to "label" properly, if a "call to action" is to be effective.[42]

Unlike Jane Gallop, who worries about preserving sexual harassment from a "sex-blind universal application" that would ensnare women as much as men, I contend that the real threat is the increasing tendency to stigmatize any "unwanted" touch, word, or even glance, as sexual harassment. Sex crimes are crimes of a sexual nature; but not all sex is criminal, a point in danger of being lost. It makes no sense to believe that only by means of draconian measures to guard them against any sexual approach can women enjoy equal opportunity at work or in school.

Controlling Women

Two serious consequences follow from the position embraced by the SHI that sexual harassment is men's way of controlling women. First, this view suggests that women cannot sexually harass women or men and that men cannot sexually harass other men (a proposition denied by the Supreme Court in its 1998 *Oncale* decision). Second, it would seem to imply something the SHI by no means wishes to admit: that men who hold women in true affection cannot be guilty of sexual harassment, since they aim at something other than mere submission. To this, one could respond by questioning the nature of men's attraction to women. But this reply would lead us down a long path at the end of which is MacKinnon's notion of heterosexual intercourse as rape and Dworkin's throwaway comment that romance is merely "rape embellished with meaningful looks."[43]

With such feminist foremothers to guide us, we might today equally well maintain that sexual harassment is "meaningful looks without the rape." From the official radical feminist perspective, what may appear as men's innocent attraction to women becomes part and parcel of their plot to subjugate and control women. Such contentions move us clearly to the terrain of heterophobia (to which I will turn in chapter 6), where the focus of discussion is no longer on alleged male wrongdoing but on male interest in women as itself an objectionable expression of sexual domination and a will to rape. In fact, this was made explicit in MacKinnon's early writings about sexual harassment. And precisely this view seems to be what many agents of the SHI espouse.

The situation, however, looks quite different from the perspective of a man. One does not need to be well versed in MacKinnon's writings to quickly recognize the trap her view of things has sprung on men. As

Michael Mills, a professor of psychology at Loyola Marymount University, comments:

> Men are currently in a situation "set up" for failure. The burden of making virtually all explicit, unambiguous first moves (first time kissing, asking for a date, initiating first-time sexuality, and so on) is on men. This makes males a target if they initiate in a way that a *particular* woman finds offensive (since a particular woman gets to decide what is or isn't offensive). Until women start taking responsibility for making unambiguous, risky first initiatives, they should lighten up when men do a clumsy, or offensive, job of it. Until then, men [take] the initiatives, women evaluate, choose, and sometimes sue. The only way to be sure attention is "wanted" is to wait for the woman to move first. *Any* male word or gesture of interest can, after all, be construed as sexual harassment if all it takes to enact this transformation is a woman's say-so.[44]

But even such patience would not guarantee safety, since any woman can change her mind *after* she has made the first move. When the labile category of "unwanted" attention is the essential criterion, men are paralyzed. As long as vigilantes are allowed to regulate hurt feelings and sexual overtures that are not, in fact, sexual assaults, we will remain stuck in an increasingly nightmarish situation in which all words and gestures have frightening potential consequences. Thus, the ultimate logic of the present rhetoric of sexual harassment leads us right back to feminists' attack on male expressions of heterosexuality, regardless of who is the initiator.

I believe Jane Gallop fails to see that the present threat to female sexual autonomy in the name of feminist correctness is a by-product of the general attack on heterosexuality that feminism has unleashed. The problem is not the "fringe" feminism that, as Gallop notes, is rejected by most women. The problem is the general antagonism toward men that has been part of feminism from its very beginning. Today this antagonism functions as a simplified version of the more complex social vision that was articulated by writers such as MacKinnon in the early stages of the Sexual Harassment Industry. Linked to the very successful movement against sexual harassment, it has brought us to the present heavy-handed and ever-expanding definitions of what even Gallop refers to as "a loathsome crime."[45]

By apparently gaining widespread support for what is in fact an extraordinary cultural shift, one that puts men permanently on the defensive in their expression of interest in women, feminists have already won some major battles. Or lost them, depending on one's point of view. As Helen Garner wrote of the Australian case of alleged harassment mentioned in chapter 4 above, feminism has turned "priggish, disingenuous, unforgiving."[46] This is a direct result of the SHI's unwillingness to distinguish between serious and trivial cases of sexual harassment, between genuine instances of abusive behavior and petty everyday occurrences, between attacks and clumsy overtures.

Jane Gallop makes the interesting observation that unlike pornography, "sexual harassment has produced no real debate within feminism."[47] She is right, and this should surprise us. But she herself does not encourage that debate. This is no accidental oversight. Nadine Strossen, president of the American Civil Liberties Union, has written about the connection between the two feminist campaigns: against pornography and against sexual harassment. She points out that sexual harassment law has provided an alternative strategy by which "MacDworkinite" and other procensorship feminists can pursue their goals:

> Although pornophobic feminists have not succeeded in purging pornography from our public sphere, as the Dworkin-MacKinnon model law would do directly, they recently have made significant strides toward that goal through an alternative strategy. They have used the concept of sexual harassment as a Trojan horse for smuggling their views on sexual expression into our law and culture. By influencing the legal and societal understandings of this concept, procensorship feminists have been alarmingly successful in effectively outlawing *all* sexual expression in many sectors of our society, even without any claim that the particular expression is subordinating or degrading.[48]

Although Gallop wants to question the assumption "that sexuality per se is harmful to women,"[49] she carefully avoids defending heterosexuality. She sees bans on consensual relations as symptomatic of this "antisex position," but she fails to identify them as a logical result of the sort of tool sexual harassment quickly became: a means of controlling male expression of sexuality, a way to put men on notice, while dressing up the attack on them as the pursuit of equality and social justice for women.

I do not like Gallop's style. She is an intellectual flasher. But as a critic of the Sexual Harassment Industry's failure to draw distinctions, I now have to argue that there is a significant difference between intellectual flashing and the real thing. Thus I have to defend Gallop's right to conduct her classes and treat her students in a way I personally find tasteless and egomaniacal. Even more reprehensible, in my view, is her specious defense of her own indulgences, while she adheres to the feminist worldview that does not condone identical conduct on the part of a man. This opportunism strikes me as more intellectually disreputable (and more potentially damaging to her students) than her exhibitionism.

But here, too, I have to grant Gallop's right to conduct her classes as she sees fit; I must distinguish between actual assault and the creation of a teaching environment that assaults one's intellect, preconceptions, or sense of good taste. And I do this because the principles of academic freedom and freedom of speech are indispensable in higher education and should not be sacrificed for the sake of curbing the occasional performance artist.

Unfortunately, Gallop is not alone in her feminist-inspired defense of her behavior. In a revealing review of *Feminist Accused of Sexual Harassment*, Professor Valerie Jenness, whose own case we encountered in chapter 4, supports Gallop's praise of an "erotics of pedagogy," as well as her effort to distinguish between sex and sexual discrimination.[50] Jenness praises *Feminist Accused* for its utility "as a rethinking of the ways in which feminist[-]inspired and [-]implemented social control policies . . . can be appropriated and used in non- or anti-feminist ways," that is, can be deployed against women.[51] The facts remain, however, that sexual harassment charges are overwhelmingly brought by women against men and that feminist defenders such as Gallop and Jenness, despite having themselves gone through painful parallel experiences, waste no sympathy on this reality.

Like Gallop, Jenness supports sexual harassment charges when they involve discrimination and not simply sex, a distinction with which Gallop credits feminism. But as we will see in part 3, it is feminism itself that muddied the waters from the beginning—and continues to do so with feminist discourse about women's inability to give meaningful consent. Gallop has to protest against such rhetoric in order to protect her own position; it would be too absurd, even for her, to declare that female students attracted to her are capable of giving consent while those attracted to male professors are not.[52]

Jenness repeatedly states that once sexual harassment is separated from the concepts of gender and discrimination, women can be "differently targeted" as harassers[53]—but to the extent that this is true (and I admit that I know of no nationwide figures on this issue), it means precisely the opposite of what Jenness claims it does. Women appear to be treated more leniently—as the difference between Gallop's punishment and Adam Weisberger's underscores. The problem is that when women like Valerie Jenness are fired without due process, they think this is merely a misuse (or abuse) of sexual harassment charges as defined by feminists. When men are fired, on the other hand, these men know that the basic framework is flawed. I have never heard of a man who has suggested that women should be targeted while they themselves should not be—and yet that is the essence of the Gallop–Jenness defense.

Jenness quotes Gallop: "University administrators who piously intone against teacher–student sex, citing the student's impossibility to freely grant consent, would be shocked if they knew their position was based in a feminist critique of the institution of marriage."[54] Indeed, this is a good illustration of the recognition among feminists (though not among male administrators) that these are feminist definitions that have prevailed in academe. Jenness concludes that "an increasing number of feminists find themselves dissatisfied with the way in which the content and implementation of sexual harassment is appropriated and differentially deployed within the context of patriarchal institutions"[55]—a blatantly biased claim that can only mean: Keep sexual harassment charges targeted at men; no equal opportunity charges wanted.

"A Presumed Harasser Responds"

At the University of Wisconsin at Milwaukee, Jane Gallop's was not the only case of sexual harassment in recent years. Another, even more bizarre episode unfolded in the early 1990s. Ellen Steury, a tenured associate professor in the criminal justice department of UWM's School of Social Welfare, suddenly "recovered" a memory of having been "harassed" by a male colleague several years earlier. Supposedly he had left at her house a pornographic book whose protagonist was also named Ellen (the colleague denied this, and the book was never produced). To this tale was added Professor Steury's anger at her department's support of a male faculty member for tenure. Claiming this action would increase the male vote in the department (those very males, incidentally, had earlier voted to grant tenure to her), Steury alleged that a hostile work environment had been created for her.

Increasing antagonisms led, in early 1992, to charges of sexual harassment against three male professors in the program, including the one originally accused. Not a shred of evidence ever emerged to support Steury's charges, which were eventually dropped. But these events took two and a half years out of the lives of the three professors, as well as costing them fifty thousand dollars in legal fees. Like Jane Gallop, these men discovered that merely to be accused is to be presumed guilty.

Meanwhile, the university, already under pressure from Labor and Justice Department investigators for alleged cover-ups of past discrimination, was hard put to demonstrate its new responsiveness to charges of sexual harassment. In its eagerness to comply, it proceeded to deprive the alleged harassers of any semblance of due process.

Eleanor Miller, head of the Office of Affirmative Action and a friend of the complainant, granted each respondent only one interview and one opportunity to make a written response. In contrast, rather like Susan Hippensteele in Hawaii, Miller untiringly aided Professor Steury in a careful search for some evidence to support her complaint[56] and allowed her to revise the allegations, notes, and witness lists for months after the filing of the original charges. These revisions, of which the accused were not informed, in turn played a part in the finding of "probable cause" that Steury had been discriminated against by two of the three men.[57]

The result was a civil suit brought against the university and its chancellor in late 1993 by the three professors, whose lawyer claimed that on five occasions she had requested the full files pertaining to the investigation, only to be refused access each time. The university, in defiance of its own explicit procedures, argued that the professors had no right to due process in advance of the imposition of discipline. Only by going to court did the three compel the university to turn over documents relating to their case. The court ordered the university to pay a fine for each day of the 112 during which they had been denied access to the files.

Professor Stan Stojkovic, one of the three accused professors, wrote (at my request) a statement about his experience:

> It was clear to me early in the allegation phase of my case that the university through its officials *presumed* my guilt in the matter as well as the guilt of two of my colleagues. In fact, the entire two and a half years of the case, at no point was I nor my colleagues allowed to talk directly to university administrators in a collegial way. Instead, the point was made very clear: you are guilty regardless of the evidence. In spite of policies and procedures on campus that required less intrusive and less formal procedures in the beginning [stages] of a case, university officials chose to presume my guilt and mete out disciplinary action.

It became apparent to me and others that university officials were more interested in promoting an image of being sensitive to the demands of feminists on campus, many of whom could not discern fact from fiction due to their narrow ideological viewpoints. I am convinced that for these feminists the "truth" was that if someone alleged you were a sexual harasser, you were defined as one in their eyes. No matter what the evidence indicated, no matter what the policies and procedures dictated on how allegations were to be investigated, and no matter that I too was a *person* deserving of at least a modicum of respect and dignity, to these true believers I was the enemy.

It was this denial of fundamental fairness and personhood that I found to be the most disturbing and personally upsetting in my ordeal. I was a means to larger ends, albeit different ends for different people. For the Chancellor, my colleagues and I became a *means* to quell the threat from the Department of Labor to cancel close to 350 million dollars in federal grants in the system if the university didn't do something to stop sexual harassment on campus. . . . For campus feminists, I was a *means* to send a message to potential sexual harassers and to advance a political agenda to make the campus a gender-sensitive place. . . . For the Affirmative Action officer (an ardent feminist), I was a *means* to promote her skewed and limited version of feminism. (By the way, I am a supporter of traditional versions of feminism that advance personhood and individual expression and development. Therefore, to be labeled a sexual harasser was personally devastating and in contrast to all my actions which have been to assist both men and women in my chosen academic field.)

These behaviors of others violated what I was taught as an undergraduate student concerning fairness in the treatment of others. Through this tumultuous time of my life, I kept Immanuel Kant's categorical imperative in the forefront of my thoughts: "Never simply treat a person as a means to an end." At every turn in my experience, however, university administrators, too many faculty, and my accusers all behaved as if I [were] an instrument to be used toward their specific ends. At no time in the process did I feel I was part of the university community. Instead, I was the pariah that needed to be exorcised from the academy.

More than anything else, the effects of such an environment were destructive: free speech was curtailed on campus, a climate of fear became normative, interest groups began to use sexual harassment cases to advance petty causes and ideologically driven issues, and most importantly, reasoned and rational debate became politically incorrect on campus. The long-term effect has been faculty fragmentation, indifference, and a self-centered approach where collegiality is for all intents and purposes dead. What drives the university now is a bureaucratic mentality that is akin to a Hobbesian state of affairs where political players fight amongst themselves. This atomistic philosophy has significantly altered the contours of the university. . . .

These effects, however, are reversible, but only in a climate where true university leadership exists. University officials have abdicated their responsibility to politicians, ideologues, and political interests. The future of academia rests with those who understand that rational debate, justice, and fairness are the defining principles of higher education. If the academy does not support these ideals, who will? The $50,000 in legal fees my colleagues and I spent, the personal pain and humiliation of going through an unethical and illegal process, and my removal from my professional commitments all pale in comparison to the more pernicious effect of stifling debate and discussion on campus.[58]

As chapters 3 and 4 above should also have made clear, anyone can be accused of sexual harassment, an offense that even the Supreme Court cannot define. Not a week passes without new cases being reported in the press. A newspaper search of the topic will reveal far more cases than a researcher could look into in years of work. How many of these are based on opportunistic charges will never be known. Many professors prefer to take the path of least resistance and offer apologies, submit to training sessions, take early retirement, or otherwise attempt to make amends for trivial or imagined injuries.

When we ban "asymmetrical" relationships; when we invent new categories of "third party harassment," "peer harassment," and "contrapower harassment" and even describe "stereotyped perceptions" as a "form of sexual harassment";[59] when we routinely defend demands for "comfort" in school and at work; when we build an entire industry to help us spot, label, and extirpate "sexual harassment" (starting in kindergarten and moving all the way up to the White House); when we assign "sensitivity training" for the reeducation of offending colleagues, and preventive workshops for everyone else—when we do these things, it seems impossible to escape from the fear that our universities might eventually come to resemble some dystopian parody of the well-regulated society, inhabited by docile people capable of thinking only pure and inoffensive thoughts. To see a primary objective, social reconstruction, surreptitiously advanced by means of a potent secondary instrument, sexual harassment law, should worry everyone who believes in open discussion of major social issues. All this gives an ominous ring to Jane Gallop's observation, early in *Feminist Accused:* "As the century draws to a close, it appears that the campaign against sexual harassment may, in fact, be *the* success story of twentieth-century feminism."[60]

PART III

The Feminist Turn against Men

◈

Chapter 6

Heterophobia

❧

Without (hetero)sexual abuse, (hetero)sexual harassment and the (hetero)sexualization of every aspect of female bodies and behaviors, there would not be patriarchy, and whatever other forms or materializations of oppression might exist, they would not have the shapes, boundaries and dynamics of the racism, nationalism, and so on that we are now familiar with.

MARILYN FRYE, *Willful Virgin*

Something very strange happened toward the end of the twentieth century. Heterosexuality went from being the norm to being on the defensive. By calling this phenomenon "heterophobia," I am not speaking abstractly. Rather, I am referring to a distinct current within feminism over the past thirty years, a current that has been "theorized" explicitly by feminist scholars and agitators alike as they attack men and heterosexuality. Such writings, as we shall see later in this chapter, bear all the hallmarks of what has been called a "manic" theory—that is, one that does not know its own limitations.[1] Not wishing to be guilty of precisely the same offense, I readily affirm that the attitudes I criticize are not held by all women, not even, perhaps, by many women, though certainly they are found among many feminist women. In their everyday form, they occur as "male bashing." As Karen DeCrow, former president of the National Organization for Women, has stated, "God knows, in the last twenty-five years, man as 'the enemy' has certainly emerged" within feminism.[2]

But heterophobia is not merely the work of lesbian separatists, since they, vastly outnumbered by heterosexual women, could never have imposed such an agenda were it not acceptable to heterosexual feminists as well.[3] If homophobia is still a problem for the society at large, hetero-phobia is now feminism's own predictable reversal of that problem. Certainly it is an irony of contemporary feminist extremists that to pu-rify the atmosphere as they wish to do, they must first be obsessive about the very thing—heterosexuality—they are attempting to elimi-nate; this is the typical dilemma of the vigilante.

The British lesbian separatist Sheila Jeffreys, in her 1990 book *Anti-climax,* gives a clear account of the attitude I am calling "heterophobia." The "sexual revolution," Jeffreys argues, is positively detrimental to women. The aim of women's liberation, and particularly of lesbian lib-eration (which seeks to go beyond "heterofeminism"), is "the destruc-tion of heterosexuality as a system." Heterosexual desire, Jeffreys affirms, sounding like a trainer for the Sexual Harassment Industry, is "eroticised power difference"—a view that is a shibboleth of feminist rhetoric these days. Far from being grounded in biology, heterosexual desire "originates in the power relationship between men and women"—though, she grants, power differences can also exist in same-sex relationships.[4] But where sadomasochism or role-playing occurs in a homosexual relationship, Jeffreys explains, they must be labeled "het-erosexual desire." The institution of heterosexuality is, to Jeffreys, founded upon the ideology of "difference": "Men need to be able to desire the powerless creatures they marry. So heterosexual desire for men is based upon eroticising the otherness of women, an otherness which is based upon a difference of power." What sort of sexuality, then, does Jeffreys approve of? "The opposite of heterosexual desire is the eroticising of sameness, a sameness of power, equality and mutuality. It is homosexual desire."[5]

Jeffreys's views bring together the two strands I am calling "hetero-phobia": the fear of and antagonism toward the Other—that is, male sexuality, especially as manifest in heterosexuality; and the turn toward Sameness, understood as the only kind of authentic relationship pos-sible.[6]

My point here is not that a few feminist extremists are making an all-out effort to bring down heterosexuality (though they evidently are doing this). It is, rather, that the Sexual Harassment Industry, by un-critically adopting the feminist language of "power" (which is repli-cated in virtually all academic sexual harassment codes)[7] is promoting an extremist feminist agenda, although it is not often recognized as such. Phrases characteristic of this agenda now trip off the tongues even of university presidents. Robert L. Carothers, president of the University of Rhode Island, for example, has written, "There is an inherently exploitative situation any time there is a power differential."[8] It does not seem to occur to him that having settled for such a definition, he would have to banish virtually all relationships, except perhaps those between clones raised in identical circumstances. For who is to say precisely which "power differentials" are truly damaging to human relations? Who can be sure that differences in intelligence, in knowledge, in sex appeal, in state of health, in age, in wealth, or in charm do not create damaging power imbalances?

It is, of course, true that quid pro quo harassment—sexual shakedown—presupposes some imbalance of power. All blackmail does. But even in this instance, it is absurd to say that what is going on is "really" about power.[9] After all, sex is what is being extorted, not money, not help filing tax returns. And the "power" involved may be very temporary indeed. One does not have to be unusually astute to see that when an obscure woman's charges of sexual harassment have the potential to topple the president of the United States, a major redistribution of "power" has taken place.

The moment we move away from quid pro quo situations, however, the problem of harassment deepens. In what sense is the "hostile environment" created by telling a joke, casting an aspersion, or expressing admiration about "power"? The fact is, all sorts of people say all kinds of things to one another, pleasant and unpleasant, regardless of the degree of official power each holds relative to the other.

It is not the argument about "power," then, that strikes me as new (or significant) in feminist agitation, but rather the heterophobia that lies behind it. Although heterophobia is not in itself a new phenomenon, never has it gone so far or gained such prominence as it has done in the past few decades. When the British writer Mona Caird in the 1880s argued against marriage, or when the militant suffragist Cristabel Pankhurst published *The Great Scourge* in 1913 and described men as repulsive carriers of venereal disease, these women were combatting particular social conditions. Their attacks were often immoderate, and there is in first-wave feminism a strong and well-known antisex bias. Some women engaged in purity campaigns and argued for chastity for both men and women, opposed legalization of prostitution, and called for censorship of written materials and of art work depicting nudity. They judged male politicians on the basis of sexual morality, as did Lucy Stone in opposing Grover Cleveland's candidacy in the presidential election of 1884 because he had fathered—and taken responsibility for—an illegitimate child. These are familiar events in the history of first-wave feminism.

But one thing we can say about these nineteenth- and early-twentieth-century women: They did not support any sort of double standard, which would have encouraged and promoted homosexual sex, while branding heterosex as demeaning and contemptible. Living at a historical moment when women were struggling to win basic political rights—and were resting their claims on arguments that they had the *same* intellectual and moral capacities as men—they evidently understood that heterophobia could not be a winning tactic. Their relative restraint is actually surprising, for they certainly would have been justified in taking a more aggressive stance at a time when women's relationships with men were characterized above all by women's civic inequality, their extreme economic dependence, their lack of education, and their vulnerability to constant pregnancy and its attendant dangers—increasing pauperization, ill health, and death in childbirth.

We on this continent, at the end of the twentieth century, hardly live in that sort of world. Most (though not all) women today have many options, owing principally to their access to education and birth control, and their resulting position in the labor market.[10] And it is precisely because of these shifts, which have enormously increased women's autonomy and life opportunities, that heterophobes wishing to attack men must find ever more dramatic grounds for doing so.

In thinking about the phenomenon of heterophobia, I am particularly fascinated by the question of how heterosexual feminists face being both feminist and heterosexual at a time when the two categories are often presented as antithetical. It is unquestionably the case that hetero women's sexual preferences and experiences are being redefined and debased by rather silly, but nonetheless influential, ideas put forth in the name of feminism.

What, for example, is a heterosexual woman to do when she is told that male potency is a threat? That the penis is an instrument of domination? That her own sexual fantasies may be betraying her "indoctrination" into patriarchal norms? How many hetero feminists feel guilt over "sleeping with the enemy"? How many fail to challenge heterophobia out of a misguided belief that only lesbian feminists are the "real thing"? How common is it for heterosexual women who call themselves "feminists" to find their heterosexuality complicated by their feminism? How productive are such tensions? Do they lead to inhibition and awkwardness as the "heterosexual body" comes under postmodernist scrutiny? How do women negotiate the ensuing problems? How do they compare the difficulties they encounter with the gains they feel they have made because of feminism? How frequently do they find that feminism turns them off?

Judging by a fascinating recent book edited by two lesbian feminists, Sue Wilkinson and Celia Kitzinger, *Heterosexuality: A Feminism and Psychology Reader,* prominent heterosexual feminists routinely approach the potential conflict between their feminism and their heterosexuality in an apologetic mode. They make politically correct protestations such as Mary Crawford's "I use heterosexual privilege to subvert heterosexism"[11]; Sandra Bartky's "The felt impossibility of changing one's sexual orientation is not an argument for the desirability of this orientation";[12] or Sandra Bem's explanation that though she has lived with the man she loves for twenty-six years, she is not and has "never been a 'heterosexual,' " her sexuality being "organized around dimensions other than sex."[13] They rarely challenge the presupposition that there need be, and actually is, a conflict between feminism and heterosexuality. One scholar who contributed to the Wilkinson and Kitzinger book, Shulamit Reinharz, tries to strike a reasonable balance, allowing that "[w]e cannot dismiss heterosexual women as having 'false consciousness.' " Yet even she goes on to say, "[I]t would be good for us also to empower women to understand their lesbian potential," while making no comparable suggestion to lesbians.[14] This same writer notes regretfully that when, in her gerontology classes, she has tried to talk with older heterosexual women about the possible benefits of living in a lesbian relationship, they "express very little interest."

In fact, feminists today are in a weak position to gauge how much of a role their overt heterophobia plays in alienating "ordinary" women from feminism. Far from being the product of "backlash" or bad public relations, such alienation would seem to result predictably from an accurate perception of the antiheterosexual tenor of much feminist discourse. Many feminists freely give voice to heterophobia, as we shall see, and only bother to deny it when it exposes feminism to criticism.

Somewhere along the line, then, the feminist criticism of patriarchal institutions derailed into a real, visceral, and frightening antagonism toward men and a consequent intolerance toward women who insist on associating with them.[15] I'm amazed, as I think about it, that hetero women have submitted to this stigmatizing of their sexual desires and personal relations—but without question many of them have done so. A few simple examples follow.

While interviewing students for my 1994 book (written with Noretta Koertge) *Professing Feminism,* I was told by an undergraduate in women's studies that one of her teachers habitually referred to her "partner," without ever using a pronoun. Assuming, along with the whole class, that this professor was a lesbian, the student was shocked, and felt deceived, when she accidentally discovered that her professor was in fact heterosexual, married, and a mother. My question is, Why would a women's studies teacher feel obliged to engage in such a cover-up? Another instance, small but telling: Following the publication of one of my early articles criticizing feminist excesses, I received a letter from a male academic who told me that he and his wife, also a professor, had been very active in setting up a women's center on their campus. When it came time to celebrate the center's anniversary, his wife had asked him not to attend the event, saying, "I don't want to flaunt my heterosexuality."

A final example, from my own experience as a teacher: In past years, in my courses on utopian fiction, I have regularly taught lesbian utopian novels without ever uttering a word of criticism even when their visions offered no hope for heterosexual women. Perhaps following my lead, women students in those classes, the majority of whom are likely to have been heterosexual, never volunteered any critical comments. Only after I had done some thinking about heterophobia did I begin to perceive the message I was inadvertently reinforcing to my students. And this is the message that still, far too often, is being conveyed in women's studies classes taught by doctrinaire feminists eager to teach their students all about "compulsory heterosexuality," as Adrienne Rich famously put it.[16] The new Houghton Mifflin *Reader's Companion to U.S. Women's History* contains an entry by E. Kay Trimberger on "Heterosexuality," which, while failing to note that heterosexual intercourse is the means by which the species has propagated and that it corresponds to the wishes of the vast majority of people, instead summarizes feminist dogma unproblematically:

> [S]exuality is not private, but is political and related to power. "Compulsory heterosexuality" is part of a power structure benefiting heterosexual males at the expense of women and homosexuals. This inequity is justified by an ideology that sees heterosexuality as natural, universal, and biologically necessary, and homosexuality as the opposite. The system also is reinforced by legal sanctions and violence against women (rape,

battering, incest, and murder) and against lesbians, gays, and transgen-dered persons (verbal harassment, physical assault, and murder).

In this entry Trimberger also asserts that "if our sexuality is socially constructed it can also be de- and reconstructed."[17]

How heterophobia works out at the level of social behavior is often bizarre. I remember a meeting of some women faculty who got together weekly for lunch, at a university where I was on leave in the mid-1980s. One day a member of the group announced she was going to be mar-ried. There was an absolute dead silence in the room. Obviously, as feminists (both lesbian and straight), we were far too sophisticated to shriek and gush happiness, and no one knew what response to make as an alternative. So stunned silence for far too long greeted her declara-tion. (She did, incidentally, redeem herself by getting divorced a couple of years later.) I have no doubt that if her news had been that she'd fallen in love with a woman and was about to move in with her, the reaction would have been quite different.

Much of the present passionate rejection of men is explained—the paradox being only apparent—by feminism's embrace of "difference." This embrace has led to such a splintering of identity that the category "woman" can hardly be used without embarrassment because there are so many newly emergent identities to which any one group of feminists needs to feel inferior: white women vis-à-vis women of color; hetero women vis-à-vis lesbians; Western women vis-à-vis Third World women; women of privilege vis-à-vis poor ones (though, characteristically in American society, this theme seems to be of less importance than the others). The fact is that feminism is fragmented by all these divisions, and each group is further torn by its own divisions as well, which has created a competition that, in *Professing Feminism,* my coauthor and I referred to as the "oppression sweepstakes."[18] This jostling for place creates so much tension that feminism is barely able to sustain itself as a movement in which separate identity groups keep speaking to one another. But there is *one* thing that can, apparently, draw them all to-gether, and that is antagonism (whether real or feigned) to men.

The crude attack on men as a group also appears to provide some psychological ballast for feminists otherwise pulled in different direc-tions by the highly politicized atmosphere in which we live. One lesbian I know, who deplores the heterophobic trend within feminism, has writ-ten to me in disgust that this amounts to casting men as what she calls

"the universal scapegoat." Of course, on reflection, this label, too, requires qualification, since women of color and women from other parts
of the world at times argue that their struggle is "together with our
men." From my own observations, however, I would say that the white
feminists who put up with such claims don't really approve of them,
and only the heavy hand of racial or ethnic identity politics keeps them
from voicing direct challenges. So it is white men who are indisputably
at the pinnacle of the hated heap—as dishonest as it is to put them
there, given the significant social divisions and highly variable behavior
that exist among white males as they do within any other human
group.[19]

Who Needs Men?

No one acquainted with women's studies programs or feminist circles
generally will deny that some of the most widely taught and read figures
are the notorious heterophobes Catharine MacKinnon, Andrea Dworkin, and Mary Daly. I cannot bring myself to call these women "radical"
feminists, as they are usually labeled, because I do not believe they go
to the root of anything. Instead, they manifest a pathological aversion
to men, a love of hyperbole, and an antipathy to heterosexuality that
has had a strong and negative influence on feminism, in the classroom
and out. It shouldn't surprise us that a movement that rewards with
fame and fortune a woman capable of writing of war as "male ejacula-
tion"[20] has benumbed many of its potential supporters.

One could, of course, argue that some of the more extreme feminist
pronouncements (by now turned into commonplace slogans)—such as
"All intercourse is rape" or "All men are potential rapists"—are useful
as rallying cries for necessary social change, creating an audience capable of demanding that rape should *never* happen, that *no* woman should
ever be the victim of sexual assault. And I think, in fact, that something
must be conceded to such an argument. But more than this must be
said, for how can one view with equanimity an agenda whose spokeswomen feel free to make grossly demeaning generalizations about half
the world?

Consider the following example: About three years ago, on FEMISA,
an e-mail list devoted to issues of gender and international relations,
someone announced that she was preparing a paper contending that
fathers are necessary for children's development. But, she said, "I
would be helped by arguments that proved the opposite: that men are

unnecessary for a child to grow into mature adulthood." Quite a few people were happy to oblige. One wrote, "Men, as a group, tend to be abusive, either verbally, sexually or emotionally. There are always the exceptions, but they are few and far between (I am married to one of them). There are different levels of violence and abuse and individual men buy into this system by varying degrees. But the male power structure always remains intact."

Another poster contributed a long message in the same vein: "Considering the nature and pervasiveness of men's violence, I would say that without question, children are better off being raised without the presence of men. Assaults on women and children are mostly perpetrated by men whom they are supposed to love and trust: fathers, brothers, uncles, grandfathers, stepfathers." Disregarding the ample evidence, readily available, that women, too, engage in child abuse, this message continued:

> I agree with the many feminists who have argued that the role of fathers as perpetrators of sexual, emotional, and physical violence against female children is absolutely critical to the maintenance of male supremacy. Through incest, girls learn about subordination on the most basic level, and are thus prepared for their proper roles as women in this society.

In a stunning illustration of concept-stretching, this last contributor went on to explain that when she used the word "abusive," she meant "to include the assertion of male dominance." The number of men who do not fit this profile, she wrote, is so small as to be "negligible."[21]

Though the FEMISA list is committed to maintaining an "international" perspective (and though most of the contributors to this discussion were academics), these posters did not bother to qualify their statements in any way, presumably intending them to characterize all men in every country. When a few men on FEMISA did protest against the male-bashing generalizations—which had not been considered "flames" but perfectly appropriate messages—it was they who were summarily removed from the list.

In the face of such mind-numbing caricatures of male behavior, I am often reminded of a scene I repeatedly witnessed years ago when I was living in Paris. At the post office, toward the end of the week, working-class men who were obviously immigrant laborers in France (Greek and Turkish men mostly, at that time) used to line up to send money home, often to places so remote that long discussions ensued at the counter as the clerks tried to figure out just which particular village or island was addressed. I used to stand in line behind these men, week after week, asking myself: What keeps them coming back here? Badly dressed, surely living in poor accommodations, yet faithful, determined to support their families, why do they do it? Nothing in the feminist vision articulated by FEMISA's sophisticated and international-minded subscribers allows one to understand the behavior of such men—except, of course, the gross and libelous supposition that what they were really manifesting was their economic power so that one day they would be able to return home and resume tyrannizing their wives and children.

At about the same time that I was observing and wondering about these men, a woman in the United States was composing what later became a famous "feminist" document: "Life in this society being, at best, an utter bore and no aspect of society being at all relevant to women, there remains to civic-minded, responsible, thrill-seeking females only to overthrow the government, eliminate the money system, institute complete automation, and destroy the male sex."[22] This statement is by Valerie Solanas, whom some readers may remember as the author, in 1968, of the *SCUM Manifesto,* whose opening paragraph this is. By being SCUM (members of the Society for Cutting Up Men), Solanas argued, women could quickly take over the country. Foreshadowing the intense animosity between many feminist women and their nonfeminist sisters, she pinpointed the real conflict as not between females and males, but between SCUM (women who are dominant, secure, proud, independent) and those she contemptuously labeled "approval-seeking Daddy's Girls,"[23] SCUM will "couple-bust," Solanas ominously announced; it will "barge into mixed (male-female) couples, wherever they are, and bust them up."[24]

And in case anyone should remain in doubt as to what SCUM had in mind for men, Solanas spelled it out (showing that Mary Daly and Andrea Dworkin are mere latecomers):

> SCUM will kill all men who are not in the Men's Auxiliary of SCUM. Men in the Men's Auxiliary are those men who are working diligently to eliminate themselves. . . . A few examples of the men in the Men's Auxiliary are: men who kill men; . . . journalists, writers, editors, publishers and producers who disseminate and promote ideas that will lead to the achievement of SCUM's goals; faggots who, by their shimmering, flaming example, encourage other men to de-man themselves and thereby make themselves relatively inoffensive.[25]

SCUM would conduct "Turd Sessions," at which men were to open their speeches with the confession, "I am a turd, a lowly, abject turd."[26]

As these passages suggest, Solanas can probably be dismissed as part of the lunatic fringe. Others have tried to deal with the problem her manifesto posed for feminists by labeling it satire. But this benign view is belied by Solanas's own actions. She is, after all, the woman who, in June 1968, shot and nearly killed Andy Warhol (and one of his associates) over Warhol's apparent lack of interest in a film script entitled "Up Your Ass" that she had submitted to him. Solanas did not lack feminist champions for her exorbitant gesture, as evidenced by the two representatives of NOW, Ti-Grace Atkinson and attorney Florynce Kennedy, who accompanied her to court. Atkinson said on that occasion that Solanas would go down in history as "the first outstanding champion of women's rights," while Flo Kennedy called her "one of the most important spokeswomen of the feminist movement."[27]

Solanas was indicted for attempted murder, declared incompetent to stand trial, committed to a mental institution, and then, in June 1969 (in view of Warhol's refusal to press charges), sentenced to three years for "reckless assault with intent to harm." She died some twenty years later and was recently resurrected in a film directed by Mary Harron, entitled *I Shot Andy Warhol*.

It is revealing that far from expressing alarm at the manifest unity of theory and praxis in Solanas's violence against men, some reviewers of this film have treated Solanas as a free spirit and see this celebrated in the movie.[28] They thus echo the opinion voiced a generation earlier by feminist Vivian Gornick. In her long introduction to the 1970 edition of the *SCUM Manifesto*, Gornick called Solanas a "visionary" who "understood the true nature of the struggle" for women's liberation.[29] One can well imagine what the reaction of feminists would be if a male who had gunned down women were lauded in this way.

But even if one grants that Solanas is an extreme and atypical case (and the film about her does, in fact, clearly portray her descent into madness), what shall we make of Sally Miller Gearhart, a professor of communications who, nearly fifteen years after Solanas, contributed an essay entitled "The Future—If There Is One—Is Female" to a volume called *Reweaving the Web of Life*? This essay makes a simple argument, one that recalls Solanas's manifesto. The future, it contends, must be in female hands; women alone must control the reproduction of the species (with men given no say in it whatsoever); and only 10 percent of the population should be allowed to be male.[30]

Like Gearhart, I myself used to believe that women should run the world. Even if we could not be sure what women would do, it was reasonable, I once argued, to expect that women would make no worse a job of it than men had done. That was before I spent ten years in a women's studies program and saw for myself how, in practice, women dealt with large and small conflicts. It was an experience that convinced me that women are in no way superior to men in political virtue, fairness, or even plain good sense. It also persuaded me that we should muddle on toward equality between the sexes, arguing over and clarifying ultimate political and social goals, and that the best way of pursuing the aim of equality is to avoid the language of hate.

Gearhart's essay makes it perfectly clear that the future she has in mind is not one that all women will share equally. How will conflict among women be resolved in the female future? She has nothing to say about this. But as a lesbian-feminist activist, she allows no doubt that only "non-male-identified women" should exercise power. Most women will be amenable to the changes she promotes, she presumes, for "[h]istorically, [women] have . . . exhibited a more group-oriented and less violent attitude toward human beings and the world in which we live than men have done."[31] Concerning matters of reproduction, only women are to have the right to make decisions. Men have no say in it at all. "Lesbians and other independent women are already moving in that direction," she assures us.

As for women not inclined to go along with her vision, they are, she says, "enslaved by male-identification and years of practice within the system." No consideration need be given to their political or other preferences. Along with men, they will receive "education" in what Gearhart calls the "voluntary and vast changes that must take place."[32] How does Gearhart deal with the historical evidence that women in power have not always been models of a kinder, gentler society? By the predictable ploy of considering such women "puppets of men behind the scenes."[33]

But there is more. Like Valerie Solanas in her *SCUM Manifesto,* Professor Gearhart calls upon men to participate in their own demise by willingly assisting in a program of reducing their numbers (reassuringly, she makes clear that mass murder is not contemplated, but, rather, slow attrition through new reproductive technologies and support from men for feminist goals). And from what I see on some feminist e-mail lists and in the published work of some men (to which I will soon turn), there are indeed accommodating males who would gladly embrace even this policy for the sake of maintaining their cherished, but never entirely secure, status as "feminist men."

Gearhart's confident vision of the feminist future is pointedly countered by another contribution to the volume in which her essay appears. This is Rachel Bedard's account of her experiences in all-female groups. Following a failed marriage and a feminist awakening, Bedard moved into a lesbian separatist house "with tremendous expectations of feminist support and nurturance. But within weeks [the women] were divided over everything from dinner hour to cats to who owned which soap in the bathroom."[34] When the household broke up before long, Bedard accompanied a woman friend to New Zealand. There she met a peaceful, caring, vegetarian man who grew his own food and tried to live in harmony with the planet. His example made her wonder whether such a way of life might not be more useful than lesbians marching and screaming obscenities. She became involved with him, all the while tormented by the thought that she was "betraying all women" by being "in complicity."[35] Still, knowing now that women too have what she calls *"human"* problems, she "could begin to move back to the personal from the political,"[36] which for her included marriage to a man. Predictably, she was ostracized for this by former friends. Tolerance has never been a notable characteristic of feminism—the "nurturing" quality of women notwithstanding. Bedard's account of these experiences is entitled, appropriately, "Re-entering Complexity."

For yet another example of the connection between feminism and heterophobia, consider Mary Daly, who in her famous 1978 book *Gyn/ Ecology: The Metaethics of Radical Feminism,* described males' need for "female energy" as "necrophilia"—"love for those victimized into a state of living death."[37] Or consider Joyce Trebilcot, who teaches philosophy and women's studies at Washington University in Saint Louis. While asserting, in a 1984 essay, that "[a]s those familiar with feminist theory know, feminists advocate lesbianism on a variety of grounds," Trebilcot is generous to feminist sisters with a heterosexual past, asking only that they take responsibility for what their sexual orientation "is now and what it will be in the future."[38] To her, the process of coming out means, among other things, "deciding not to participate in the institution of heterosexuality," which she sees as entirely a product of social construction. Thus, for Trebilcot and her like-minded colleagues, the denial of the biological basis of heterosexuality is part of the defense of lesbianism. And Trebilcot isn't shy about letting us know that "pluralism," which holds all alternatives as "equally okay," is not something she can abide.[39]

For women who claim not to be sexually aroused by women, Trebilcot provides this advice: Get your desires in line with your reason. After all, "sexuality is socially constructed." By thinking about the social and economic advantages gained from heterosexuality—so this argument goes—a woman may recognize that this choice has been "pushed upon her," and her sexual identity may change as a result.[40] All women can in fact achieve this, Trebilcot assures us, and the desirable result will be fewer heterosexuals and less lesbophobia (her word) and heterosexism. She seems not to notice that heterophobia and homosexism have simply been substituted for them in this zero-sum game that passes for "theorizing" lesbianism.

A similar approach is taken in the 1993 essay collection *Heterosexuality: A Feminism and Psychology Reader*, discussed earlier in this chapter. In the book's many short narratives, most striking is the tone of self-criticism adopted by the heterosexual women, almost none of whom considered her heterosexuality a nonproblem. One of the contributors, Doris C. DeHardt, a feminist therapist, tells us that she used to believe she could facilitate her clients' heterosexual relationships. Now, however, she thinks that "feminist marriage is, like military intelligence, an oxymoron."[41] While the heterosexuals (with rare exceptions) apologized, most of the lesbian contributors took no pains to conceal their sense of superiority at living perfectly coherent feminist lives. Without meaning to do so, the volume paints a disturbing portrait of the heterophobia that is now part and parcel of second-wave feminism.

Yet when, several years ago, I gave some public lectures on the subject of heterophobia, women's studies faculty in the audience accused me of having scraped the bottom of the barrel to come up with obscure and obsolete extremist claims that in no way applied to today's feminism. That this is a disingenuous charge is made evident by much current feminist writing.

Let me cite here, as a further example, the work of a well-known feminist and professor of women's studies, Marilyn Frye, who teaches at Michigan State University. In an essay published in 1984, Frye stated that she was disinclined to argue for criminalization of specific sexual acts (the case in point was adult–child sex) but was inclined, instead, to favor social pressure against both sexual acts and sexual relationships "in any case of marked difference of social and economic power between the parties." More pertinently, she added, "For this principle not to rule out heterosexual relations between adults, perhaps we should have to bring about the feminist revolution. If so, so be it."[42]

Some years later, in an essay entitled "Willful Virgin, or Do You Have to Be a Lesbian to Be a Feminist?" (from which I took the epigraph to this chapter), Frye again revealed the continuity of her vision with that of Solanas in the 1960s, MacKinnon and Dworkin in the 1970s, and Gearhart and Trebilcot in the 1980s. The essay is a polished bit of sophistry, attempting to present itself as a reasoned "no" to the question posed by its title but in fact endorsing a "yes" in every particular. Thus: "I believe that all feminist theory and practice eventually conveys one to this proposition: that a central constitutive dynamic and key mechanism of the global phenomenon of male domination, oppression and exploitation of females, is near-universal female heterosexuality." Should any reader still fail to get it, Frye clarifies: "The point is that virtually all women in patriarchal cultures are rigorously required to be sexual with and for men."[43] Illustrating what passes for sophisticated feminist analysis these days, she continues:

> For females to be subordinated and subjugated to males on a global scale, and for males to organize themselves and each other as they do, billions of female individuals, virtually all who see life on the planet, must be reduced to a more-or-less willing toleration of subordination and servitude to men. The primary sites of this reduction are the sites of heterosexual relation and encounter—courtship and marriage-arrangement, romance, sexual liaisons, fucking, marriage, prostitution, the normative family, incest and child sexual abuse.[44]

To any feminist imagining herself capable of consciously choosing a male partner with whom to share her life, Frye offers this advice: If you wish to "embody and enact a radical feminism," you can't be heterosexual in any "standard patriarchal meaning of that word." You must learn to be "a heretic, a deviant, an undomesticated female, an impossible being. You have to be a Virgin."[45]

Biology is irrelevant to Frye, whose argument blatantly denies that female heterosexuality has any natural roots in biology: "A vital part of making generalized male dominance as close to inevitable as a human construction can be is the naturalization of female heterosexuality. Men have been creating ideologies and political practices which naturalize female heterosexuality continuously in every culture since the dawns of the patriarchies."[46] In case there are still some readers who have not absorbed the lesson of Adrienne Rich's 1980 essay that gave us the term "compulsory heterosexuality,"[47] Frye spells it out anew:

> Female heterosexuality is not a biological drive or an individual woman's erotic attraction or attachment to another human animal which happens to be male. Female heterosexuality is a set of social institutions and practices defined and regulated by patriarchal kinship systems, by both civil and religious law, and by strenuously enforced mores and deeply entrenched values and taboos. Those definitions, regulations, values and taboos are about male fraternity and the oppression and exploitation of women. They are not about love, human warmth, solace, fun, pleasure, or deep knowledge between people."[48]

Nearly ten years ago, Alice Echols, in her book *Daring to Be Bad: Radical Feminism in America, 1967–1975,* noted the confusion between essentialism and social constructionism characteristic of "radical feminists" who, while indignantly proclaiming that they are not essentialists, see male dominance as "eternal and unchanging." This stance makes "social constructionism, in their hands, virtually indistinguishable from essentialism," Echols pointed out, for if the social structure is "as impervious to change as [radical feminists] suggest, it might as well be biologically fixed."[49]

Far from considering such inconsistencies mere symptoms of confused thinking, I take them as indicators of the blatant opportunism of much feminist writing. Whatever works in a given context is good to use. Most illuminating about this kind of theorizing about men is how closely it mirrors (i.e., reflects an inverted image of) some equally cracked views of women, those of Otto Weininger, for example. Where Frye sees men as forcing heterosexuality upon women in order to serve their own interests, Weininger (to whom I will return later in this chapter) sees women as forcing heterosexuality upon men in order to drag them down from the intellectual and moral heights that males alone can scale. And Weininger, too, promotes the spiritual ideal of the Virgin, the male virgin.

Constructing the Feminist Future

In the above passages from Frye, readers will have noticed the identification of heterosexuality, allied to patriarchy, as the root of all evil. A corollary of this idea is the assumption that women's independence from men would necessarily lead to the establishment of peace and order in the world. This is a childish dream, perhaps a touching one, but still nothing more than a dream. It is also a staple of feminist utopian fiction. Let us ignore, for the moment, the fact that women as a group do not hold identical ideas about things (how could they?). And that they are not natural socialists, or born egalitarians (though many feminist writers like to pretend that they are). What do we find when we investigate how women actually handle conflict?

If even a self-selected group living in one small household, such as Bedard's, encounters insurmountable obstacles to a harmonious common life, imagine what would happen if an entire country were to be run by women. Shall we trust our feminist leaders in the future to "somehow" make peace between groups as deeply divided as pro-choice and anti-choice women? Between those who want conventional religion in the schools and those who will allow none—or perhaps only Goddess worship? Can anyone honestly believe that conflicts would inevitably abate?

If we reject, as it seems obvious we must, the notion that a world ruled by women would necessarily be superior, we have the right, even the obligation, to ask what sorts of political processes feminists would set in the place of the much-despised masculinist ones. And how would the feminist future deal with dissenters? It seems that feminist utopian fiction should have something to tell us on this subject. But it does so only too rarely. Even my undergraduate students notice that Charlotte Perkins Gilman's utopian novel *Herland* (1915), which describes an all-female society, *presumes* lack of conflict, and so offers no mechanisms for coping with it. And they recognize, too, the coercive manipulations that subtly underlie Gilman's society, the pressure brought to bear, for example, on women who are not—by Herland's eugenic standards—deemed worthy of reproduction (accomplished through parthenogenesis in the novel). When social pressure fails, more stringent steps are taken, but these are not described in the novel, leaving us to wonder: Do the uncooperative women undergo forced abortion? Are they killed off, as all dangerous animals have been?

Not surprisingly, feminist extremists often exempt themselves from the behavioral norms they wish to impose on all other women. They carve out little pockets in which *their* particular personal lives and tastes can continue untainted and undisturbed, and it is only other women whose lives need to be scrutinized, regulated, and if they do not measure up, scorned. How else explain that Andrea Dworkin, with her notoriously hateful writings about men and heterosex in general, has also written lovingly about her own father, a feminist man to whom she says she owes her passion for writing and her independent spirit? How else explain Catharine MacKinnon's apparent belief that while *other* women cannot give informed consent, she herself can?[50] This seems a fair inference to draw from those affectionate photographs seen a few years ago of MacKinnon arm in arm with her then-fiancé Jeffrey Masson. Clearly, these women are prepared to impose their views on others, while for themselves, they maintain the rights belonging to autonomous adults. This is the standard tactic of authoritarian leaders.

Faced with the inconvenient fact that many women who are economically independent nonetheless seem to like living with men, heterophobes have had to bring out their heavy artillery to combat so stubborn a resistance. The older of the two main weapons they deploy is the language of hate against men. So much abuse is heaped on males that it becomes difficult for self-respecting women who consider themselves feminists to associate with them. This is the approach that is epitomized in such expressions as "sleeping with the enemy" and in the labeling of "heterosexual feminist" as a "paradoxical identity."[51] As a result, heterosexual feminists, put on the defensive, often attempt to remain in good standing with their lesbian friends by insisting that while they have no use for most men, their own husbands or lovers are rare profeminist paragons. This is a coward's defense, similar to that of the racist who acknowledges knowing some "good niggers" here or there, while vilifying Blacks in general.

The second, and newer, armament in the heterophobes' arsenal is the postmodernist obfuscation that "problematizes" not only gender but also sex. It represents both as entirely imaginary constructs, which—once they are clearly seen for what they are—will cease enslaving us. In other words, as we learn that our "sexual preference" and even our "sexual identity" are the products of a social conditioning that forces us to limit our lovers to a particular group of people, heterosexual relations as we know them will come to an end, along with all questions of sexual "identity" and "preference." For as seen in this new light, not only gender but also sexual identity is performance, is ideology, but certainly is not an essential part of the reality of human beings who actually are born female and male.[52]

On one feminist e-mail list not long ago, a professor who said she was teaching her students that all sexual identity is a social construction pronounced herself thrilled to come upon the work of Anne Fausto-Sterling, who has written that as many as 4 percent of newborn infants are hermaphrodites who are then surgically conformed to either male or female bodies.[53] Like other postmodern feminists, this professor was happy to extrapolate from such research that the other 96 percent of us, too, have not only our gender roles but our sexual identity forced upon us. This led her to the further conviction that a less patriarchal society would encompass many more sexes than the two into which we are all molded.[54]

Though fun to play with in theory, such ideas (which, among other things, display an extraordinary hubris in assuming that human beings can finally and definitively be cut off from the rest of the natural world) seem in practice designed not so much to add fascinating diversity to the already exuberant human scene as, quite specifically, to decompose the maleness of men and neutralize heterosexual women's orientation toward it. Not surprisingly, they never impugn the femaleness of women-loving women.

Some proponents of these extraordinary arguments may honestly think that it is not possible to gain civil equality for gays and lesbians except by stigmatizing heterosexuality, or at least by "interrogating" it. In this view, gay-rights activism, like feminism, is a zero-sum game: Whatever I win, you lose. But as a strategy, this proposition seems doomed, since such theorizing will have little effect on the vast majority of people, who will no doubt go right on being stubbornly heterosexual, while feeling nothing but estrangement from (if not ridicule for) the sort of feminists who tell them sternly they shouldn't be doing what they are doing, much less consider it "natural" and enjoyable.

An egregious example of the "problematizing of sexuality" is offered in an article by Deborah C. Stearns entitled "Gendered Sexuality: The Privileging of Sex and Gender in Sexual Orientation." Here the author solemnly undertakes to show that all "sexual orientation," whether homosexual, bisexual, or heterosexual, is socially constructed. She argues that a partner's sex should be no more significant than any other personal characteristic that makes us prefer one individual over another.[55] I highly doubt that such reasoning—surely unconvincing to most homosexuals and heterosexuals alike—will be successful in permanently separating women from men.[56] In fact, I have often wondered why, given the failure even of truly repressive and homophobic societies to wipe out homosexuality, we should believe that redefining heterosexuality as "compulsory" would dissuade anyone from it.

Many such arguments rest on John Money's famed (now notorious) research stating that it is learned gender roles, rather than biological sex, that determine sexual identity. Money's most publicized case, of a male infant who was raised as a girl, was not long ago exposed as signifying precisely the opposite of what both Money and his feminist supporters have been asserting for a generation. In fact, social conditioning failed to override biology, nor did it determine sexual orientation. John, who suffered traumatic loss of his penis at the age of eight months, was reared as a girl, Joan, on the advice of Money. At the age of fourteen, and with no knowledge of his own medical history, John began to openly rebel against his imposed femaleness, which he claims never felt right. Eventually, he went back to his original, and apparently biologically programmed, male identity. He married a woman and today has a family. Money, it appears, for years tried to cover up the collapse of his most famous case, despite the repeated doubts about it raised by other researchers—in particular by Milton Diamond, who held that gender identity is "hard wired" into the brain and thus creates a predisposition within the limits of which the environment works.[57]

In any case, Money's claims about the John/Joan case were useful for the feminist agenda from the outset. In Catharine MacKinnon's early work on sexual harassment, for example, Money is a prominent figure, whose research is used to justify MacKinnon's attack on heterosexuality. The point of these attacks in the context of sexual harassment is that sexual overtures (or what is now increasingly called "sexual harassment") can then be claimed to have nothing to do with biology or sexual attraction as a natural phenomenon, and everything to do with patriarchal power. As MacKinnon wrote in her 1979 book on sexual harassment, "social factors aside, a female sexual identity does not feel intrinsically out of place in a biologically male body and vice versa." MacKinnon was glad to be able to state with certainty that the "effect of biology on the behavior of the sexes, so often accepted as primary, has been found to be largely secondary."[58] After a generation of indispensability to feminist arguments about the social construction not only of gender but of sexual identity itself, the John/Joan case will now stand as a monument to the flaws of this theory.

But the question that needs to be asked is this: Why was Money's and others' similar writings on gender identity so important to feminist theorizing? The answer appears to be that despite all the talk of social constructionism, there lies at the heart of much feminist writing a secret belief that as long as two sexes exist whose identities, natures, and in some measure behaviors are governed by biology, women can never gain civic and social equality. What else could explain the now decades-old battle, on the one hand, against sex differences as a fact of nature and, on the other, against men as men? In an inversion of Blackstone's famous dictum about married women's status, many feminists seem to want to believe that male and female are one and this one is—or at least should be—female. The incoherence of the two positions (social constructionism when that is most useful; biological essentialism the rest of the time) seems not to have produced any terminal discomfort among feminists, since they are able to shift from one position to the other without difficulty. And in fact, the news of Joan's reversion to a male identity in the John/Joan case did not cause a major upheaval in feminist circles. Just as I predicted when the news first became widespread through an article in *Rolling Stone* magazine, feminists shrugged off the entire episode. The whole point of being an ideologue, I observed at the time, is that new information does not disturb one's worldview.[59]

Another dismal instance of the feminist antibiology approach to sexuality—and a textbook case of heterophobia at work—is provided by an article entitled "The Medicalization of Impotence: Normalizing Phallocentrism," by Leonore Tiefer. Its abstract summarizes the argument as follows:

> Today, phallocentrism is perpetuated by a flourishing medical construction that focuses exclusively on penile erections as the essence of men's sexual function and satisfaction. This article describes how this medicalization is promoted by urologists, medical industries, mass media, and various entrepreneurs [offering treatments for impotence]. Many men and women provide a ready audience for this construction because of masculine ideology and gender socialization.[60]

In this author's perspective, nobody really needs an erect penis. Presumably, she would prefer to live in the world of Sally Miller Gearhart's 1980 feminist utopia *The Wanderground*, where the women's only male allies (of whom women are nonetheless suspicious) are the gay men, called "gentles," who have voluntarily accepted impotence. The only good man, it would appear, is an impotent man. The feminist failure to treat as a serious act of violence Lorena Bobbitt's severing of her husband's penis, and the general lack of public interest in other, similar, cases, merely confirms this particular manifestation of heterophobia.

Groveling Men

Should it surprise us that some feminist men have themselves accepted the view of maleness expressed by feminist extremists? After all, even ordinary men these days fear to challenge feminist perspectives. As psychotherapist Laurie Ingraham comments, "The 'in thing' is to totally support women no matter what."[61] Many men do this only passively, through failure to challenge feminist assertions and aspersions, like the men Ingraham describes at a professional meeting of therapists: They sat quietly while demeaning comments about men, made by the women running the event, were greeted with much laughter by the predominantly female audience,[62] the kind of reaction I, too, observed at the Yale conference described in the introduction, above. But some men feel compelled to go much further than silent assent.

John Stoltenberg, long-term live-in companion of Andrea Dworkin, has evidently not succeeded in overcoming the innate dualism that much feminist writing denounces as a characteristic masculinist approach. Though he believes he has rejected sexual dualism by "refusing to be a man" (the title of his first book and of his political program), he in fact embraces the duality of body and soul, invoking the "fundamental dichotomy between manhood and selfhood."[63] Stoltenberg's work represents a staggering disregard for biology in its claim to have reconceptualized life in such a way that "manhood"—defined in strictly negative terms—is accepted as inimical to "selfhood," the entity he is trying to develop. Labeling men "penised humans," Stoltenberg judges them to be nothing more than the product of a flimsy assignment made at birth because some humans are born with "a bit of flesh" (an "exterior genital tubercle," as Stoltenberg likes to call it) that the attending physician judges to be "long enough."[64] Females, he asserts, are thereby relegated to the category of the "not penised."

Stoltenberg cannot be defended on the grounds that he is speaking of gender, not sex—that is to say, of social construction, not of biology. If he were, he would not go on to describe the penis (as does his roommate Dworkin) as a weapon. His project is to urge men to give up maleness for "selfhood": "That bit of flesh [the male baby's penis] then bears an awesome burden as the human to whom it's attached begins believing that with this anatomic organ comes a separable sphere of sexual sensation that is, unambiguously and unquestionably, male."[65] Elisabeth Badinter, after reading Stoltenberg's *Refusing to Be a Man*, commented on the "self-hatred" evident in his work, in which male identity is equated with rape.[66] This is the message of his subsequent *End of Manhood* as well: Manhood equals injustice.

In an effort to make these views more palatable, Stoltenberg enthusiastically quotes Andrea Dworkin's affirmation: *"We are, clearly, a multi-*

sexed species which has its sexuality spread along a vast continuum where the elements called male and female are not discrete."[67] Such a claim would seem to lead to a recognition that somewhere along this continuum there is something unproblematically called a male. But that is not the conclusion Stoltenberg and his confreres come to. Rather, they see the "continuum" metaphor as a means for denying and undoing sexual dimorphism as a *fact* of mammalian life. This is part of the scenario promoted by those who use Fausto-Sterling's notion—that there are "five sexes," rather than two—not to expand the number of sexes to include the very few people born with sexual anomalies but to deny sexual difference altogether and, specifically, to deny the "naturalness" of a male/female polarity and complementarity.

But Badinter is onto them. "Beneath its liberating guise," she writes, "the idea of a 'multisexed species' is, here, a denial of sexual identity and especially of male identity." She points out that Stoltenberg has adopted Dworkin's "terrifying denigration of the penis."[68] He declares, for example: "Nothing is less an instrument of ecstasy and more an instrument of oppression than the penis."[69] Andrea Dworkin was adamant on this subject years earlier, when she wrote that men's "phallic identities" must be sacrificed and that no part of the "male sexual model itself" could survive. As she put it, "For men I suspect that this transformation begins in the place they most dread—that is, in a limp penis. I think that men will have to give up their precious erections and begin to make love as women do together."[70] One can imagine her reaction to the development and marketing of Viagra.

The point is clear: MacKinnon, Dworkin, Stoltenberg, and the others are not necessarily antagonistic to sex. They are not puritans. Perfect embodiments of heterophobia, they denigrate, quite specifically, heterosex and male sexual desire as manifest in erections.

In *The End of Manhood,* Stoltenberg lists "Ten Ways You Can Fake It If You Fear Your Manhood Act Is Shaky":

> Believe in a very butch god.
> Start a war.
> Rape someone.
> Lynch or gas someone.
> Force someone to have a baby.
> Whack off to a picture of someone being hurt.
> Whack off inside someone you're hurting.
> Hit or have sex with a child.

Leave a mess.

Laugh at a guy's joke.[71]

In its crudeness and simple-mindedness this catalog is merely an outrageous example of a technique found regularly in the writings of both feminist extremists and the Sexual Harassment Industry: the failure to draw distinctions between wildly disparate things. Most men do not rape and do not start wars, but they do laugh at raunchy jokes. Hitting and having sex with a child are hardly comparable. But to Stoltenberg they are all the same. One of his typifying tales is the story of a little boy who by the age of six had learned to practice the strategy of "sibling battery" on his little sister so as to feel good about being a boy.[72] Has Stoltenberg no friends who can tell him about all the little girls who beat up their younger brothers? He and his followers admit no such possibility.

Stoltenberg, alas, is having an influence on other men. One of my e-mail correspondents, a young professor of journalism, Robert Jensen, generously (knowing how I would use them) sent me several of his articles describing his transition from heterosexual, to homosexual, to celibate man now exploring impotence as the ultimate response to the apparent inescapability of "patriarchal sex," in whatever context sex is pursued.

Jensen's writing is a good distillation of the Dworkin–Stoltenberg message about heterosex. "Patriarchal sex," Jensen tells us, is defined by the axiom "Sex is fucking."[73] That is why his goal (evidently inspired by Stoltenberg) is "to be a traitor to [his] gender, as well as to [his] race and [his] class." Jensen gave up sex "with other people (including the people in pornography)" after realizing that he could not have sex of any sort without recreating "patriarchal sex." He explains, "I was the man, and I was in control because men 'naturally' take control of sex."[74] Even converting to homosexuality did not save him from these dilemmas, for he found that gay sex, too, was contaminated by patriarchal values.[75]

Reading Jensen's essays, which are largely autobiographical explorations of his engagement with radical feminist ideas, I found it hard to avoid a sense of both the pathos and the grandiosity of his situation. Here is a man who honestly seems to believe he has a kind of magical power over women by virtue of being a "penised person," and who furthermore holds that sexual relations are manifestations of his need for control (including, he says, control "either of the woman or the woman's pleasure").[76] Perhaps he has never encountered a take-charge woman in bed, or does not know what Carol Queen tells us in her book *Real Live Nude Girl: Chronicles of Sex-Positive Culture,* which is that large numbers of the men who sought her services as a prostitute wanted to be dominated.[77] Nor has Jensen developed the sense of humor without which sexual activity quickly turns ludicrous. With his constant breast-beating (perhaps the metaphor is not located quite correctly), Jensen's work suggests a blinkered egocentricity. Of course, he could retort that my view of him merely proves him right: Men *are* like that. Still, in our correspondence on e-mail, Jensen seemed to me a sympathetic, and certainly a cooperative, person. I am therefore struck by the sad and grotesque quality of the fantasy of power evident in his writing, the fantasy of which he reassures himself by grandly abdicating it, sacrificing sexuality on the altar of feminism. Jensen quotes his hero, Andrea Dworkin: "The normal fuck by a normal man is taken to be an act of invasion and ownership undertaken in a mode of predation; colonializing, forceful (manly) or nearly violent; the sexual act that by its nature makes her his."[78] Evidently his masculine control is no match for the tough-talking Dworkin, who browbeats her readers with her rhetoric. As Elisabeth Badinter shrewdly comments (about Stoltenberg), "The aggressivity of a feminist becomes masochism in a man's writings."[79]

Jensen repeats the sorts of observations on the word "fuck"[80] that were made by a little-known feminist jurist, Thomas Baty, more than fifty years ago. When Dworkin wrote in this same vein more recently, she was celebrated by feminists such as Mary Daly for being the first person in history to understand that women are humiliated by the sexual act itself. But this is not so. The magnificently eccentric Thomas Baty used this very argument, for decades, starting in 1916.[81]

Writing in his persona of "Irene Clyde," Baty quoted from classical and contemporary sources pointing to the power element in sexuality. He gave colloquial examples such as the exclamation of the French officer who, after a humiliating military defeat, had cursed, "Nous sommes F——!"[82] (*Nous sommes foutus*). Foreshadowing many contemporary feminists, he viewed such expressions as transparent reflections of the way in which the human race has habitually regarded heterosexual intercourse.

Only in the twentieth century, Baty contended, had people thought to deny or minimize the fact that women's physical relation to men was one of subjection and humiliation. The outward physical relationship was only the symptom of an inward spiritual disease—and it was the

latter that was the ultimate target of Baty's attack: "The willing acceptance of inferiority is the root and essence of all evil: it cankers character."[83] It was not "filth" that was the fundamental vice of sex, as some
nineteenth-century sexual reformers believed; rather, it was the "willing acceptance of inferiority," "the wallowing in a moral deformity—
the acceptance of a stunted life which might have been a complete one.
. . . The sting of sex is contemptibleness."[84]

The conclusion was inescapable: "The creature who resigns herself
to be a stunted character is a Fool: no greater exists in this universe."[85]
Nonetheless, Baty was careful to distinguish between biology and social
construction (although lacking the vocabulary), which made him speculate that some day heterosexual intercourse might well be free of the
connotations of domination and submission, superiority and inferiority, that he felt it had in his time.[86] He did not, in other words, blame
the penis.

But even in Baty's own time, feisty women were not ready to accede
to the suggestion that heterosexual intercourse degraded them. Naomi
Mitchison, for one, attacked the antisex brigades by drawing an important distinction. Commenting on the "possession" of women by men,
Mitchison, in her 1934 book *The Home and a Changing Civilisation*, argued that women's guilt at being overwhelmed and "possessed" by a
man is due to confusion of two sorts of possession:

> One's historical mind gets at one, pointing out that one is the "weaker
> sex", for this reason oppressed and exploited, and one mixes that up with
> what ought to be the very pleasant feeling of being gripped by muscles of
> a different strength and texture to one's own, and, hating the one, one's
> hatred is transferred to the other. One wants, passionately, *not* to be the
> weaker, and this is understandable considering the history of the last sev-
> eral thousand years, but why on earth should one bother? Men are
> weaker than elephants and less able to do lots of things: but elephants do
> not oppress them.[87]

The sort of "possession" associated with being in love, Mitchison argued, adds something to, rather than takes it away from, each of the
two partners and should not be confused with the unacceptable and
demeaning social possession of women by men.

Recent sex reformers such as Carol Queen, a performance artist and
bisexual agitator, write in a very similar vein. Queen analyzes her earlier difficulty in coming to terms with the fact that she liked sexual
submission. Such desires, she says, caused her guilt not because "they

were kinky, but because they were unfeminist." But it was submission to a man (as opposed to a woman) that "was *really* perverse." Sounding like Naomi Mitchison sixty years earlier, Queen writes, "Sexual submission never meant that I wanted to be nonsexually submissive."[88]

Robert Jensen, by contrast, seems mired in a belief in the superiority of his own genitals, a condition for which he is constantly apologizing. All men are raised with rapist ethics, he maintains, whether or not they are all rapists in legal terms.[89]

Like other feminist extremists (though differently bodied from most), Jensen affirms, once again, the very domination he claims to want to relinquish. What else should one conclude about a "confession" that second-guesses all men and women who do not share his view of heterosex? Quite obviously, along with MacKinnon and her supporters, Jensen assumes that his truth-telling is the real thing, while others wallow in illusion, unable to confront their humiliating submission in the sex act, if they are women, or their will to power, if they are men. Yet another feminist supporter, Allan Hunter, identifies himself as a "heterosexual sissy" and argues for the posture of "sissy" as an appropriate role for men like himself who want to help usher in a feminist age.[90]

Such ideas are, as it turns out, a mere reversal of Otto Weininger's. In his 1903 book *Sex and Character,* Weininger, an anti-Semitic Jew who committed suicide at the age of twenty-three, contrasted women and Jews with men and Aryans. On the most positive reading, Weininger was driven by a desire for spiritual wholeness that the body prevented him from realizing. While discussing "male" and "female" as ideal types, he in fact parodied actual women and their behavior, just as Solanas, Dworkin, Stoltenberg, and Jensen parody men. Seeing women as embodiments of sexuality who lack all spiritual and moral traits in their own right, Weininger blamed them for drawing men into a debased relationship. Although the Jews in Weininger's scheme of things are the lowest of the low, even "the woman of the highest standard is immeasurably beneath the man of [the] lowest standard."[91]

At the heart of Weininger's extraordinary catalog of supposed female characteristics lies the essential nothingness of women; devoid of a soul, incapable of greatness or genius, women are possessed by their sexual organs and hence dangerous to men. "Women have no existence and no essence; they are not, they are nothing. Mankind occurs as male or female, as something or nothing. Woman has no share in ontological reality, no relation to the thing-in-itself, which, in the deepest interpre-

tation, is the absolute, is God."[92] After explaining why women have no
real existence, Weininger, in all seriousness, wondered, "At this stage it
may well be asked if women are really to be considered human beings
at all, or if my theory does not unite them with plants and animals?" To
Weininger, who considered sexuality immoral, "Woman requires man
to be sexual, because she only gains existence through his sexuality."[93]
In this way, woman keeps man from attaining his true moral potential.
Weininger concluded that fecundity was loathsome and that the education of mankind must be taken out of the hands of the mother. As noted
earlier, such views are mirrored by feminist extremists such as Valerie
Solanas, who in her *SCUM Manifesto* described men as "incomplete females," forced to constantly seek out women in order to achieve some
sort of existence.[94]

Feminist scholars have traced and denounced ideas such as Weininger's, which, in less-heated rhetoric, go all the way back to Aristotle. But
it is astonishing to note the extent to which Weininger's misogynistic
perspective has been inverted in the writings of feminist heterophobes
over the past few decades. For feminists who hoped something positive
would arise from feminism, it is particularly disturbing to observe the
reemergence of ancient stereotypes—even if they now go against men
rather than women. Moreover, while Weininger's was an idiosyncratic
voice, feminist extremists today have a considerable following for their
flagrant misandry and enjoy respectability in many circles.

Sex reformer Carol Queen, who criticizes our culture for being "sex
negative," writes about the importance of "honoring desire."[95] Robert
Jensen, by contrast, argues, rather like Joyce Trebilcot, that we all have
an "epistemic responsibility" to get over our corrupt sexual tastes, those
tastes that make mutually desired heterosexual intercourse indistinguishable, in his view, from rape. Jensen's own effort to live up to this
epistemic responsibility has led him into "not-sex," which he defines as
"intimacy that resists or transcends oppression." Masturbation, also, is
a problem, Jensen concedes, since "the fantasies that fuel that masturbation are almost exclusively scripted by patriarchy."[96] He embraces,
instead, the perspective, offered him by a friend, that when erection is
not achieved, "something new becomes possible." Thus, Jensen concludes, he now strives for impotency.[97]

Jensen's and Stoltenberg's perspective brings to mind Sharon Olds's
poem—which strikes a very different chord—"Outside the Operating
Room of the Sex-Change Doctor":

Outside the operating room of the sex-change doctor, a tray of penises.

There is no blood. This is not Vietnam, Chile, Buchenwald. They were surgically removed under anaesthetic. They lie there neatly, each with a small space around it.

The anaesthetic is wearing off now. The chopped-off sexes lie on the silver tray.

One says *I am a weapon thrown down. Let there be no more killing.*

Another says *I am a thumb lost in the threshing machine. Bright straw fills the air. I will never have to work again.*

The third says *I am a caul removed from his eyes. Now he can see.*

The fourth says *I want to be painted by Géricault, a still life with a bust of Apollo, a drape of purple velvet, and a vine of ivy leaves.*

The fifth says *I was a dirty little dog, I knew he'd have me put to sleep.*

The sixth says *I am safe. Now no one can hurt me.*

Only one is unhappy. He lies there weeping in terrible grief, crying out *Father, Father!*[98]

The desire to cast off the body is found in the religious traditions of many cultures, not just the Western. It is hard to avoid a sense of sympathy for the desperation that drives this sort of quest, and the hubris involved in rejecting human biology. It brings to mind the image that George Orwell found so repulsive in the work of such futurists as H. G. Wells: "the brain in the bottle." For feminist misandrists, however, males alone should relinquish their bodily existence, not females, for whom, on the contrary, bodies may still be sources of pleasure (via food, other women, the external world generally). They would surely see it as a misogynistic plot were anyone to suggest that females too should give up the pleasures of which their biology makes them capable.

Whenever sexual difference is denied or suppressed for political purposes, there is an implication that admitting the existence of biological differences entails some important social consequences that must be resisted. When we erase difference, we seem not to overcome it but rather to reduce one thing to another (in this case, male to female) and to pretend that nothing has been lost in the process. In fact, we are left with half the human picture, not, as feminist rhetoric might have it, with all of it in a newly "theorized" whole.

The Costs of Heterophobia

Am I making too much of an admittedly minority position within feminism? I do not wish to suggest or imply that heterophobes are taking over and that men will soon be in danger of elimination—through being either physically wiped out or simply thought out of existence by the ultimate politicization of everything. No, I do not want to go that far. But I am saying that the language of heterophobia, which is prevalent in feminist writings, *should* be taken seriously. Cultivating hatred for another human group ought to be no more acceptable when it issues from the mouths of women than when it comes from men, no more tolerable from feminists than from the Ku Klux Klan.

One might retort that there really is little cause for alarm. Heterophobes today are not generally in positions of authority. They do not occupy posts that let them enforce their ideas. In one sense, this is obviously true. No leading politicians have run on a platform of heterophobia. But consider the kinds of prominence actually achieved by feminist ideas. These ideas are now repeated and assented to by people who certainly do not regard themselves as feminist extremists, and who perhaps do not even realize where their rhetoric originates, so successful has it been in mainstreaming itself as reasonable and warranted protection of women.

Sexual harassment legislation and regulations, in school and in the workplace, are clear demonstrations of the real power feminist theorizing has acquired in daily life. The relations between men and women have indeed become "problematized," so much so that any word, any gesture, may these days give offense to women. If in the old days women's complaints against men's abusive behavior were seldom taken seriously, today things have moved 180 degrees. Nor is this just a matter of a turnabout in social norms, or a change in office etiquette. As we have seen in part II, people have lost their jobs because of flimsy or entirely false allegations of sexual harassment. In many instances, men (and some women) are being deprived of due process. And there are feminists who quite explicitly and seriously consider that this is a justified course. In their view, due process is one of the patriarchy's power tools, like freedom of speech.

Feminism has in fact been remarkably successful in creating a climate in which men's words and gestures are suspect, and in which it is now women's charges that are given prompt credibility, or at least the benefit of the doubt. Tell a man such as Leroy Young, who lost his university position because of a barely investigated charge of sexual harassment, that feminists do not possess power. But it is not only men who are the victims of such accusations. Women in academe, too, though much more rarely, are being accused of sexual harassment—sometimes with charges that are quite absurd—when it suits the agenda of other women, even of so-called feminists.

Still—and I want to state this explicitly—the fact that women, too, are caught in the net should not be our sole reason for protesting against the Sexual Harassment Industry. We ought not to ignore that it is men who are the intended targets of feminists planning their brave new heterosex-free world. Even without attributing a conspiracy to the SHI, it is apparent that the feminist struggle against "sexual harassment" has indeed been successful in enacting a whole series of feminist aims. Women's revenge, in other words, is no longer merely a fantasy. The writings of the most notorious and least responsible among heterophobes have enormously contributed to the creation of a "gotcha" atmosphere in which individual autonomy and its sexual manifestations in particular are under attack.

Heterophobia (despite its apparent relationship to the long tradition of sexual repression in America) should not be mistaken for a nostalgic return to Victorianism. On the contrary, its best fit is with the dismaying history of twentieth-century totalitarianisms. A tendency toward totalizing pronouncements and an absence of respect for the political process—the heart of which, after all, is compromise—are blatant among feminist extremists.

But at the moment, the dominant trend within feminism seems still remarkably resilient to any self-criticism. When in May 1996, I sent the Women's Studies E-Mail List a message relating to my heterophobia project, inviting reactions, scores of hostile replies poured in.[99] Women told me that my project was dangerous, ill conceived, and methodologically flawed; they seemed about evenly split between those who denied there was any heterophobia within feminism and those who said men deserved it. Quite a few objected to the term "heterophobia" itself (evidently unaware that the "radical feminist" Robin Morgan herself used the term, and at times deplored the tendency, in a 1982 book).[100] As one put it:

> The very word "heterophobia" suggests, as its opposite, "homophobia," when in fact "heterophobia" is to "homophobia" as "white-male bashing" is to "gay/lesbian-bashing"—a manipulative and reactionary appropriation of terms and experiences that only belong, properly speaking, to the minorities whose experiences of prejudice and brutality they were originally coined to describe.

Even the feminist novelist Marge Piercy, who, I assume, would not take kindly to suggestions that she recast her writing according to someone else's views, urged that I reconsider or redefine my project.

A few men were heard from, too, identifying themselves as male feminists and affirming that they had had nothing but positive experiences with female feminists. I hope they were not pained by some of the women who posted explanations of why as women they could never quite trust even male feminists.

By contrast, most of the handful of supportive responses were sent to me privately, not to the entire list. These led to some fruitful exchanges. Some women observed that their heterosexual women's studies professors seemed to be the most heterophobic of all. This is the phenomenon of "male bashing" familiar to many who have taken women's studies courses but ardently denied by defenders of the faith, who insist it is merely an invention of those promoting the "backlash" against feminism.[101]

It is astonishing that decades of progress for women, decades of denunciation of misogynist ideas, should have brought us to the point where a mere reversal—misandry instead of misogyny—should count as serious feminist thought and should be taught and promoted in the name of feminism. Although it is not difficult to match crazed feminist pronouncements of our time with crazed masculinist assertions from the past,[102] there are two important differences. The first is that—apart from collections of misogynistic rants across the centuries (the sorts of material professors like to hand out to their students to shock them into sudden awareness of the long history of male disdain for women)— few of us today, least of all in the academy, are exposed to persistent hysterical denigrations of women. For the writings of feminist extremism, on the other hand, there does seem to be a large and apparently insatiable market, and their authors are without question among the best-known names in contemporary feminism.[103] The second difference is that no one ever believed or claimed that the old misogynistic ravings could pave the way to a better life for humankind, whereas somehow heterophobes have gained acceptance for many of their prejudices, precisely because they are being proclaimed in the name of an ideal female future.

On the one hand, feminist extremism has brought about very negative results, such as the exorbitant and paradoxically inevitable sexualization of all interactions between men and women that occurs when the vigilante mentality is unleashed; the vocabulary of sexual harassment even at the kindergarten level; the denial of due process to those accused of sexual misdeeds in universities and the workplace; the attack on the rights of fathers; the madness of "recovered memories" of child sexual abuse; and so on. On the other hand, this vindictive brand of feminism has nowhere to go because it alienates many women—and, of course, men, too.

Which is it, then, readers may wonder: Has heterophobia succeeded, or is it doomed to failure? The two possibilities can, I think, be reconciled. We need to acknowledge that the negative consequences are real and are being felt—in unjust and frivolous accusations against men (and against women too); in a strained atmosphere between the sexes; in assaults on freedom of expression and association. But these are short-term results. They lead so obviously to a worse world for us all that they cannot possibly endure. Other, more tyrannical and much more powerful, ideologies have self-destructed; so will this.

When that happens, the damage done to feminism in the eyes of millions of potential supporters will be clearly felt. For the feminism that aimed at promoting justice and equality, not anger and revenge, will have been tainted by the male-bashers, the deniers of biology, the ideologues—who are indeed often the loudest among feminist spokespersons. Enormous effort will then be required to restore feminism to the dignity without which it cannot succeed in improving women's status in those locations and situations, at home and abroad, where such improvements are still much needed.

Having said this, however, I must go on to clarify that I am not arguing against heterophobia merely because "it's bad for feminism," though it surely is that. The power of feminism as an orthodoxy is made evident every time someone limits a critique of feminism to this argument, for this reveals how illegitimate it is thought to be to attack feminism for the harm it is doing to men and to nonfeminist women. Yet such a criticism is richly deserved and needs to be voiced. A political movement that holds half the human race in contempt, a movement whose adherents meet any and all criticism by pretending it is the work of enemies at the gate, a movement grounded in gross caricatures and distortions, cannot seriously aspire to succeed in the long run—unless, that is, it resorts to undemocratic means. That many feminists today call for precisely such methods should not, then, surprise us.

Chapter 7

The Authority of Experience

cᴈᴠᴈᴐ

If there were no authority on earth
Except experience, mine, for what it's worth,
And that's enough for me, all goes to show
That marriage is a misery and a woe.

CHAUCER, *The Canterbury Tales*

The "authority of experience" has been invoked by feminists since early in the second wave.[1] Beginning modestly as a challenge, as Adrienne Rich put it, to "a culture which validates only male experience" while denigrating or ignoring women's,[2] the claim to experiential authority has, in the space of twenty-some years, moved to a position of centrality in feminist thought. When the "reasonable woman" standard was abstracted from this authority and incorporated into jurisprudence, the proposition that men and women inevitably see things differently and according to some gendered pattern became codified in law. As Catharine MacKinnon writes, "The law against sexual harassment is the first law to be written on the basis of women's experience, as well as the first to recognize that sexual abuse can violate equality rights."[3]

The U.S. Court of Appeals for the Ninth Circuit established this view in *Ellison v. Brady* (1991) when it rejected a gender-neutral "reasonable person" standard. Such a standard, the court held, ignores women's particular experience of sexual harassment.[4] We need to be very clear about the meaning of the "reasonable woman" standard in relation to sexual harassment litigation. It means that what is actionable is not the *intent* to offend or discriminate, as determined by a hypothetical reasonable person, but rather whatever a "reasonable woman" *feels* to be offensive and discriminatory, that is, what she claims to spontaneously *experience* as offensive and discriminatory. This apparently innocuous change, in addition to shifting the burden, has another important implication. In the old definition, the emphasis was on the word "reasonable." In the new dispensation, it clearly falls on the word "woman."[5] Women's thoughts and reactions are thus accepted as differing from men's in some essential ways.

In sexual harassment law, therefore, the "authority of experience" has been given a place of honor. Such a move should have caused feminists everywhere to rejoice, for a fundamental tool of feminist analysis—the concept of subjective experience—was thereby elevated to law.[6] But feminists have raised two types of objections to the premises underlying the "reasonable woman" standard. One, expressed by liberal feminist scholars such as Barbara Gutek, rejects the "essentializing" inherent in the *Ellison v. Brady* decision. In an essay written with Maureen O'Connor, Gutek makes a strong critique of the notion that there exists a gendered "perceptual gap" in men's and women's assessments of sexual harassment. Gutek and O'Connor therefore suggest that a more valid standard might be that of a "reasonable *victim*," whether male or female. Such a shift would, they argue, preserve the emphasis on power differentials that the notion of "victim," of either sex, implies.[7]

The second type of critique rests on the notion that positing a hypothetical "reasonable woman" is insufficient. Because some feminist scholars wish every woman's individual "experience" of harm to be grounds for legal action, they argue that the "resonable woman" standard homogenizes all women and fails to recognize the particularity of their positions and responses. Thus the standard has the effect—so they claim—of taking the heat off the harasser's actions.[8] Such a critique attempts not to broaden the concept of "victim" to include men but rather to make it easier for any woman's perception of victimhood to be validated.

In addition to some courts' acceptance of the "reasonable woman" standard, the broadening of the word "discrimination" is of great importance, for it is this that has allowed offensive behavior to be considered actionable regardless of the agent's intent, which may be entirely benign, and regardless of the severity of the harm actually suffered. Since the law cannot (yet) compel people to be "nice" to one another, much less force them to behave according to the moment's feminist creed (even if all feminists could agree on this), feminist activists have resorted to the next best thing; they have expanded the definition of "discrimination" far beyond anything originally envisioned in the 1964 Civil Rights Act, which explicitly stated that intent to discriminate would have to be proved by the prosecution.[9] The Civil Rights Act of 1991 removed the requirement of discriminatory intent and wrote the concept of "disparate impact" (i.e., effects, not intent) into statutory law for the first time. It also gave plaintiffs in Title VII discrimination cases the right to a jury trial and to monetary damages. This set the stage for the elevation of women's word to the level of law—which was precisely the goal of feminist activists.

A whole series of consequences comes into view as a result of these changes. Foremost among these is the enthronement of female subjectivity. Since by all accounts male subjectivity lags far behind, perhaps mired in some Neanderthal stage, it follows that if men do not realize their behavior is in fact (and in law) offensive, they obviously require "reeducating." And indeed, training in the new gender-appropriate behavior is an instrument much favored by the Sexual Harassment Industry.

Consider the case of one professor's reeducation, enthusiastically described by Jan Salisbury and Fredda Jaffe in a recent essay, "Individual Training of Sexual Harassers."[10] The authors distill the experiences of three "trainers" (who eschew the label "counselors" because the term raises an expectation of confidentiality that does not suit the needs of organizations trying to protect themselves from lawsuits). These trainers worked with twenty-five individuals (one of them female) in an effort to "rehabilitate" workplace harassers. Salisbury and Jaffe offer as an emblematic instance of how trainers "manage harassers" the case of an archaeology professor. A female student complained that he had made sexist comments, inquired into her private life, made abusive comments about her class performance, and given her an unsolicited hug on a field trip.[11] Because this was the second complaint against the professor, "the college felt he needed individual training." Recourse to this corrective measure seemed urgent, as the professor, while admitting to most of the alleged acts, insisted on seeing context and intent very differently.

> Rather than admit to a pattern of discrimination, Dr. Stevens [not his real name] talked about isolated incidents "taken wrong," such as referring to female students as "girls" and male students as "men," stating the opinion that archaeology fieldwork may be very hard on women who want

relationships and children. He acknowledged he was gruff and highly critical with *all* students on occasion and that during field trips he did ask about students' families and dating as a way of getting to know them. The hug was done in a group of people as a spontaneous reaction to his joy in finding an important relic. Finally, he stated to the investigator that he felt aggrieved [considering] the time he had spent mentoring the complainant.[12]

Consultation with the affirmative action officer and department chair resulted in "a formal letter of reprimand stating that termination could result if the [alleged] behavior continued. It was agreed that the professor would meet [with the trainer] for two sessions of two hours each."[13]

The authors tell us what goes on in such sessions. Through reading and soul-searching discussion, the offending party is brought to the point where he agrees to spend time learning about, and even leading, activities related to women at the college. He also undertakes (we are not told whose idea this was) to write a letter of apology to the student, expressing his esteem for her abilities and detailing what he has learned from his training. The trainer suggests that this letter (to be submitted first to the trainer for "review") also be approved by the department chair and the university's EEO office.[14]

I doubt that I am the only person to be revolted by this spectacle of an open threat of loss of employment, followed by a process of "reeducation" and an abject act of public contrition. In no way should such rituals be seen as innocuous dispensations of appropriate information and mild correction. In fact, they amount to a bold and ruthless attempt at restructuring the relations between men and women, beginning with the humiliation of men. This conclusion is borne out by the spate of books on sexual harassment now available to administrators; these books tell them not so much how their institutions can avoid legal liability and costly lawsuits as what they can do to reform male behavior and—toward this end—how they can train women to identify, label, and act on anything that can be construed to fall within the steadily broadening scope of "sexual harassment" understood as a form of discrimination. The kinds of injury women are to be alert to, as in the case of the hugging professor described above, need not be intended as slights—and usually they are not. They need only be "experienced" as such, at the time or *ex post facto*.

"Theorizing" Experience

"Authority of experience" does, however, come with certain inherent problems. "Experience," it turns out, is not a self-evident or self-explanatory entity, certainly not in a time of postmodernist perceptions.[15] Does the claim to experiential authority entail the demand that we each confine ourselves to our own direct experiences, never venturing to speak on those vast areas of perception mediated to us by our minds? Such a view would go a long way toward undermining feminist analyses of the male world, analyses resting on countless imputations and inferences about male thought-processes, character, and psychology. It would also circumscribe all feminist writing that is not strictly autobiographical.

Celia Kitzinger, a lesbian professor of women's studies and author of a book on heterosexuality, wants to defend the right of lesbians to "theorise heterosexuality," as she puts it. She is therefore willing to grant that heterosexuals, in turn, are entitled to write about lesbians. Noting that her students typically hold views far less liberal than her own, she makes some interesting observations about how such theorizing interacts with feminist identity politics:

> In any dispute, [the students believe that] the person who can claim the relevant experiential authority [has] the most right to speak, especially where she can also claim to be the most oppressed. So a lesbian theorising lesbianism is on safe ground, virtually unchallengeable by a heterosexual woman; whereas a heterosexual woman theorising lesbianism can be challenged by lesbians as lacking both experiential authority and an understanding of oppression. A lesbian theorising heterosexuality lacks experiential authority but, being (by virtue of her lesbianism) more oppressed, is imagined to speak in a 'purer', more 'authentic' voice. As such, the situations are not parallel: the lesbian speaks with more authority on heterosexuality than the heterosexual can on lesbianism, and it is this notion of lesbian purity or moral superiority that seems to render lesbian theories of heterosexuality so very threatening to heterosexual feminists—and hence leads to some of the more florid attacks on lesbian theorists.[16]

Given this situation, Kitzinger writes, "[i]t is important, for the development of feminism, that we judge the adequacy of feminist theories in terms of their political utility, or predictive power, rather than in terms of the author's biography and her presumed 'right' (or lack of it) to create theory."[17]

Despite the common sense evident in much of what Kitzinger says, her conclusion here strikes me as dangerous, for it means nothing other than that the ends should justify the means. Theories, she asserts, prove themselves by their "political utility." This is an ominous precept, one that will warm the heart of every zealot who does not wish to be bothered with either facts or truth and who finds, in postmodernist writing, a defense for such a posture.

Kitzinger herself demonstrates what happens when the "political utility" of a theory is used as the measure of its adequacy. She argues, plausibly, that "experience" is not *prior* to theory—since our very understanding of our experience depends on a "web of interpretation and reinterpretation." Experience is always embedded in a theoretical framework, whether this is acknowledged explicitly or remains implicit.[18] She gives some striking examples of how feminists develop new ways of thinking about their experience:

> What we may have thought of, with self-hatred and guilt, as a dirty childhood game is reinterpreted as child sexual abuse. The flattering wolf-whistle becomes sexual harassment. The pile of dirty dishes in the sink no longer occasions self-rebuke and a sense of personal failure, but rather anger at an unreconstructed husband. It is not simply that the *interpretation* of the experience changes: the very experience and the emotions associated with it are different too.[19]

Thus, she concludes, experience "is always already theorised."

Kitzinger here recognizes that what is called "sexual harassment" is a relatively recent social construction; it is not a simple fact of male malfeasance toward women. But she does not see the other side of this coin, which is that women can also be taught to take offense at things that are not inherently offensive. Unlike battery and sexual assault, where the hurt resides in the action itself, the injury in much of what is today labeled sexual harassment arises in the *interpretation* women are being taught to adopt as a guide to understanding others' words and gestures. Kitzinger's example, in the passage just cited, of the wolf whistle reinterpreted as "sexual harassment" is a perfect illustration. Theft and violent sexual assault do not depend upon hermeneutic unpacking for their effect (though some cases of date rape no doubt do). Sexual harassment—in the sweeping sense in which the term has come to be used today—does require it.

This is why MacKinnon, for example, does not hesitate to see her own understanding of "experience" as overriding that of women who don't share her view. As Judith Grant comments, in *Fundamental Feminism*: "MacKinnon knows that experiences need interpretation. The problem is that MacKinnon believes she knows in advance what that interpretation should be."[20] And to facilitate her interpretation, MacKinnon offers contradictory approaches to harassment, which between them effectively cover the field. One approach rests on the notion of difference and answers to the "but for" test: but for the fact that this person is a woman, would she have been treated in this way? The second approach focuses on inequality rather than difference. It presumes that women and men cannot meaningfully be compared because the social construction of gender in a patriarchal society invariably subordinates women to men. To these irreconcilable approaches corresponds the hopeless confusion that makes discrimination rest on differential treatment sometimes because of gender and at other times because of sexual attraction itself.

It is a sign of the extraordinary power gained by feminist perspectives that men have in some cases lost their livelihoods because a woman has interpreted something said or done (that just a few years earlier would have seemed innocuous) in accordance with new feminist dogma. In fact, much of the SHI literature is devoted to combating the suspicion that a "victim" could ever be hypersensitive, mistaken, or paranoid about an "experience." Just how rapid and drastic the move away from this view has been can be gauged by an article published a mere twenty years ago in the feminist journal *Frontiers*, entitled "Hostility and Aggression toward Males in Female Joke Telling," in which Carol Mitchell, a folklorist, analyzed jokes told by women and featuring female protagonists and male targets. Nowhere in this 1978 essay does the about-to-be-unleashed concept of sexual harassment appear.

Mitchell, of course, was aware that jokes are often used to embarrass or to express hostility. As an example, she recounted a dirty joke told by three women to their male boss. "Given the joke telling situation," Mitchell said, "the man had to laugh, but he realized he was being laughed at by the three women since he was surprised by the joke. Since the man was their boss hostility could not be expressed openly, but could be expressed by means of a joke."[21] She went on to discuss castration jokes told by women. Here, the issue of power (recognized by Freud in his discussion of "smut") is clear; women enjoy these jokes because they express power over men—something they do not generally have. Why, one might ask, should men's sexual jokes not be seen in the same light? Why are they, in the sexual harassment literature, inevitably taken as a manifestation of actual male power? There is a long and interesting history to the study of jokes as social and psychological mediators. Only in our time has this complex phenomenon been reduced to a male weapon in "hostile environment harassment," pure and simple.

There are other signs, too, that a major retraining campaign is under way—a considered effort to redefine and in fact discourage heterosexual relations. As I have repeatedly stressed, the SHI does not attempt to differentiate between instances of indisputable abuse and mere expressions of sexual interest. Each is taken to be as egregious as the other. The key concept by which male–female interactions are being redefined is "power differential," the presence of which contaminates any sexually tinged word, gesture, or look and turns it, potentially, into "sexual harassment." This persistent inability or refusal to draw distinctions cannot be taken as accidental. Male sexual interest is not simply being construed, or interpreted, as "power." It has actually been redefined as such. The slow and continuous expansion of efforts to regulate personal relations, now extending even to consensual relationships between adults, is a particularly clear example of the stigmatizing of male sexuality in and of itself. True, women and homosexuals are occasionally caught in the trap, but this seems an unintended consequence; they are not the main target—as the sexual harassment literature has made clear from its very inception. Sexual harassment is first and foremost an act committed by powerful males against powerless females. The infantilization of adult women implicit in this view does not seem to trouble many of those who profess feminism.

Whose Authority?

But what about preexisting relationships? Is the concept of "consensual" associations safe at least there? Apparently not, to judge by the opinions of feminist law professor Robin West. She thinks that such a concession would leave out of bounds (meaning out of regulatory reach) the entire murky area of what used to be known as the private sphere. As West insists in her essay "A Comment on Consent, Sex, and Rape" (published recently in the journal *Legal Theory*), the sex to which women "consent" is often what "men want and women agree to but don't particularly desire."[22] In the tradition of MacKinnon, Dworkin,

Jeffreys, and Frye, West is out to challenge the "legitimization" of consensual sex that occurs when only *non*consensual sex is stigmatized.[23] To
succeed, she needs to redefine "consensual sex" (in quotation marks) so
as to highlight its damaging effects on women.

In her earlier work, West argued that women's subjective lives are
unlike men's: "The quality of our suffering is different from . . . men's,
as is the nature of our joy." Categorically, West declared, "[W]omen
suffer more than men."[24] The phrases "date rape" and "sexual harassment" (which she calls oxymoronic) capture these differences: Men experience the first term ("date," "sexual"); women, the second ("rape,"
"harassment"). When West wrote these words, in the mid-1980s, she
could still complain that women's "suffering for one reason or another
is outside the scope of legal redress."[25] This is no longer true.

It seems, however, that not enough female suffering could be
brought into the discussion through the existing vocabulary of date
rape and sexual harassment. West must therefore aim at the redefinition of heterosexual intercourse itself. This has been done before, in
the writings of feminist extremists starting in the late 1960s, as we saw
in chapter 6. What is of interest now is how their loudly proclaimed
antagonism toward men is being recycled to yield sophisticated theoretical pronouncements.

West's more recent work is part of the effort to reconceptualize sex
itself as the real problem. In an essay entitled "The Harms of Consensual Sex," she makes her position clear. "I want to argue briefly that
many (not all) consensual sexual transactions are [harmful to
women],"[26] she writes, her parenthesis inviting gratitude for a small
concession. Making the typical authoritarian-feminist move of telling
other women that they misunderstand their own experience (a claim
contradicted, one would think, by the very doctrine of "authority of
experience"), West does not hesitate to inform us that the woman who
experiences no such harm is actually the one who is most harmed.
Why? Because such a woman has incorporated a sense of self-negation
that makes her fail to recognize the injuries she suffers. "Women who
engage in unpleasurable, undesired, but consensual sex may sustain
real injuries to their sense of selfhood"—in ways West goes on to enumerate.[27] Her argument seems to evoke an implicit model of sexual
desire as spontaneous, pure eroticism uncomplicated by real-world factors. Against this ideal, West sets "consensual sex" and the injury done
to women's sense of autonomy by participating in it when the decision

to do so is contaminated by "their felt or actual dependency upon a partner's affection or economic status."

But is it only sexual compliance that threatens "selfhood" in this way? What about all the many things people do that may not, at each and every moment, represent their own authentic and spontaneous desires? Should one abolish these from life? Or only from one's sex life? The result, if one were to do it, would be a totally egocentric universe in which no one would have regard for another's interest or needs. Meanwhile, paradoxically, men are still being instructed in some quarters that they must pay attention to women's desires (including women's different paths to sexual fulfillment). Even accepting West's very limited understanding of what constitutes "desire" and "pleasure" in an intimate relationship, we should ask whether feminists really wish to argue for a new double standard, by which men do what is necessary for women's pleasure and happiness while women should refrain from any reciprocal actions.

West's strictures against "consensual sex" involve the familiar transformation of sex into power. And as usual, it is not all varieties of sex that are meant. Her redefinition focuses specifically on heterosex, which West seems to believe is always pleasurable for men and rarely so for women.[28] It is this discrepancy, West argues, that explains men's insistence that "voluntariness alone ought to be sufficient to ward off serious moral or political inquiry into the value of consensual sexual transactions."[29] Here West is onto something that earlier feminists might have missed: Judging rape as "bad" merely because it is "not consensual" clearly implies that consensual intercourse is "good." It thus "legitimizes" consensual heterosexual transactions—the very thing West wants to challenge.

Thus does the heterophobic view of the world, in which women under patriarchy cannot give meaningful consent to intercourse with men, slowly extend its reach, in defiance of the notion that women's "authority of experience" must be respected. In her recent essay on rape, West explicitly embraces such a view:

Women have a seemingly endless capacity to lie, both to ourselves and others, about what gives us pain and what gives us pleasure. This is not all that surprising. If what we need to do to survive, materially and psychically, is have heterosexual penetration three to five times a week, then we'll do it, and if the current ethic is that we must not only do it but enjoy it, well then, we'll enjoy it. We'll report as pleasure what we feel as pain.

It is terribly difficult to get to the bottom of these lies, partly because we convey them not just with our words, but with our bodies. It is now a commonplace that women don't "feel at home" with male language—but this is no wonder, when what we've mainly learned to do with it is lie.[30]

West evidently believes she has disarmed her opponents by explaining any possible disagreement with her views as lies: Women lie to protect their version of reality, and it is this self-delusion that motivates lack of acceptance of West's harsh "truths."

When I tried out West's idea, that women's lives are characterized by pain and self-deception, on several (feminist) women I know, they first responded with disbelief and then tried to figure out a context in which she might possibly be right. Could she be writing about the eighteenth century? About women in some very peculiar circumstances? I simply repeated West's words, which in her essay are unqualified and evidently intended to stand as general truths about women. In the face of my interlocutors' incredulity I explained that West would probably reply that women are "liars," unable to face the truth about their condition, committed to tolerating unpleasant "consensual" intercourse and to pretending they enjoy it. The older of the two women then brought the discussion to a close by commenting that such statements do feminism no service.

But thinking again about all this somewhat later, I realized that the important thing in West's work is not its substance. It is, rather, her mastery of coercive discourse. Feminists have for long told us that women have no language, that they are silenced by phallogocentrism (a contention taught in some women's studies classes and repeated, as I have often observed, without embarrassment by some very articulate women students). How striking, then, to encounter in a feminist author, writing in the name of feminism, a sequence of overdetermined arguments that literally attempt to take the words right out of any respondent's mouth, leaving nothing but assent as a possible reaction.

It is ironic that, by adopting this strategy, feminist heterophobes are actually replicating the very relationship they claim existed between women and words in the rejected past. Only now it is feminists who claim that women lack the ability to understand their own reality. Given this imbecility on the part of women, leaders are indispensable to act as a feminist vanguard for mobilizing the unconscious masses.

And such leaders are not hesitant to step forward, with their supposedly sophisticated theoretical analyses in support of the new heterophobia. One such figure is Dee Graham, a psychology professor who claims to be able to explain the very existence of heterosexuality in women by invoking what she calls the "Societal Stockholm Syndrome." In a 1994 book entitled *Loving to Survive,* Graham expounds her theory in minute detail.[31] As in the famous Stockholm bank-hostage episode in 1973, in which four hostages bonded with their captors and came to see the police as their common enemy, women—so the argument goes—are eternally held hostage to men by the four "interlocking" conditions identified as the Stockholm Syndrome: threat to survival, isolation, inability to escape, and dependence on the oppressor's kindness.[32] According to Graham's scenario—a version so fantastic it assumes mythic proportions—male abuse of women, in all its forms, is the reality of everyday life. Only "radical feminist theorists have recognized the centrality of men's violence to women's lives."[33] The point of all male behavior is domination (women, by contrast, "as a group abhor violence").[34] Heterosexual behavior thus becomes a "survival strategy" for women, as do "feminine" characteristics, which result from women's need to ingratiate themselves with their "captors."[35]

How does Graham sustain such an extravagant claim? She does so by citing primarily extremist arguments and feminist scare statistics concerning women's sorry plight. Her discussion of mass murderers is an example. "[V]irtually all" are male while their victims are mostly female, we are told, which leads to the comment: "These findings indicate that women's survival is threatened by male violence,"[36] and to the opening sentence of the following section, on wife abuse: "Even women who are not murdered by their battering partners find their survival continually threatened."[37] Thus does the exceptional become the typical. The torture of women in Latin America and the burning of witches in Europe hundreds of years earlier are all brought in to teach the same lesson.

The latter example incidentally serves to show up the kind of spurious scholarship on which Graham's thesis rests. Graham repeats the long-discredited fable about the 9 million victims of the European witch-hunts over a three-hundred-year period,[38] further noting that as some scholars say witches were persecuted for six hundred years, the real number of martyred women may actually be twice that high. By contrast, Robin Briggs, in his recent meticulously documented *Witches and Neighbors: The Social and Cultural Context of European Witchcraft,* tells us that the best-informed recent estimates of the total number of executions for witchcraft in Europe are between forty thousand and fifty thousand, of whom about 25 percent were men.[39] The 9-million figure, so beloved of feminist writers (Graham is hardly alone in this vast exaggeration), is an overestimate by some 18,000 percent! But this is no accident. Graham refers to witches for precisely the same reason she discusses male mass murderers: Women are in dire peril of their lives. "This history [of witch persecutions] and others like it in other parts of the world should leave no doubt in today's women's minds that men are capable of killing women, of using violence for the social control of women, and that men will settle for the flimsiest reasons as rationalizations for the killings."[40]

Such rhetorical excess, however, has its own logic. Any woman who contests Graham's interpretation, who insists on the authority of her own experience (not to mention of her own reading) to argue that Graham's view is slanderous and that the men she has known are no worse than are the women, who affirms heterosexual desire as a good thing, not the terrorized adjustment of a prisoner—any such woman is, by that very insistence, demonstrating that she is in thrall to the Stockholm Syndrome. In the preface to her book, Graham warns her readers that they will need to "work through their initial shock and resistance" to her argument.[41] As with other such inflammatory writing, Graham's thesis makes it impossible to distinguish in a meaningful way between situations of genuine abuse and the ordinary life of heterosexual women. And that is precisely the point. Men are women's captors. Women are men's hostages. Heterosexuality is the form of their subjugation.

Like Robin West, then, Dee Graham is part of the current trend to redefine heterosexuality along extremist feminist lines.[42] Increasingly, heterosexuality is presented as deviance, a kind of mental illness, a state of mind produced by terror. And this frame of reference is then used to reconstruct heterosexuality across the life span, representing it as "coercive sexuality," as explained in a recent article by Wendy Patton and Mary Mannison. Their project, the authors say, "is concerned with documenting a broad continuum of unwanted sexual experiences, including those that appear 'normal' within the dominant heterosexuality discourses," in women's lives from childhood to adulthood. The point of the term "continuum" is clearly spelled out: "The concept of a continuum assists women to identify links between typical and aberrant behaviour, and enables women to locate and name their own experiences."[43] Thus, just as consensual becomes "consensual," alarmingly set off by scare quotes, so the concept of normal sexual interactions is transformed into "normal" sexually intrusive behaviors.

Authorizing the Experience

For a less extreme vision of heterosexuality, motivated by the desire to shift from some inarticulate authority of experience to an explicitly articulated authorization of experience, consider the contribution of Lois Pineau, who wishes, modestly, to make "communicative sex" the norm for heterosexual relations. In a prize-winning essay, Pineau has proposed that something similar to Antioch College's rules (requiring explicit requests for permission at every step of sexual intimacy) should become the legal standard for sexual consent.[44] Once again, heterosexuality is presented as something men want and women reluctantly assent to. Others have pointed out that ambiguity on women's part in responding to men's sexual overtures may be not only a cultural habit but an evolutionary strategy, designed to maximize women's reproductive success. By giving ambiguous responses (traditionally called "playing hard to get"), women test men's level of interest and commitment and evaluate their fitness as long-term partners. Men, for their part (so the analysis goes), seek to ensure their own reproductive success by not investing heavily in women whose behavior demonstrates their ready availability to other men.[45]

It is intriguing to contemplate such explanations and to play out scenarios that both challenge and confirm such a view of heterosexual behavior. But feminist reformers have a well-known antipathy to sociobiology—at least whenever it might reinforce heterosexuality and conventional gender roles. In any case, that "communicative sex"—seeking explicit permission for each stage of sexual intimacy, each time—would enormously narrow the expressive behavior of both men and women is self-evident. Looks, gestures, sighs, hints, the back-and-forth of sexual play—all would be delegitimized if explicit verbal consent were to become the sine qua non of "legal" sex.

It needs to be noted that, as Pineau recognizes, her argument assumes that women are indeed able, contrary to the views of MacKinnon and others, to give meaningful consent. Women simply need to do it explicitly and verbally, not by gesture or implication. (She has some muddled ideas about long-standing relationships in which this explicit communication might not be necessary, but she recognizes that this concession gets her into the dangerous terrain of seeming to condone marital rape.)

Pineau has another rather daring suggestion. With the advent of the "communicative sex" model, date rape (defined as nonaggravated sexual assault) should be reduced from a felony to a misdemeanor, both so that women would be more likely to report it and so that the conviction rate would increase: "My hypothesis is that a higher conviction rate would actually provide more protection for women, and that the increased probability of getting a conviction would lead more women to report sexual assaults and to prosecute their assailants."[46]

What is fascinating about this suggestion is that it clearly rests on a view of date rape as a fundamentally *different* phenomenon from "real" rape, a distinction that feminists have denounced for years. Pineau treats men's fears of false accusations of rape as proof of the many injustices they perpetrate on women, who thus have reason to seek revenge.[47] She conceives of communicative sex as a reasonable alternative because, she says, those who wish to have sex that is not communicative, and do not want to complain, are free to proceed.[48] But are they? In such a situation, men would always be taking a risk if things did not work out just as the woman desired—and Pineau's strategy clearly is designed so that men would seek women's permission, not the reverse. As Pineau says, evoking a traditional "patriarchal" model of heterosexual relations, "Mind you, a man who has noncommunicative sex with a woman would do so at his peril, just as a man who helped himself to my property would do so at his peril."[49]

The analogy is instructive. Pineau argues that men must give up the assumption that "no" might mean "yes." Women's behavioral repertoire would thus be controlled in a new way, by feminist dictates. This, Pineau is saying, is a small price to pay for offering women more protection from rape. Furthermore, she makes the readiness to pay this price the key feature that, to her, differentiates feminists from nonfeminists.[50]

Nor is Pineau particularly sympathetic to women who might not agree with her ideas. True, she acknowledges, like women who didn't want the vote, some women might not want the "right to communicative sex." But, she says, "[t]here is no more force to such a position than there is to that of a slave who is opposed to the abolition of slavery."[51] Once again, we see that feminists, rhetoric notwithstanding, need not grant authority to every woman's experience.

Pineau and her defenders do not see her model of communicative

sex as an inappropriate intrusion of the state into the most private
sphere. One of these defenders, Matthew R. Silliman, is, in fact, scorn-
ful of the notion that rules such as those of the Antioch College policy
would make intimacy "artificial." He doubts that any "thoughtful person" in our time could possibly believe that there is anything "natural"
or normative about sexual relations.[52] An interesting reflection, this, on
the ideological underpinnings of new intrusions into the private
sphere. The presumed social construction of sexuality, itself a highly
contested claim, thus emerges as a "fact" ready to do service in the
support of still further social constraints.

A dogged stupidity pervades much feminist writing about sexuality.
It is obvious when dealing with acquaintance rape—a murky area that
feminist discourse has attempted to make unmurky via the pretense
that it is as simple an arena as the violent-attack-by-a-stranger. The
1993 edition of *Get Smart!*, designed to be a resource book for female
students, uses the familiar analogy of a mugging victim who, whatever
poor judgment she exercised, would never be made to feel responsible
for the crime.[53] The book spells out the standard current line about
rape: Lack of consent is the appropriate definition, and because society
tends to blame the victim (as if this were still the case), women are
unlikely to make false accusations of rape.[54]

This strikes me as an odd conflation of old and new ways of looking
at things. All the advantages to be gained by asserting that women are
blamed for rape, are disbelieved, and are on the defensive and therefore unlikely to make false allegations—all these advantages are still
claimed. At the same time, changes in the law and in public consciousness mean that the situation is not as it was, women are not vilified for
charging rape, accusations are not readily dismissed, and so on. Thus,
the weapon of current law and custom is wielded while the old, nearly
obsolete standard is still appealed to in an effort to lend credence to a
woman's claims of helplessness.

But the main thing this entire discussion overlooks is the ambiguity
of sexual situations. The same women who believe in the authority of
bodily experience, who talk about the "truth of the body," who say the
body "doesn't lie" and the "body remembers," are eager to disregard
the body when it acquiesces, responds, moves in for another caress,
while the mouth whispers "no." In this instance—which is, in fact, the
very definition of seduction—the "truth of the body" counts not at all.

Thus, attacks on heterosexuality become indistinguishable from attacks on rape—not because heterosexual intercourse *is* rape (or akin to

it), as MacKinnon and Dworkin would have us believe, but because the ambivalence of sexual desire, the play of approach and withdrawal—all this has to be delegitimized if the case against men is to prevail. The problem is built in once "acquaintance rape," along with an assumption that active verbal consent is the only meaningful kind, becomes an accepted concept, as is rapidly occurring.

Saying and Doing

Catharine MacKinnon employs speech-act theory to defend her view of words as deeds ("performatives," in the terminology of British philosopher J. L. Austin, who by this term distinguished words whose utterance conveys a new reality, whether psychological or social, from utterances that simply convey information, which he called "constatives").[55] But words are not simply deeds, even in speech-act theory. "I thee wed," said to a stranger in the street, is not the "performance" of marriage. It is a phrase that, when embedded within certain actions and legal requirements, becomes an essential part in the performance of marriage. Perhaps a better example is "I promise to do this," by which one performs the act of promising. The promise is not, however, the doing; it is a statement of intent. In both examples, something other than uttering the words themselves is necessary. That something is what the philosopher John R. Searle calls "appropriateness," or "felicity" conditions, which represent the rules language-users assume to be operating in their verbal dealings with one another.[56]

MacKinnon cannot possibly believe that saying "I'm imagining that I am raping you" is the same thing as raping someone (though she did seem to take that position in the pages of the *Nation* a few years ago).[57] She could not seriously maintain that "I hate you, dumb cunt" is the same thing as killing a woman in a misogynistic rage. So why is she pretending to hold such beliefs? Perhaps it's because her entire case rests upon precisely such a muddling of the issues. She has to make words seem like deeds, has to claim they are *as damaging as* deeds. The sociologist Joel Best, in explaining how a social problem comes to prominence through the work of individuals who expand its definition and find ever more instances of it, labels this procedure the "just another example of X strategy"—where "X" is the problem that is being dramatized. Thus, he contends, the "domain" of the identified problem inexorably "expands," as greater and greater claims are made for the problem's pervasiveness.[58]

MacKinnon wants to claim maximum harm for women from the practices she is attempting to end. This is the reasoning that lies behind her well-known views of pornography. Exaggeration is part and parcel of her feminist representation of the world. Without it, her own measures would stand out more starkly as what they are: extremist descriptions of (some) male behavior, designed to edge out distinctions and clear thinking.[59] Andrea Dworkin assaults clear thinking by her catatonic writing style, which aims to numb the reader into submission; MacKinnon does it by the tone of simple and straightforward certainty with which she makes highly problematic assertions such as: "Unwelcome sex talk is an unwelcome sex act."[60] Is welcome sex talk, then, a welcome sex act? Tell that to the partner of an impotent man. But such erasure of what would seem to be self-evident distinctions is an important move in feminist writing today, which thus comes to have an authoritative ring that discourages questions.

Speech-act theory teaches us that, as John Searle stated in *Speech Acts: An Essay in the Philosophy of Language,* "[s]peaking a language is engaging in a (highly complex) rule-governed form of behavior."[61] Speech act theorists distinguish several kinds of "illocutionary" acts, such as promising, warning, threatening, greeting, or informing (as distinct from "perlocutionary" acts, intended to create a certain effect in the hearer). One type of illocutionary act, called a "declaration," brings about the state of affairs it refers to. Examples include firing someone, baptizing a baby, or passing sentence on a convicted person. But for no type of speech act is it enough simply to utter words. Speech acts are "correctly or felicitously performed only if certain conditions obtain."[62]

From this point of view, it becomes clear that when MacKinnon attempts to use speech-act theory to justify her claim that words are deeds, she is either grossly simplifying the theory's fundamental insight (yes, speech is a kind of behavior) or intentionally distorting the theory (as if nothing distinguishes speech from other kinds of behavior). In either case, it appears that what she is really after is to make her definition the prevailing one within both the legal system and popular consciousness. In other words, she wants to create a situation where so many women claim that to be called a name or to hear a discouraging word at school or at work *is* to "be violated," that this becomes true.

How could this happen? It is, in fact, already happening, under our very eyes, as speech that was once considered unpleasant, rude, vulgar, or even deeply offensive comes to be redefined as "just another example" of the prohibited thing: harassment, which in turn, thanks to

MacKinnon's pioneering efforts, has been defined as sexual discrimination depriving women of their civil rights. This new definition, after all, has some additional advantages: It is shrouded in a breathtaking simplicity, such that one need no longer trouble to draw distinctions in male behavior. What else explains how calling a college student a "girl" can be viewed as an offense requiring the professor's reeducation, as described above? The fact that other women—even women who have experienced genuine male violence—disagree with the new dispensation matters not at all. These are presumably not reasonable women. Their experience simply carries no authority.

Let us consider more closely some of the implications of the rhetoric of sexual harassment, in which even verbal expressions of sexual interest are transformed into exercises of power. When gay men pursue other men for casual encounters, is this an expression of "power" or of the search for "pleasure"? When lesbians pursue other women, how is this to be construed? Unless sex reformers want to open themselves to accusations of being antisex (not to mention homophobic), they would have to admit (along with Jane Gallop) that their analyses of sex-as-power are intended to apply, above all, to the world of heterosexual relations. And, in fact, early "radical feminists" did openly admit this. Ti-Grace Atkinson, for example, is credited with the comment, "Feminism is the theory, and lesbianism the practice."[63]

Do feminists seriously wish to claim that gay men may pursue other men out of desire while straight men pursue women only out of a wish to oppress them and demonstrate male power? Such a claim would be obviously flawed; yet it is implicit in the sexual harassment literature, which, as we have seen, rarely mentions homosexuals but treats male-to-female words and gestures as prototypical cases of objectionable behavior.

Some feminist critics, however, have made it clear that the actions they find culpable rest on a heterosexual model even when practiced by homosexuals. Andrea Dworkin, as Nadine Strossen comments, is well known for her "long-standing antipathy" toward *any* expression of male sexuality, including gay male sexuality.[64] Nor is lesbianism necessarily exempt from criticism by other lesbians. Janice Raymond excoriates sadomasochistic lesbians (such as Gayle Rubin), who, in her judgment, are assimilated "very forcefully into a leftist and gay male world of sexuality." Raymond opposes this kind of "sexual liberation," just as she opposes the 1960s sexual revolution, which, in the extremist feminist view, merely made women more accessible to men. In her sexual

scenario, the "forceful and often violent sex performances" that characterize lesbian sadomasochism are sorry substitutes for proper feminist
"ardor and intense passion," which presumably do not focus on "genital sex."[65]

Although some feminists have attempted to maintain a liberal attitude toward lesbian sadomasochistic activists, who are, after all, exercising consenting adults' authority of experience, feminist extremists tend
to see in this attitude only what Janice Raymond labels a "dogmatism
of tolerance" (she has a good ear for the effective oxymoron) or a "tyr-
anny of tolerance," which, she claims, has infected the women's movement and promotes a value-free know-nothingness leading to the
"unexamined life."[66] As it happens, I agree with Raymond that feminism, above all, cannot be value free (if it were, it could not promote
gynocentric values over androcentric ones, just to mention an obvious
example). But this view is a far cry from embracing Raymond's sort
of dogmatism. Surely there are positions available along the spectrum
between value-free neutrality, at one end, and dogmatic conviction, at
the other.

Like other critics who don't for a moment grant the authority of the
average woman's experience, Raymond argues that "hetero-relations,"
like heterosexuality itself, are not biologically ordained but forced onto
women by tearing them away from the "Gyn/affection" to which they
naturally are heirs.[67] Not content with merely questioning the status of
normative heterosexuality, Raymond declares it to be "unnatural."
Why, she asks, if women were "naturally" heterosexual, would men
need to use so much physical abuse and coercion to make them comply
with male desires? The obvious answer is that contrary to Raymond's
defective initial premise, massive evidence suggests that women do engage in heterosex voluntarily. One could just as easily turn her proposition on its head and ask: If women were "naturally" inclined toward
same-sex relations, why would heterophobes, over the past few decades,
have had to mount a huge propagandistic effort to separate women
from men and turn them instead toward other women?

Another question arises in this context. Lesbian feminists use the
persistent but hidden history of lesbianism as a challenge to the norm
of heterosexuality. They argue that because, in the past, lesbians risked
a great deal in acting against the norm of their time, it follows that
lesbians alone experienced an authentic sexuality. But that very history
works in the opposite direction as well, as experience once again rears
its head. Do these feminists ask us to believe that no heterosexual

woman ever took risks? Even when it has been most dangerous for them, women have faced dishonor, pregnancy, and death, for the sake of coupling with the men they desired.

And, in the lighter vein of popular culture, women have even initiated dirty jokes. Twenty years ago this could still be acknowledged. "Many of the sexual jokes that women and men tell can be used as real attempts at seduction," folklorist Carol Mitchell wrote in the article cited earlier in this chapter. Indeed, she described a woman's report of telling a joke to a male friend with such an aim.[68] Today, the Sexual Harassment Industry is so caught up in its heterophobia that it must reject this reality and concentrate only on the hostility and power differentials that it tirelessly insists govern male and female interactions.

Should the vast literary and historical record be discarded as mere propaganda for the unnatural condition of heterosex? Should it all be reinterpreted as a cover-up for the ugly facts of rape and constant assault, as though the latter were the millennia-long true story of relations between the sexes?[69]

And if so, does there not remain the problem of male sexuality? Are we really to believe that it, too, is a deception, an artifact created for the sake of a display of power, not an expression of genuine sexual desire and of the pursuit of pleasure—itself no negligible an aspect of life? The pleasure of sex (even leaving love out of the equation for the moment) seems to make people—of all types and all inclinations—take considerable risks. And one of the measures of social progress has been the human individual's increased autonomy in choosing his or her own partner based on personal preferences as against the claims of family, property, and convention. Seen in this light, the attempt to legislate "communicative sex" as the new norm for legal consent, like the attempt to closely regulate sexual relations in school and workplace, is a throwback to the days of excessive state regulation of the private sphere, the days that gave us prohibitions against interracial marriage and sodomy. It is but one more step into the past, now brought to us by feminism as it claims to be leading us into a better future.

Chapter 8

"There Ought to Be a Law"

ᘏᘏ

Nothing is more likely to be abused than the power of officials who think they are doing the right thing.

ANTHONY LEWIS, PBS's *Firing Line* (1995)

Years ago, "There ought to be a law" was a frequently heard phrase. The wish that our own idea of what is right and what is wrong should be the law of the land is a common response to the awareness that life is not always as we want it to be. Of course, it is one thing to express such a desire casually and quite another to try to make it come true. But the latter is what is happening at the moment, in ways that should alarm us. In the light of sexual harassment law, speech codes, and similar efforts to regulate behavior, does it still make sense to say, "There ought to be a law"?

The Drive for a Perfect Future

I have been studying utopian and anti-utopian literature for over twenty years and teaching it for nearly that long. In the past, I assumed that anti-utopian works such as *Brave New World*—seemingly intended to warn us about the dangers of attempting to construct perfect futures—were expressions of the authors' conservative politics. This supposition affected my entire perspective on the warnings they were sounding. Thus when, in the early 1980s, I read some nineteenth-century antisocialist satires depicting societies in which the demand for equality has run out of control, I took them to be nothing more than mean-spirited attacks on socialism and the ideal of equality and gave them little further thought.

But as the years went by, I discovered that life was beginning to imitate art. I saw colleagues I had long considered on my side politically supporting speech codes, embracing vague or exaggerated definitions of "harassment," and arguing for administrative control of personal relationships between professors and students. Out of the depths of my memory, those long-forgotten anti-utopian stories, depicting the collision course between equality and freedom, came rushing back to my mind.[1] And now I find them hovering over me as I watch universities struggling with (it often looks more like capitulating to) demands for intervention in all areas of campus life—the very restrictions that, back in the sixties, students had been trying to persuade university administrations to abandon.

Some examples might prove instructive here. In 1873, Bertha Thomas published a story about a futuristic society committed to rectifying the "Iniquitous Original Division of Personal Stock."[2] The remedy includes such measures as preventing athletes of above average strength or agility from participating in sports; reducing the over-healthy to the standard set by the infirm; making beautiful people wear ugly clothes; granting honorific titles to people with physical defects (the graver the defect, the grander the title); actively restraining good-looking girls from "appropriating the affections of the whole youth of the Commune"; and purposefully neglecting the education of the handsome and witty.

In 1891, the British satirist Jerome K. Jerome imagined a similar society, in which absolute harmony and equality have been achieved by allowing no one to engage in "wrong" or "silly" behavior.[3] All are now equal, but this is not enough. All must also look the same: identical hair color for men and women; the same clothes for everyone. But even this is incomplete equality. In Jerome's "new utopia," the tallest have an arm or a leg lopped off, and surgery is performed to reduce brains to average capacity. Beauty, of course, is abolished because of its long and ignoble history of preventing full equality.

More recently, Kurt Vonnegut's short story "Harrison Bergeron" depicted a U.S. "Handicapper General" who, with her team of agents, metes out disabilities and impediments, guaranteeing equality by doing away with all competitive advantage and its attendant demoralization for the not-so-advantaged.[4]

Fantastic? Ridiculous? These days, it seems, reality has overtaken

satire. In 1995, the Chancellor's Office of the University of Massachusetts at Amherst, where I teach, circulated a proposal for a new harassment policy, which—negotiated over an eighteen-month period by the
administration and the Graduate Employee Organization, without consultation with either lawyers or faculty—seemed perilously close to satire. Aiming to prohibit harassment, the policy defined it as

> verbal or physical conduct that a reasonable person, with the same char-
> acteristics as the targeted individual or group of individuals, would find
> discriminatorily alters the conditions under which the targeted individual
> or group of individuals participate(s) in the activities of the university, on
> the basis of race, color, national or ethnic origin, gender, sexual orienta-
> tion, age, religion, marital status, veteran status, or disability.[5]

Still dissatisfied with this catalog of protected categories, the university's Graduate Employee Organization proposed to expand it to include
"citizenship, culture, HIV status, language, parental status, political af-
filiation or belief, and pregnancy status." The administration's response to this addendum was to declare that it "believe[d] such
categories [were] already protected under those previously listed."[6]

Undeterred either by judicial decisions that had struck down comparable policies at private and public universities such as Stanford, Wisconsin, and Michigan or by negative publicity,[7] Chancellor David K.
Scott made it perfectly clear, when four critics of the policy, I among
them, met with him, that he aspired to nothing less than success for
our university where other institutions had failed. That is, he meant to
carve out an exception to the First Amendment by crafting a rule that
would stand with existing restrictions on free speech such as libel and
"fighting words."[8] In practice, as the chancellor further indicated, the
policy would require a "double standard" of application: Historically
oppressed groups would be protected from offensive speech, while historically powerful groups would not be.[9] In the face of greater opposition to this proposal than it had foreseen, the administration put the
entire harassment policy on a back burner, where it has been left to this
day.

Of course, the University of Massachusetts is not alone in attempting
to make language do the work of social engineering. The question is
only, How far are reformers prepared to go? In 1995, the Women's
Studies E-Mail List featured a message posted by a feminist philosophy
professor who asserted that she could no longer in good conscience use
the word "intellectual," for to do so would imply that some women are

better than others. Later that same year, when a professor expressed her interest in starting a women's studies honor society, the idea aroused strong opposition from some respondents, who declared themselves alarmed at the "hierarchical" values present in any designation of honors for some students and not for others. In late 1997, a similar proposal was once again aired on the list, with precisely the same effect. Leveling is apparently a recurring impulse among some academic feminists.

Readers should not imagine such views to be insignificant or marginal. Prominent feminists often pursue their agenda unrelentingly, with no regard for its academic consequences. Take the case of Annette Kolodny, former dean of humanities at the University of Arizona at Tucson and a well-known feminist. Kolodny recently published *Failing the Future: A Dean Looks at Higher Education in the Twenty-first Century*. Lurking behind this book's innocuous title is an intriguing proposal for the expansion of womanpower in the academy. This proposal, in turn, depends upon a highly peculiar understanding of the meaning of academic freedom.[10]

In 1991, at the annual meeting of the Modern Language Association, the Commission on the Status of Women sponsored a forum, "Antifeminist Harassment in the Academy," for which Kolodny was asked to define "anti-feminist *intellectual* harassment" as a specific and independent category of discrimination. The stress was to be on the word "intellectual," to set it apart from other encroachments such as "sexual harassment, emotional battering, and physical threats" (an interesting string of associations, incidentally).

In an effort to come up with a workable definition, Kolodny, at the 1991 MLA Convention, suggested the following:

> Anti-feminist intellectual harassment, a serious threat to academic freedom, occurs when (1) any policy, action, statement, and/or behavior has the intent or the effect of discouraging or preventing women's freedom of lawful action, freedom of thought, and freedom of expression; (2) *or* when any policy, action, statement, and/or behavior creates an environment in which the appropriate application of feminist theories or methodologies to research, scholarship, and teaching is devalued, discouraged, or altogether thwarted; (3) *or* when any policy, action, statement, and/or behavior creates an environment in which research, scholarship, and teaching pertaining to women, gender, or gender inequities is devalued, discouraged, or altogether thwarted.[11]

Quite an astonishing definition, this. Adhering to the early legal precedents set under Title VII of the 1964 Civil Rights Act, where "intent *or*
effect" is stressed, rather than intent *and* effect (because, as Kolodny
points out, intent is difficult to prove),[12] she proposes a truly sweeping
entitlement: anything, regardless of its intent, that discourages a woman's thought or expression is to be held discriminatory. And the definition doesn't stop there. It would also ban anything that creates an
environment that discourages, devalues, or thwarts either research
about women or gender or the "appropriate" application of feminist
theories or methodologies. Kolodny's definition would be likely to prohibit the kinds of criticisms I have made throughout this book (and
elsewhere) of feminists and feminist-inspired work, because such critiques might well "discourage" the authors of that work or their supporters. Would it encompass all criticism of women and women's
scholarship (as well as of men and their scholarship when it touches
on questions of gender)? Would a new standard, perhaps that of the
"reasonable feminist," need to be created to settle conflicts among critics? What would be an inappropriate "application of feminist theories
or methodologies"? And who would be left to judge it?

Kolodny tells us that she went at her task with a desire to preserve
"academic freedom undiminished by bias, prejudice, or discomfort
with difference."[13] But, she observes, since women and minorities have
had no role in forming the concept of academic freedom, their interests
are protected by this concept only "insofar as their products and activities *conform to the accepted products and activities of the past.*"[14] A key question emerges from this formulation: Is Kolodny suggesting that women
and minorities are—and should be—beyond any criticism? Or only that
they ought to be protected from special criticism addressed explicitly
to them?

Most amazing of all, as in Professor Ann Ferguson's defense of the
"Vision 2000" plan, discussed in chapter 2 above, Kolodny's feminist
assault on academic integrity is being undertaken in the very name of
"academic freedom"—with the special meaning that term is acquiring
on some feminist lips, a meaning perilously close to an open declara-
tion to the effect that no criticism of feminism and feminists shall be
tolerated.

Kolodny makes it clear that this new level of harassment protection
is to apply to both men and women, as objects and subjects. Her aim,
she says, is to raise awareness by identifying a complex problem.[15]
Thus, promotion and tenure procedures could be seen as "harassing"

if they failed to recognize and reward new kinds of scholarship, such as the interdisciplinary work often done in women's studies, writing computer programs instead of books, and so on. Kolodny does not explain how her definition will distinguish between those treated unjustly and those whose work is simply found to be poor. It appears as though certain identity groups (women) and certain subjects (women and gender) are to be beyond reproach.

The problem with Kolodny's definition is this: Women may indeed at times be treated unfairly, as men may be; but how could one possibly prove that "intellectual harassment" is at work? And even if one could demonstrate such discrimination, why should it be prohibited *only* when anti-feminist? Why not outlaw every form and variety of it—anti-Christian or anti-Republican (these also occur) or anti-philological or, inclusively, anti-old-fashioned? But Kolodny is not writing dystopian satire. Her point is not to imagine amusing scenes that would unfold as charges and countercharges flew through academic hallways. Surely her object is to preventively inhibit any serious criticism that might be made of women and feminism. And no one should doubt that such a broad new definition of harassment, if it were widely adopted, would have this very result. After all, it is in precisely the same indirect way, by urging better-safe-than-sorry attitudes in school and workplace, that sexual harassment regulations have had a profound effect.

Two important Supreme Court decisions handed down in the last week of the 1997–98 term are likely to be of great help to the feminist agenda (even though they might not satisfy Kolodny), by increasing employers' and employees' awareness of sexual harassment liability as a powerful weapon. In *Faragher v. City of Boca Raton,* the Court held that employers are potentially liable for the sexual misconduct of a supervisor toward an employee, even if the employer had no knowledge of it. The *Faragher* case was watched closely by both feminists and employers, since it was hoped that the Supreme Court would finally resolve the question of whether an employer can be held liable for actions of which it was unaware. The 7-to-2 decision made it clear that employers are indeed responsible for policing the workplace (and their "agents" within it) in order to prevent sexual harassment. Thus employers will be obliged, even more than in the past, to demonstrate their compliance with federal law not only by having in place sexual harassment policies (as the city of Boca Raton did) but by publicizing and enforcing these policies effectively. At the same time, the Court left employers one way to avoid liability. In a second 7-to-2 ruling (again with Justices

Thomas and Scalia dissenting), issued the same day, in the case of *Burlington Industries v. Ellerth,* the Court declared that, although an employer can be liable even if an employee suffered no adverse job consequences for refusing a supervisor's advances, such an employer could successfully defend itself against liability by showing that the employee had failed to take advantage of the employer's complaint policies.

It should be obvious that these two rulings (which said nothing to clarify the definition of sexual harassment) give both employers and employees a powerful incentive to act in a defensive way. But this they can only accomplish by cultivating an untiring alertness to potential sexual harassment in all possible situations, each now having a stake in taking preventive measures. An employee who until now might merely have wondered whether an annoying word or gesture had risen (or might eventually rise) to the level of sexual harassment, is now, by this ruling, encouraged to complain immediately, so as not to risk being later found delinquent in utilizing the existing policies. The employer, in turn, will be motivated to prove that it has a strong anti–sexual harassment program and complaint procedure in place, by taking even more stringent precautions than in the past to prohibit all possible words and deeds that might eventually approach the level of actionable behavior. For this is the only kind of affirmative defense it has available.

Most commentators on the rulings believe that they will make it much easier for complainants to win lawsuits. And this can only increase the pressure on everyone involved to create sex-free workplaces. In conjunction with the *Oncale* decision of March 1998,[16] in which the Supreme Court unanimously adhered to a single standard for same-sex and opposite-sex harassment cases, the two most recent decisions make it unsafe now for anyone to engage in any sort of sexual behavior at work. As Jeffrey Rosen pointed out, the *Oncale* case provided the Supreme Court with an opportunity to put a stop to "creeping MacKinnonism" by insisting that Title VII—the intent of which was to protect members of one sex from disadvantages to which the other sex was not subjected—was meant to curtail discrimination, not sexual behavior.[17] Instead, it appears that MacKinnon's view is winning out. Sexual expression, when it occurs in the workplace, is tantamount to sex discrimination. Following the Supreme Court decisions, the *Washington Post* advised companies that they should first declare a policy of zero-tolerance for sexually offensive behavior, then establish the usual preventive measures including sexual harassment training, and lastly launch yearly anonymous surveys to bring latent problems to light.[18] Obviously, every one of these measures will heighten a sense of vigilance and intolerance. Just as obviously they will increase the role and scope of the Sexual Harassment Industry.

The Comforts of Prohibition

At my own university, I have watched in dismay as professors and students who consider themselves progressive have increasingly advocated the censorship of language and the monitoring of behavior and attitudes, and called for rules and regulations to govern virtually all aspects of academic life. To my ears, their demands sound ominously like foreshadowings of all-too-familiar dystopian visions, which, alas, I can no longer dismiss as reactionary grumblings. Granted, the dystopian fantasies of Bertha Thomas and Jerome K. Jerome are programmatically antisocialist in objective. But this fact no longer tells me all I need to know about them. Nowadays, I view them as dire warnings or—worse—as analogs to equally zany but unfortunately very real events happening before my eyes.

By now, even Hollywood has noticed the trend and got into the act. The 1993 film *Demolition Man* (directed by Marco Bramvilla), clearly based on Huxley's novel, is set in the year 2032, precisely one hundred years after *Brave New World* was published, and has a heroine named Lenina Huxley. Extending Huxley's satire of a perfectly managed future to the point where total and constant monitoring of individuals touches every aspect of life, the film envisions nothing so crude as Orwell's telescreens. Rather, organically bioengineered microchips are sewn into everyone's skin, and these devices "code" people so that they can be tracked wherever they are.

Police have become almost entirely unnecessary because "things don't happen anymore," as the warden of a cryogenic prison says with satisfaction. People can go to "compu-chat" machines on the street for instant therapy and words of encouragement. Life is kept pleasant by the omnipresent computers that automatically fine any user of offensive language one or more credits and announce it publicly in a monotonous computer voice. In this future California, no one has died from unnatural causes in sixteen years, and the police don't have the vaguest notion of how to respond to a Code 187—a "Murder Death Kill," as they call it—when, following the demands of the plot, it occurs for the first time in decades. Attempting to deal with a killer from our time who escapes from his fast-frozen imprisonment, the computer provides the police with such pieces of advice as: "With a firm tone of voice, command maniac to lie down, with hands behind back." This is, of course, ineffective, which is where Sylvester Stallone, in the role of renegade cop John Spartan, comes in. Using a defamiliarization technique typical of utopian novels, in which a person from our own time reacts with amazement to the newly encountered future, the film makes our hero inadvertently contravene all the norms of the perfect society.

In *Brave New World,* Aldous Huxley had written: "There isn't any need for a civilized man to bear anything that's seriously unpleasant."[19] *Demolition Man* extends that principle as we learn that whatever is not good for people is considered bad and for this reason has been made illegal. The list includes alcohol, caffeine, contact sports, meat, offensive language, chocolate, anything spicy, gasoline, uneducational toys, and abortion—but also pregnancy if you don't have a license. Not only is reproduction state-controlled and managed hygienically in laboratories, but, as a result of AIDS and other epidemics, body contact has been proscribed. Sexual pleasure is achieved through direct brain stimulation via matching headsets. At one point, Lenina Huxley exclaims with disgust at John Spartan's outmoded idea of sex: "Don't you know what the exchange of bodily fluids leads to?!" He replies, "Yeah, I do: kids, smoking, a desire to raid the fridge." So successfully does the film convey the sense of life in a completely regulated society that, on hearing this line, I actually felt a touch of nostalgia.

The attraction of literary and cinematic utopias, in contrast to the political treatise or essay, is that they set in motion before the mind's eye how life might actually be lived in another—usually very different— kind of society. They also make us see our own society in a new light. Thus, when I first came across some very nasty novels depicting a world ruled by women—books such as Edmund Cooper's novel *Who Needs Men?* (1972),[20] renamed *Gender Genocide* when it was published in the United States, no doubt because of its lively descriptions of newly graduated female "Exterminators" hunting down the few remaining men in their society as a rite of passage called "first blooding"—I took them for misogynistic rants, inspired by contempt for women and fear of their domination in the future. To be sure, some of them do deserve such a reading. But I was puzzled that women, too, had written such books. For example, Pamela Kettle published, in 1969, *The Day of the Women,*[21] which describes how a female political party comes to power in England and develops into a tyrannical antimale oligarchy, complete with spying, selective breeding, and the killing of male babies.

In time, however, what I had formerly taken as literary exaggeration began to look uncomfortably real and familiar. With something of a shock, it came to me that venomous women spewing hatred of men and displaying contempt for heterosex were no longer pure fiction. I had been reading their words for some years, written not by male misogynists but by women calling themselves feminists.

Sensitized as I now am to this subject, it is obvious to me, as I have argued throughout this book, that much of the zealotry we are seeing in the university (and out of it) on the issue of sexual harassment should be construed as an attack, quite specifically, not only on men but on heterosexuality itself. It is, of course, true that women, too, are occasionally caught in the web spun by feminist zealots. But this does not alter the facts that men are the main target and that the cessation of heterosexual expression—or even interest—seems to be the chief agenda of many feminists. Perhaps most surprising is the fact that so many heterosexual women who identify themselves as feminists have stood quietly by as their own tastes and preferences have become the subject of grotesque and demeaning caricatures set forth in the name of feminism.

Nowadays I can observe the new heterophobia almost on a daily basis as I read of one or another effort meant to make the world a comfortable place for women, never mind the cost at which such comfort will be obtained. A recent example was the recommendation—which I have absolutely no doubt would win the support of many of my feminist colleagues—that construction crews in Minneapolis should cease engaging in "visual harassment" of women passing their building sites.[22] And what about the absurd charges that massive sexual harassment is going on in school yards, and the demand of adult women that little boys be made to face up to it and reform?

I do not think we should assuage our outrage over such infringements of people's rights with the assurance that the most egregious encroachments will be dismissed by the courts. Before that happens, they will certainly have contributed to a climate in which men will have become "the universal scapegoat."

For another example, consider a much publicized incident several years ago at the University of British Columbia. At that institution, a report costing a quarter of a million dollars was produced that indicted the entire Department of Political Science for sexism and racism. The document included an appendix of several pages listing allegations of misconduct so astonishingly trivial that it is hard to believe any of it was meant seriously.[23] Professors were charged with criticizing their students' work, or bestowing more praise on one student than on another; of being aloof, or not being aloof enough; of failing to engage students in discussion of new ideas; of being dismissive of students' marxist perspectives. They were also accused of making the kind of personal comments that one might well argue professors should not make. But these, too, turned out to be so trivial, so far from giving serious offense, that the only conclusions a "reasonable person" could draw from the report is that professors must watch their every word and every gesture, that silence is no less dangerous than speaking, that attention and lack of attention are equally suspect, and that students are weak and pitiful children the fragility of whose egos must at all times be foremost in professors' minds.[24]

Is it, therefore, out of what John Fekete calls "moral panic,"[25] that professors themselves now call for regulations or at least are willing to tolerate them? Has life in academe become so hazardous that, for their own safety, professors ask for explicit rules by which to gauge their every move? Have they, and the students demanding such action, given any serious thought to precisely what life would be like under such an inquisitorial regime?

I do not evoke the term "inquisition" lightly, or as a throwaway insult. I believe we need to consider closely what it is that distinguishes an inquisition from our usual adversary judicial procedures. Adversary proceedings involve real controversy, with each side getting as much attention as the other and having as much opportunity to present its case in a neutral forum. When an inquisitorial process replaces or weakens the adversary one, certain characteristic shifts appear. The presumption of innocence is diminished; the role of investigating officials is vastly enlarged; there is less protection of the rights of the accused; a zealous promotion of vigilance and enforcement measures occurs; and of course, there is a presumption of pervasive malfeasance in the behavior of the targeted group. An inquisitorial mind-set is evidently central to the Sexual Harassment Industry. Paying lip service to "due process" now and then, as the SHI literature does, and making brief references to the "rights of the accused" do not suffice to make the SHI proceedings described in this book just ones.

In our book *Professing Feminism: Cautionary Tales from the Strange*

World of Women's Studies, Noretta Koertge and I wrote about the dangers of an ethic rooted in identity politics (whether of gender or race):

> The greater feminism's success in raising our feelings of moral outrage at sexual harassment, date rape, or insensitive remarks in the workplace or classroom, the more likely it is that members of a protected group will find it in their interest to make a false or frivolous accusation. In a rape trial, for example, it is now ironic that, as we—properly—destigmatize the woman accuser, we simultaneously undermine the feminist argument that the process of accusing someone of rape is so self-vilifying that no woman would ever intentionally make a false accusation.[26]

The result of this reversal is evident in the growing Sexual Harassment Industry. As we have seen, to justify its existence the SHI has to inflate the problems, engage in domain expansion, intensify the needs for its own services, discredit opponents, assume male guilt, and ignore its own inconsistencies. It must also show extreme partiality in its response to laws, as is apparent in the tendency of SHI activists to disdain the First Amendment as mere masculine privilege, while enthusiastically endorsing increasingly broad definitions of, for example, hostile-environment sexual harassment.

Several things strike me as remarkable about the present desire for intervention on the part of people who used to be considered liberals, even civil libertarians. First, when comparing today's activists with some of their distinguished forerunners, I find it hard to ignore their utter lack of concern for true economic and political reform. Today, the changes we talk about relate primarily to the realm of culture and, one might well say, to a particularly narrow segment of culture at that: the realm of manners and behavior, principally sexual behavior. The feminist slogan "The personal is political" has transmuted into its opposite, "The political is personal," which in turn has come to mean that where everything is political, nothing is.

It is my belief that many of the individuals displaying this kind of zeal today do so out of a lack of experience with totalitarian systems. They have become so accustomed to individual liberties that these rights are a matter of indifference to them. Only young women who have grown up with relative sexual freedom would be so ready to believe that "all intercourse is rape" and that men, in general, are their enemy. Had they been brought up by repressive parents, who kept them away from their boyfriends or washed their mouths out with soap, they would, I have no doubt, today be hippies reenacting the Berkeley free-speech movement and celebrating "free love."

Still, it shocks me to meet students today who take their right to utter any opinion and say any word so much for granted that they actually support censoring speech and behavior even in an academic setting—always assuming, of course, that this will above all affect *others*, and not themselves (supporters of harassment codes invariably seem to see themselves as sensitive individuals, in no need of correction; I, on the other hand, know I am likely to say unpopular things and therefore keenly feel the need for unfettered speech). Again, I believe only lack of any actual experience with censorship can explain their facile embrace of the censor's mentality and their naive belief that it can lead to good things.

It is this state of affairs that psychology professor John Furedy refers to as "velvet totalitarianism"— the kind that does not depend on physical torture and fear for one's life (only one's livelihood). Furedy identifies five basic features of "velvet totalitarianism": (1) unclear laws—so that, for example, no one is quite sure whether something is or is not harassment, and the offense is likely to be in the eyes of the complainant rather than in the act itself; (2) the presence and power of unqualified pseudoexperts, made necessary by the vagueness of the laws; (3) a climate of "freezing fear" because engaging in public discussion of controversial but fundamental issues becomes dangerous; (4) status-defined ethics, whereby the rightness or wrongness of an act is determined by who does it to whom, not by the act itself; and finally (5) the demonization of dissidents.[27]

But all this has happened before, and not wrapped in velvet. One of the most astonishing features of the present climate is that today's zealots live in utter disregard of cautionary examples from the history of our own twentieth century. There is no shortage of descriptions of Mao's Cultural Revolution, to take just one notorious example (of special pertinence to the realm of education.)[28]

Not long ago I read the autobiography of Anchee Min, a Chinese woman who came to America in 1984. She describes an incident that occurred when she was fifteen and belonged to the Little Red Guards. Convinced by a local party leader that she had been "mentally poisoned" by a beloved and dedicated teacher of English, she witnessed this teacher being ritually humiliated in front of two thousand people but refusing to confess her guilt. Anchee Min recounts how she, identified as a "victim" of the teacher, stood up and read a speech she had prepared. She accused her teacher of having attempted to turn her students into running dogs of imperialism by giving them Hans Christian Anderson's stories about princes and princesses and other enemies of the people. The teacher tried to talk to her pupil before the crowd, urging her to tell the truth, but Anchee Min stuck to her denunciation. The episode ends thus: "I was never forgiven. Even after twenty-some years. After the Revolution was over. It was after my begging for forgiveness, I heard the familiar hoarse voice say, I am very sorry, I don't remember you. I don't think I ever had you as my student."[29]

Perhaps most interesting to me about this memoir is the sense it conveys (postmodernism notwithstanding) that certain aspirations are indeed universal: the right to a private life, to personal happiness, to an intimate sphere not invaded by the state and organized according to political demands; the desire for love; the discovery of an inner self at odds with the "official" society; the small everyday transgressions sprouting under the posture of outward conformity.

In her book *Red Azalea,* Anchee Min also writes of the conflict between desire and politics—the former controlled and outlawed in the name of the latter, but springing to life anyway, despite enormous dangers. She describes a collective farm where all sexual relations are suppressed. When one young woman is found making love in the fields, she is "saved" by the farm commander, who urges her to claim that she was raped. She complies. The young man involved is executed, and the woman goes mad. The book is filled with telling examples and illustrations of what happens when a culture is in thrall to politics, when those much-maligned "liberal" values that teach respect for the rights of the individual are treated with disdain.

See-Through Worlds

All this calls to mind the lesson of *Brave New World,* summed up by Huxley's Director of Hatcheries, who says, "That is the secret of happiness and virtue—liking what you've *got* to do."[30] Huxley's fictional world, with its ectogenesis, neo-Pavlovian conditioning, and hypnopedia, makes this lesson possible. In fact, it makes any other attitude impossible.

Most fictional utopias (especially the ones portrayed in dystopian satires) regulate personal life in order to achieve the maximum social harmony. Typically, they do this by decreasing the range of private interactions, within which behavior occurs unobserved by the watchful eyes of the state. Transparency and visibility emerge as important social values, justifying the lack of a personal space in which private words and gestures can take place.

But transparency is also an intuitively understood image of exposure. Consider the following dream, recounted to Charlotte Beradt by a Jewish doctor in Germany in 1934:

> It was about nine o'clock in the evening. My consultations were over, and I was stretching out on the couch to relax with a book on Matthias Grünewald, when suddenly the walls of my room and then my apartment disappeared. I looked around and then discovered to my horror that as far as the eye could see, no apartments had walls any more. Then I heard a loudspeaker boom, "According to the decree of the 17th of this month on the Abolition of Walls . . ."[31]

The meaning of this nightmare is not hard to grasp. The image of total exposure recalls Jeremy Bentham's model prison, the Panopticon, which he designed in 1786, in the spirit of prison reform, not of torment. It is a circular structure that can be managed by one governor-general, who can see all the cells from a single central location—though the prisoners are invisible to one another. One need not have read Foucault to recoil, instinctively, from visibility and transparency or to note how readily they become tools for the management of a given populace.

Where everything is visible, where all actions are observed, where there is no distinction between inside and outside, the entire society has itself become a prison. Transparency is a step toward this, an emblem of the prison of the mind, bound first by perceptible and tangible force, then by its own fears, and finally (in slow stages) by invisible and, for all one knows, nonexistent barriers. They are nowhere and everywhere, intangible and internalized.

Feminism today, in its erasure of the boundaries between public and private, is writing a new chapter in the dystopian tradition of surveillance and unfreedom. It thus reinforces, perhaps without realizing it, the dystopian theme of transparency, whereby one's every gesture, every thought, is exposed to the judgment of one's fellow citizens.

In Zamiatin's *We,* the brilliant Russian novel that served as a model for Huxley's and most subsequent twentieth-century dystopias, people have numbers, not names, and virtually all aspects of life have been brought under state control. Sexual conflicts, competitiveness, and per-

sonal attachments have all been done away with by the great, historic
Lex Sexualis, which states, "A Number may obtain a license to use any
other Number as a sexual product."[32] One need merely sign up for
such use during the personal hours, the only time when curtains can be
lowered on the glass walls of the huge dormitories in which everyone
dwells. Zamiatin's narrator initially looks forward to the time when even
these personal hours will have been abolished and all life will have
come under the control of the perfectly regulated world-state.

Huxley uses a similar approach. In his future society, promiscuity is
encouraged, and orgies are a routine part of orchestrated pseudo-
religious rites. Orwell, whose future England makes no pretense of
being organized for the happiness of its citizens, opts for suppressing
sexual passion altogether, though not very successfully, as it turns out.
What is important to recognize is that it matters little whether sex is
prohibited or promiscuity encouraged. Either way, the management
of sexuality is a key element in these dystopias, which through such
manipulation attempt to erase the private sphere (either by turning it
into a commodity, as does Huxley, or by prohibiting it altogether, as
does Orwell) and refocus their citizens' attentions and emotional ener-
gies on the collectivity and its leader.

But Orwell does resemble Zamiatin and many other utopian writers
both before and after him in his recognition that from the perspective
of the ruling state, the private sphere—the sphere of personal attachments—is a potential source of social disruption and a permanent
threat to state power. Love, family life, and particularly sexual passion
shift one's allegiances from the public to the private domain. This is
why they are eliminated in the dystopias of Zamiatin, Huxley, and Orwell, a result all these writers protest. Private attachments and loyalties
can undermine and endanger public commitments and duties; this is
clearly the point of the control and redefinition of the private sphere
that one finds in totalitarian regimes and in their fictional analogs. Orwell's thought police, whose very presence is designed to make
"thought crime" impossible, are complemented by the image of the
"place where there is no darkness," the place toward which Winston
Smith is attracted, not knowing that it will be the torture chamber
where the last vestiges of his private, concealed self will be stripped
away.[33]

In going into such detail about the dystopian literary tradition, I am
not contending that feminists consciously opt for a transparent world.
Rather, I am arguing that a fundamental lack of respect for the private

sphere has developed side by side with the standard feminist critique that sees private heterosexual life, and heterosexual interactions in school and workplace, as a patriarchal imposition that must be resisted and transformed. Not enough attention is being paid to the costs of this transformation—as is evident in the astonishing success of the Sexual Harassment Industry. This is the usual problem of utopias: how to bring about the goals one identifies as desirable without incurring a great many negative consequences along with them.

The feminist discourse on sexual harassment, as we have seen, is explicitly embedded in a view of it as part of the vast patriarchal effort to keep women down. To the extent that this discourse has been adopted as a framework by the society at large, it has led to an impossible situation, in which boundaries between the public and the private sphere become ever more porous, a situation worthy of the great dystopian satires of the past. I am not, of course, arguing that what goes on in universities should simply be construed as part of the "private" sphere, exempt from the harsh light of public attention. I appreciate the importance of the feminist critique of the public/private dichotomy. This critique has helped to expose abuse in the private sphere as a matter for public concern.[34] Rather, I want to call attention to the fact that even in the public sphere of the workplace and the school, relationships have a private dimension and we intrude on that dimension at some peril. When teachers refuse to close their office doors during a conference with a student, out of fear of charges of impropriety of one sort or another, their private selves are under attack. This is also the case when they must watch every word they say in class, lest someone be made "uncomfortable" by it (paradoxically, itself an odd importation of a private value into a public setting). It is disingenuous to claim that such heightened awareness leads to more responsible "professional" behavior. More regimented, more impersonal, more guarded, yes; but also less open, less generous, less friendly. Certainly, behavior is transformed. And that, I have argued, is precisely what the obsession with sexual harassment is meant to achieve. Whether we celebrate or deplore this result depends, no doubt, on what we take its larger significance to be.

Proponents of a policy of banning, in particular, seem to have an intense, and perhaps bizarre, preoccupation with sex. It cannot genuinely be "power differentials" that concern them, since these are manifest in many forms quite unrelated to sex and most of these forms are not objects of concern to the social engineers proliferating in academic offices. Is anyone (yet?) claiming that it should be prohibited, say, for a professor to give time and attention to a particularly promising student? That it should be illegal to coauthor a paper with a talented student, as happens in many fields, and not with all members in this cohort? Would such preferment not also subject the student to the professor and increase the risks of painful rejection later? Would it not be "grooming" her for who knows what demands to come? Clearly, the work of regulating academic life is far from over. And it does appear to be the fear of sexual awareness and sexual involvement specifically that elicits concern over the "power differentials" supposedly making intimate relationships between students and teachers illegitimate.

Instead of protecting the concept and practice of academic freedom, which to my mind includes not only freedom of speech but also freedom of association between consenting adults, many academics today appear to view this freedom with alarm. They seem to see it as "academic license," license, presumably, to exploit and abuse, hence requiring curtailment. Once again, it appears that their concern is, above all, with regulating the behavior of *others,* not of themselves, since professors are perfectly able to decide, individually, *not* to engage in personal relationships with students. But supporting such regulations presupposes a massive distortion, on the banners' part, of the supposed "power" of professors, as well as of the "powerlessness" of students, who are, by this attribution, infantilized or suspected of a dependency that would make them into replicas of psychiatric patients in need of both therapy and protection from unscrupulous therapists.

Where does it all come from, this lack of confidence in ourselves and our fellows, and this desire to *force* adults to "do the right thing"? Perhaps here, too, we have literary and historical precedents to guide us.

The Burden of Freedom

Many of the famous dystopias written in the twentieth century feature what has been called a "Grand Inquisitor" scene—in which the leader of the fictional society explains to the rebellious protagonist that people are happier now that they have been relieved of the burden of freedom and have been told what to do, what to think, how to behave, and, of course, what to read. What they are allowed to read, in many cases, turns out to be nothing, for these societies all strive for conformity, and books and ideas tend to make people dissatisfied with their condition.

The danger of reading is a major theme in Ray Bradbury's 1953 novel *Fahrenheit 451* (the temperature at which books burn). Books lead to reflection and even conflict: This is what the fireman Montag, the novel's protagonist, hears from Faber, a former English professor thrown out of work when the last liberal arts college closed its doors decades earlier due to lack of students and patronage. Books have to be destroyed because they convey the "texture" of life, Faber says. They "show the pores in the face of life. The comfortable people want only wax moon faces, poreless, hairless, expressionless."[35] But by now, Faber explains, the firemen are rarely necessary: "So few want to be rebels any more."[36]

Writing more than forty years ago, Bradbury earlier in the novel created a Grand Inquisitor scene that sounds uncannily familiar to readers today. Captain Beatty, the Fire Chief, explains to Montag:

> "Bigger the population, the more minorities. Don't step on the toes of the dog lovers, the cat lovers, doctors, lawyers, merchants, chiefs, Mormons, Baptists, Unitarians, second-generation Chinese, Swedes, Italians, Germans, Texans, Brooklynites, Irishmen, people from Oregon or Mexico. . . . It didn't come from the Government down. There was no dictum, no declaration, no censorship to start with, no! Technology, mass exploitation, and minority pressure carried the trick, thank God. Today, thanks to them, you can stay happy all the time, . . .
>
> "You must understand that our civilization is so vast that we can't have our minorities upset and stirred. Ask yourself, What do we want in this country, above all? People want to be happy, isn't that right? Haven't you heard it all your life? . . .
>
> "Colored people don't like *Little Black Sambo*. Burn it. White people don't feel good about *Uncle Tom's Cabin*. Burn it. . . .
>
> ". . . If you don't want a man unhappy politically, don't give him two sides to a question to worry him; give him one. Better yet, give him none. . . .
>
> ". . . We [the firemen] stand against the small tide of those who want to make everyone unhappy with conflicting theory and thought. We have our fingers in the dike."[37]

Bradbury's Grand Inquisitor scene, like others in dystopian fiction from Zamiatin on, is based on Dostoyevsky's prototype in *The Brothers Karamazov*. There, Ivan Karamazov relates a parable of Christ's return to sixteenth-century Seville, where he is imprisoned by the Grand Inquisitor. In a long monologue, the Grand Inquisitor explains to Christ why he will be burned as a heretic. It has taken the Roman Catholic

Church centuries to vanquish the freedom that Christ bequeathed to men. Freedom of conscience is a burden of which people beg to be relieved, the Grand Inquisitor says. The Church has accepted this burden on their behalf, giving them instead what they crave: miracle, mystery, and authority.[38]

We, today, are witnessing a latter-day version of the Grand Inquisitor's vision, as ordinary people (in the academy, these are, of course, intellectuals) demand social salvation by turning power and control over to some force beyond themselves. Hence the call for rules and regulations, or the quasi-legal codes instituted on college campuses—anything to save us from the messiness and possible unpleasantness of everyday human interactions; from disappointment and bitterness in love; from unsuccessful sexual encounters; and from work environments filled with the tensions of human beings still capable of having private selves, still free to make unkind comments on our foibles or to criticize our efforts.

Do our students really want the safety and security promised by a Grand Inquisitor? Some certainly do—or, in the absence of such a sense of security, imagine that they do. In my course on women's utopian fiction, for example, I was surprised to discover that many of the young women in my class found the safety of women as depicted in Margaret Atwood's *Handmaid's Tale* a very appealing prospect. True, the novel, which envisions a takeover by religious fundamentalists, institutionalizes rape (strictly for the sake of reproduction) in a carefully orchestrated monthly ritual that involves the handmaid (who is fertile), the commander (her master), and the commander's infertile wife. If only the role of handmaid were abolished, some of my students argued, the scenario wouldn't be so bad. Atwood's vision of hysterical women tearing a man limb from limb for allegedly committing the crime of rape did not seem to bother many of them. In the same class, these women expressed approval of the flogging of an American youth in Singapore for defacing walls with graffiti. A really safe and clean society, they said, may be worth such brutality.

I was struck by their fears and anxieties, caused, it appears, not so much by the real problems of American life as by the inflamed portrait of life's dangers promoted by feminists. On one of the stalls in the bathroom right outside the classroom in which I was teaching, I read that one out of every two women will be raped in her lifetime. Such statistics did not seem questionable to the young women in my course, who claimed to be willing to give away much in exchange for the security they felt they lacked. Far from appreciating freedom (academic or other), they acted as if they were living in a society in which others' words and actions were a constant threat. Having no personal experience with societies where speech is regulated, where speech codes are the norm, where personal behavior is highly regimented and there is no freedom of association, these students have no trouble thinking they might like such a society if only it made them feel safe. An atmosphere of panic, bolstered by atrocity tales, is clearly a prerequisite if zealous solutions are to win support. And in my experience, a great deal of the feminist teaching that goes on, particularly in lower-level women's studies courses, is designed to induce precisely such feelings of panic.

To be effective, education should promote the play of the imagination. But I see few signs of creativity at work as students and colleagues not only fail to defend the academic freedom they take for granted but actively assail it. I am not sure there is enough imagination around at the present time to let them even learn from the experiences related by others. Consider, for example, the views of Kate Zhou, a Chinese political scientist now working in the United States, contributed to a discussion on FEMISA (the e-mail list devoted to gender and international relations, mentioned in chapter 6 above). I was in a distinctly minority position when I argued on that list for the importance of free speech, which—in that particular context—meant tolerating the messages of male contributors who were making themselves unpopular (by now, this would probably be labeled "electronic harassment"). I contended that even obnoxious males should not be struck from the list and that intolerance of ideas we don't like can quickly move into the prohibitory mode, as if the people with whom we disagree had no right to speak freely. Pursuing such a course, I said, we would soon find ourselves instituting censorship, public humiliation, shunning, ganging-up-on, and so forth, so as to protect the orthodoxy of a few.

Kate Zhou posted the following response:

Dear Sisters:

I am a feminist from China. For many years, sexist language was banned by the Chinese state (at least in the urban public sphere). Urban Chinese women were very much "free" from sexist verbal attacks. Many women including myself were willing to give up freedom for some degree of protection and security. When everyone lost the freedom to speak, women's independent voice was also gone. When women's voices were silenced, women suffered.

Yes, we did not have to be bothered by sexist language and pornography. But we could not complain that we had to line up two or three hours for basic food. We had to take less interesting work because we had to take care of the family. It was not politically correct to complain about the double burden.

Is it clear to feminists that there has been no feminist movement in those countries that practice state censorship?

My experience in China seems to suggest that women are often victims of any kind of censorship. As a feminist, I believe that women have the ability and power to defend their interests if given a chance. We should welcome complex and diversified debates. Difficult and complex debates help to train us. If we try to shut someone up because we dislike what he has to say, we just confirm our weakness and sexism.[39]

FEMISA did not take this sound advice. After more postings from argumentative men (who sometimes were merely pointing out that women's hateful antimale language was routinely posted on the list, while their objections and criticisms were treated as intolerable "flames"), the list-owners proved those men's point by barring various men from the list and moving the entire list onto "moderated" status, the better, it appears, to control its discussions.

I believe that we must heed the experiences of people in societies where individual freedom has been construed as inimical to the greater social good and hence has been restricted by the state and its institutions.[40] We often seem to gravitate toward what is absent from our own historical situation. When free speech is missing or seems constrained, we want a free-speech movement. When there is censorship of reading material, we get protests such as those that arose around the obscenity trial of Radclyffe Hall's *Well of Loneliness* in England in 1928, or around that of D. H. Lawrence's *Lady Chatterley's Lover* in this country in 1959. When girls (but not boys) must be in their dormitories by a certain hour and a couple must have three feet on the floor (common dormitory rules when I was an undergraduate in the early 1960s), it is these regulations that cause resentment and rebellion. And when all such rules are gone, as they are today, why should it surprise us that people cry out to be saved from themselves and from one another?

But for adults who have enjoyed freedom of expression and association to throw it away so cavalierly certainly suggests they are unaware of either the abundant literary models or the actual societies in which restrictions such as they advocate have been in force. Does it make a difference whether the rules and constraints (which no supporter has been able to demonstrate are actually likely to lead to a better society) are demanded by feminists or by—say—fundamentalists? I do not believe so. Once set in motion, where will such curtailment of freedom stop? Whom should we trust to define the good society for us?

There have, of course, always been sane feminists, who have seen the dangers of either sex dominating the other. One such figure was the British writer Katharine Burdekin, who, in the 1930s, wrote a series of remarkable feminist-inspired eutopian and dystopian novels. In a novel called *Proud Man,* originally published in 1934 under the male pseudonym "Murray Constantine," Burdekin outlined her critique of a world run by women. The narrator of the novel, an androgynous being from a future that it calls "human," observes life in England in the 1930s and comments on the behavior of all the "subhumans" of the period, still living in "the childhood age." This is what the narrator says:

> If women retain their biological importance, and become pleased with themselves from birth, and learn to associate power with the womb instead of with the phallus, a dominance of females over males is not only possible but likely. Their self-confidence, which would be rooted as deep as the old male jealousy, would cause in them a tremendous release of psychic power with which the males would be unable to cope. Naturally a female dominance would make the race no happier, nor bring it a whit nearer to humanity. The privilege would merely be reversed, and possibly it would be more oppressive and more cruel.[41]

Twenty years ago, I would never have suspected that we, today, would need to hear such a warning. The fact that heterophobes, at the moment, are still struggling to achieve political power should not deceive us about the kind of world they clearly want to bring about—and would if they ever gained the means to do so. They have succeeded, by means of sexual harassment legislation, in introducing an element of genuine paranoia into the relationships of ordinary men and women, and this achievement should not be taken lightly. Their ideas need to be seen for what they are: a project posing as utopian that, were it ever to become reality, would turn out to be a nightmare.

A Feminism for the Future?

A Feminism for the Future?

❧

Imagine that you live in a world in which for millennia your kind has had fewer rights and opportunities than the dominant group. Imagine that a struggle lasting several centuries changed that inequity, enabling you to live with far greater freedom—personal, political, and professional. Imagine that while you were learning the history of your own group's subjugation, the marks of that oppression increasingly slipped away, replaced by egalitarian practices. Although your anger at past injustice is kept alive by the gnawing sense that perfect contentment still eludes you, indignation becomes ever more redundant as the external conditions of your life continue to improve.

Imagine, further, that harmony between your group and those who formerly dominated has become a real possibility but that this unprecedented rapprochement demands of you the relinquishing of ancient grievances. Is it possible that faced with this break with the passions of the past, you will feel the need for a fresh cause that will let you replenish your frustrations and act out old and hard-to-give-up resentments? Realizing that the workaday settings in which people spend most of their time foster close relations between members of the two groups, might you not see opportunities here for discovering a new sense of outrage? For if you were to closely observe every word, gesture, and glance exchanged in the ordinary situations of daily life, would you not be likely to find in these casual interactions a host of possible transgressions against your group that a legal apparatus, responsive to your sensibilities, would deem actionable? Imagine, then, the boost to your sense of righteousness offered by this newly discovered arena of action, and the fervor with which you now feel compelled to instruct others in the detecting of offenses that you have learned to see proliferating everywhere.

Imagine that you will call your discovery "sexual harassment" and that you will make this the touchstone of all relations between your group and those who used to dominate you. Imagine your satisfaction as former oppressors see them-

selves placed in a situation in which every detail of their passing behavior is put under scrutiny. What if there were now to come into being a class of people claiming expert credentials and authorized to examine that behavior, invite complaints about it, and oversee the resulting adversarial struggles in school and workplace? Imagine the revitalizing anger you could draw from this spectacle, and the renewed faith that with this problem on the way to being solved, life might at long last be as it should be.

Imagine, in sum, that you are living at the end of the twentieth century in North America.

Then look around. Stop imagining and start observing.

I have written this book in the hope that it will contribute toward restoring balance and a bit of sanity to the relations between men and women, in the academy and beyond it. I find it frightening to see a society unleash against its own citizens codes of speech and behavior that can ensnare anyone and that often have as their underpinning nothing more than a woman's sense of "discomfort" about certain words or actions. It took a complex ideological apparatus to get us to this point, and it has been my aim to unravel some of the strands of that apparatus. I have done so believing that to conflate much of what today is labeled "sexual harassment" with serious forms of sexual assault and abuse is to invite authoritarianism into our lives—the hand of the state everywhere in the private sphere, until there is virtually no private sphere left.

To those of my readers who feel personally affronted by this book, I say: It has been my purpose to disrupt your intellectual comfort. To those predisposed to dismiss my arguments as reactionary or as an example of "backlash," I respond: Unassailable ideas create totalitarian policies. I urge all readers to think about the consequences of the course currently pursued by the Sexual Harassment Industry. Consider the social and human costs of the relentless pursuit of purity and comfort. Contemplate the many ways the SHI has led perhaps not to the destruction but surely to the imperilment of intellectual and political freedoms hard won by Americans over centuries.

Finally, ask yourself this: Is the SHI working to create a world that can stand as the realization of feminist aspirations? I do not think so. A feminism deeply compromised by hatred and scorn, pious and narrow, scurrilous and smug, dismissive of those it injures and derisive toward those who dare to disagree—this is not a feminism with a future.

Notes

Notes

Preface

1. Maria D. Vesperi, "A Sexual Harassment Charge, a Teacher's Suicide," *Sacramento Bee*, July 2, 1993, p. B7. For a troubling account of a comparable case in the workplace, see Christopher Byron's excellent article "The Joke That Killed," *Esquire* (January 1995): p. 84. Byron, in describing the suicide of an AT&T employee accused of sexual harassment, explains that the Department of Labor's Office of Federal Contract Compliance investigates approximately four thousand companies a year. If evidence is lacking that charges are being brought under Title VII, the company is suspected of being "soft on discrimination and harassment, which could lead to the revocation of contracts."
2. Mimi Ko Cruz, "No Hugs?" *Los Angeles Times*, February 12, 1998, p. B1.
3. CNN News, February 13, 1998.
4. Anne Gearan, "Sex Charges against Nine-Year-Old Dropped," *Daily Collegian* (Pennsylvania State University), June 26, 1997, p. 7.
5. Cited by Linda Vaden Gratch, "Recognizing Sexual Harassment," in *Sexual Harassment on Campus: A Guide for Administrators, Faculty, and Students*, ed. Bernice R. Sandler and Robert J. Shoop (Boston: Allyn & Bacon, 1997), p. 283.

Introduction

1. Daphne Patai, "Beyond Defensiveness: Feminist Research Strategies," *Women's Studies International Quarterly* 6, no. 2 (1983): 67–89, reprinted in M. Barr and N. D. Smith, eds., *Women and Utopia: Critical Interpretations* (Lanham, MD: University Press of America, 1984); and in R. L. Dudovitz, ed., *Women in Academe* (Oxford: Pergamon, 1984).
2. Until the Supreme Court spoke on the issue, many divergent lower-court decisions had been made regarding same-sex harassment. See Hayden Coleman, "Same-Sex Harassment: A Survey of the Application of Federal Law" (prepared for the Lamda Legal Defense and Education Fund); Joan Biskupic, "Court Says Law Covers Same-Sex Harassment," *Washington Post*, March 5, 1998, p. A1.

3. From my verbatim notes taken at opening session of Yale University's conference, "Sexual Harassment: A Symposium," February 27, 1998.

4. Ironically, later in his own comments, Judge Calabresi wistfully referred to "what women have stood for," which might be lost if equality meant assimilation into male patterns.

5. Lin Farley, *Sexual Shakedown: The Sexual Harassment of Women on the Job* (New York: McGraw-Hill, 1978).

6. Valerie Solanas, *SCUM Manifesto* (New York: Olympia Press, 1968).

Chapter 1

1. Lin Farley, *Sexual Shakedown: The Sexual Harassment of Women on the Job* (New York: McGraw-Hill, 1978), p. xi.

2. Farley, *Sexual Shakedown*, pp. 82–84.

3. Lynne Eisaguirre, *Sexual Harassment: A Reference Handbook*, 2d ed. (Santa Barbara: ABC-CLIO, 1997), p. 27. Farley and two Cornell colleagues, Susan Meyer and Karen Sauvigné, located a lawyer for Wood and invented the name "sexual harassment" for her claim.

4. Bernice R. Sandler, " 'Too Strong for a Woman': The Five Words That Created Title IX," *About Women on Campus* 6, no. 2 (Spring 1997): 1 (italics in original).

5. Sandler, " 'Too Strong for a Woman,' " p. 2.

6. Sandler, " 'Too Strong for a Woman,' " p. 3.

7. Sandler, " 'Too Strong for a Woman,' " p. 4.

8. Sandler, " 'Too Strong for a Woman,' " p. 5.

9. Sandler, " 'Too Strong for a Woman,' " p. 5.

10. U.S. Department of Education, *Digest of Education Statistics* (Washington, DC: National Center for Education Statistics, 1997), Table 207, "Undergraduate Enrollment, Fall 1995."

11. U.S. Department of Education, *Digest of National Statistics* (Washington, DC: National Center for Education Statistics, 1997), Table 265, "Bachelors' Degrees Conferred, 1994–95."

12. Reported in Bernice Sandler's own journal, *About Women on Campus* 6, no. 2 (Spring 1997): 7 (citing U.S. Department of Education data).

13. Karin Winegar, "Subtle Sexism More Insidious than Outright Discrimination, Study Shows," *Minneapolis-St. Paul Star Tribune*, November 16, 1994, metro edition, p. 1E.

14. Sandler, *About Women on Campus* 3, no. 3 (Summer 1994): 9.

15. Jean O'Gorman Hughes and Bernice Sandler, *Peer Harassment: Hassles for Women on Campus* (Washington, DC: Project on the Status and Education of Women, Association of American Colleges, 1988; Washington, DC: Center for Women Policy Studies).

16. Farley, *Sexual Shakedown*, p. 16.

17. Catharine MacKinnon, *The Sexual Harassment of Working Women* (New Haven: Yale University Press, 1979).

18. MacKinnon, *Sexual Harassment of Working Women*, p. 1.

19. MacKinnon, *Sexual Harassment of Working Women*, p. 3.

20. MacKinnon, *Sexual Harassment of Working Women*, p. 2.

21. MacKinnon, *Sexual Harassment of Working Women*, p. 6.

22. MacKinnon, *Sexual Harassment of Working Women*, p. 221 (italics in original).

23. MacKinnon, *Sexual Harassment of Working Women*, p. 220.

24. *Meritor Savings Bank v. Vinson*, 106 S.Ct. 2399 (1986).

25. The University of Massachusetts at Amherst, for example, hired Fran Sepler's firm, Sepler & Associates (formed in 1991) to provide $26,000 worth of training in sexual harassment "risk management" and prevention, at rates ranging from $1,250 to $1,800 per trainer per day, plus consultations at the rate of $180 per hour. In addition, the university provided over $10,000 to cover travel, hotels, and meals. "Contract for Services between University of Massachusetts at Amherst and Sepler & Associates" (for a total payment of $36,395, signed by Deputy Chancellor Marcellette Williams on May 14, 1997).

26. Mane Hajdin, "Why the Fight against Sexual Harassment Is Misguided," in *Sexual Harassment: A Debate*, by Linda LeMoncheck and Mane Hajdin (Lanham, MD: Rowman & Littlefield, 1997), p. 154; the following discussion is from page 155. Hajdin's analysis and critique of current sexual harassment law (especially of its failure to explain the "wrongness" of what is now considered sexual harassment), a model of clarity and insight, leads him to the conclusion that the fight against sexual harassment "is unjustified and ought to be opposed" (p. 161).

27. Mane Hajdin, "Response," in *Sexual Harassment: A Debate*, by LeMoncheck and Hajdin, p. 221.

28. *Harris v. Forklift Systems, Inc.*, 114 S.Ct. 367 (1993).

29. *Ellison v. Brady*, 924 F.2d 872, 879 (9th Cir. 1991).

30. In my attempt to understand the effects of the law on manners and mores, I owe much to the writings of Eugene Volokh on sexual harassment in the workplace. See especially his essay "What Speech Does 'Hostile Work Environment' Harassment Law Restrict?" *Georgetown Law Journal* 85, no. 3 (February 1997): 627–48. An updated version of this essay is available at http://www.law.ucla.edu/faculty/volokh/harass/breadth.htm.

31. Michael S. Greve, "Sexual Harassment: Telling the Other Victims' Story," *Northern Kentucky University Law Review* 23 (1996): 528.

32. Jeffrey Rosen, "Men Behaving Badly," *New Republic*, December 29, 1997, p. 19. By contrast, Mane Hajdin misses the logic of the feminist framing of sexual harassment discourse when he makes comments such as "[E]veryone would agree that there is nothing wrong with being a heterosexual." "Why the Fight against Sexual Harassment Is Misguided," in *Sexual Harassment: A Debate*, by LeMoncheck and Hajdin, p. 129. As I demonstrate in chapter 6 below, many feminists do indeed disagree with precisely that view.

33. "Sexual Harassment" (brochure produced by Personnel Services, Southern Illinois University at Carbondale, October 1993). Cathy Young, in chapter 4 of *Ceasefire: Beyond the Gender Wars* (New York: Free Press, 1999), illustrates with a large number of sexual harassment cases the mas-

sive consequences of harassment law's inability to distinguish between the trivial and the grave. See also Cathy Young, "Groping toward Sanity," *Reason* (August/September 1998): pp. 24–31.

34. William Petrocelli and Barbara Kate Repa, *Sexual Harassment on the Job*, 2d ed. (Berkeley: Nolo Press, 1995), p. 3/3 [*sic*].

35. See Harvey Wallace's recent textbook, *Victimology: Legal, Psychological, and Social Perspectives* (Boston: Allyn & Bacon, 1998), which has a section on sexual harassment.

36. Linda LeMoncheck, "Taunted and Tormented or Savvy and Seductive? Feminist Discourses on Sexual Harassment," in *Sexual Harassment: A Debate*, by LeMoncheck and Hajdin, p. 58.

37. Experimental psychologist Margaret A. Hagen, in *Whores of the Court: The Fraud of Psychiatric Testimony and the Rape of American Justice* (New York: ReganBooks/HarperCollins, 1997), p. 256, argues that in actuality "there are no symptoms reliably indicative" of post-traumatic stress disorder. Hagen notes that Dr. Gerald Rosen, writing in the *Bulletin of the American Academy of Psychiatry and the Law* 24 (1996), describes the symptoms of PTSD as "subjective, well-publicized, and easy to simulate." For these reasons, the diagnosis has raised concern about attorneys coaching their clients on how to behave. Hagen, *Whores of the Court*, p. 257. See also Allan Young, *The Harmony of Illusions: Inventing Post-Traumatic Stress Disorder* (Princeton, NJ: Princeton University Press, 1995).

38. MacKinnon, *Sexual Harassment of Working Women*, pp. 217–18.

Chapter 2

1. *Books in Print*, 1997–98, lists more than 250 titles under the subject-heading "Sexual Harassment." This wave of books began after the Anita Hill–Clarence Thomas hearings. See Barbara Presley Noble, "When the Subject Is Harassment," *New York Times*, July 12, 1992, p. 25.

2. Bernice R. Sandler and Robert J. Shoop, eds., *Sexual Harassment on Campus: A Guide for Administrators, Faculty, and Students* (Boston: Allyn & Bacon, 1997). Because I analyze this book and its rhetoric in detail, page references to it are incorporated parenthetically into the text of this chapter.

3. That an orthodoxy has emerged about sexual harassment can be seen in the transformations evident in the work of psychology professor Barbara A. Gutek. In an article written jointly with Charles Y. Nakamura, "Gender Roles and Sexuality in the World of Work," in *Changing Boundaries: Genders Roles and Sexual Behavior*, ed. Elizabeth Rice Allgeier and Naomi B. McCormick (San Francisco: Mayfield, 1983), pp. 182–201, Gutek noted that what she labeled "social-sexual behavior at work"—defined as "non-work-related behaviors that have sexual content" (p. 186)—was often desirable and pleasurable for the participants; she also recognized that seeking partners at work was both common and legitimate. By the late 1980s, however, in essays such as "Sexuality in the Workplace: Key Issues in Social Research and Organizational Practice," in *The Sexuality of Organization*, ed. Jeff Hearn et al. (London: Sage, 1989), pp. 56–70, Gutek was

distancing herself from such a perspective, taking care to attribute it to some workers, without any hint of endorsement on her part. She wrote about the possibility (and did not question the desirability) of designing environments "where gender would be irrelevant and sexual overtures would not be made" ("Sexuality in the Workplace," p. 66). Sexual behavior at work, she argued, trivializes the labor of the employee ("Sexuality in the Workplace," p. 67). No critique of the increasingly Taylorized workplace accompanied these observations. Finally, in her most recent work, for example "Sexual Harassment Policy Initiatives," in *Sexual Harassment: Theory, Research, and Treatment*, ed. William O'Donohue (Boston: Allyn & Bacon, 1997), pp. 185–98, Gutek totally abandons her earlier cautions.

4. Joel Best, *Threatened Children: Rhetoric and Concern about Child-Victims* (Chicago: University of Chicago Press, 1990). See also his article, "Victimization and the Victim Industry," *Society* 34, no. 4 (May–June 1997): 9–17.

5. Joel Best, "Victimization and the Victim Industry."

6. Karin Winegar, "Subtle Sexism More Insidious than Outright Discrimination, Study Shows," *Minneapolis-St. Paul Star Tribune*, November 16, 1994, metro edition, p. 1E.

7. Best, *Threatened Children*, p. 187.

8. Best, *Threatened Children*, p. 188.

9. Best, *Threatened Children*, p. 65.

10. By contrast, see Jaimie Leeser and William O'Donohue, "Normative Issues in Defining Sexual Harassment," in *Sexual Harassment: Theory, Research, and Treatment*, ed. O'Donohue, pp. 29–49, who analyze and refute the feminist conception of sexual harassment and argue for a clear definition rooted in respect for persons, a definition capable of distinguishing sexual harassment from cases of poor etiquette or unprofessional behavior. Unfortunately, many of the subsequent essays in O'Donohue's volume are by "experts," such as Michelle Paludi, whose views, unlike O'Donohue's, echo those of the SHI. It is interesting to note that Harvey Wallace, whose *Victimology: Legal, Psychological, and Social Perspectives* (Boston: Allyn & Bacon, 1998) entirely embraces the feminist rhetoric on sexual harassment, misses much of its political content. Thus, he writes, "Sexual harassment continues to be a form of sexual violence in the United States and will continue as long as men view women as sexual trophies or playthings instead of equals" (p. 142). On the same page, he defines sexual harassment as "the imposition of any unwanted condition on any person's employment because of that person's sex." Compare this with Vicki Schultz's argument in "Sex Is the Least of It: Let's Focus Harassment Law on Work, Not Sex," *Nation*, May 25, 1998 (cover story), that sexual harassment as currently understood is "both too narrow and too broad"—too narrow because courts often disregard nonsexual forms of harassment, and too broad because sexual interactions that do not threaten "women's equality on the job" are also often banned. The problem, Schultz asserts, "isn't sex but sexism." Title VII was intended to allow men and women "to pursue their life's work on equal terms," free of pressure to conform to gender-role expectations. Schultz argues that sexual

harassment in the workplace is a manifestation of men protecting their turf against the incursions of women. Evidently many, not always compatible, theories of sexual harassment are available.

11. More than fifteen years ago, Phyllis L. Crocker, in "An Analysis of University Definitions of Sexual Harassment," *Signs: Journal of Women in Culture and Society* 8, no. 4 (Summer 1983): 696–707, argued that definitions "must be flexible" and "must be designed from the victim's perspective" (p. 706). Her work is an important contribution to the extension of the term "sexual harassment." She warned, "[I]t is extremely difficult to encompass every dimension of a problem we are still learning about. Attempting to address the complexity of the issue by introducing elaborate distinctions merely creates an overly legalistic and mechanistic formula that allows for excuses and technical loopholes" (p. 697).

12. Linda LeMoncheck, "Taunted and Tormented or Savvy and Seductive? Feminist Discourses on Sexual Harassment," in *Sexual Harassment: A Debate*, by Linda LeMoncheck and Mane Hajdin (Lanham, MD: Rowman & Littlefield, 1997), p. 24.

13. This point is explicitly made by Billie Wright Dziech and Linda Weiner in *The Lecherous Professor: Sexual Harassment on Campus*, 2d ed. (Urbana: University of Illinois Press, 1990), p. 21: Students must know "that for behavior to be sexual harassment, it does not have to be repeated; one time can be enough. Students need to understand that harassment does not have to be of a particular type or intensity; sexual innuendos in class are as inappropriate as invitations to bed." Not only is the legal standard of "persistent and pervasive" brushed aside here, but "inappropriate" behavior is made synonymous with the most severe sexual harassment.

14. One critical scholar has written, aptly, of the "morass of research studies" employing different sampling strategies, survey procedures, and survey items to elicit information, so that it becomes extremely difficult to conceptualize experiences of sexual harassment. Results of surveys vary depending on what questions were asked and how samples were compiled. See James E. Gruber, "An Epidemiology of Sexual Harassment: Evidence from North America and Europe," *Sexual Harassment: Theory, Research, and Treatment*, ed. O'Donohue, p. 88.

Gruber's own survey of eighteen recent studies (1979–86) of sexual harassment among employees and university students in the United States and Canada concludes that from 28 to 75 percent of women said they had experienced sexual harassment. The median figure for the eighteen studies is 44 percent (p. 85). Gruber also affirms (as do most other commentators) that "sexual bribery and sexual assault . . . [are] relatively infrequent among both students and workers" (p. 89). The point is, the serious cases are few, but that is not reflected in SHI rhetoric. Elizabeth Grauerholz, "Sexual Harassment in the Academy: The Case of Women Professors," in *Sexual Harassment in the Workplace*, ed. Margaret S. Stockdale (Thousand Oaks, CA: Sage, 1996), pp. 29–50, has a table showing the tiny incidence of sexual bribery and sexual assault and depicting "comments" and "undue attention" (p. 35) as the usual problem experienced by female professors. Yet her conclusions (pp. 46–47) insist that "many faculty women are sexually harassed—some egregiously" (p. 47).

For an excellent overview and critique of sexual harassment research, see Klaus de Albuquerque, " 'Academia's Dirty Little Secret': Deconstructing the Sexual Harassment Hysteria," *Sexuality and Culture* 1 (1997): 71–105. Regarding the problem of researcher bias, Albuquerque notes, "I did not find a single study that asked students and faculty to enumerate the various problems they faced in the academy, allowing them thereby to indicate whether sexual harassment is a major or minor problem, or not a problem at all" (p. 86).

15. Dziech and Weiner, *The Lecherous Professor*, p. 43.

16. Best, *Threatened Children*, p. 80.

17. Best, *Threatened Children*, p. 26.

18. Jean O'Gorman Hughes and Bernice Sandler, *Peer Harassment: Hassles for Women on Campus* (Washington, DC: Project on the Status and Education of Women, Association of American Colleges, 1988). For the origin of the term "peer harassment," see Katherine A. Benson, "Comment on Crocker's 'An Analysis of University Definitions of Sexual Harassment,' " *Signs: Journal of Women in Culture and Society* 9, no. 3 (Spring 1984): 516–19.

19. Best, *Threatened Children*, 29.

20. U.S. Department of Education, Office of Civil Rights, *Sexual Harassment Guidance: Harassment of Students by School Employees, Other Students, or Third Parties*. Federal Register, March 13, 1997, vol. 62, no. 49.

21. Detailed descriptions of how to train people to recognize victimhood are by now a staple of the SHI. See, for a recent article exemplifying current SHI orthodoxy, Laura A. Reese and Karen E. Lindenberg, " 'Victimhood' and the Implementation of Sexual Harassment Policy," *Review of Public Personnel Administration* 17, no. 1 (Winter 1997): 37–57.

22. Benson, "Comment on Crocker's 'Analysis of University Definitions.' "

23. Benson, "Comment on Crocker's 'Analysis of University Definitions,' " p. 518.

24. Benson, "Comment on Crocker's 'Analysis of University Definitions,' " p. 519.

25. Catharine A. MacKinnon, "Sexual Harassment: Its First Decade in Court," in *Feminism Unmodified: Discourses on Life and Law* (Cambridge: Harvard University Press, 1987), p. 107.

26. OCR *Guidance* (my italics).

27. OCR *Guidance*.

28. The Violence against Women Act of 1994, which calls for civil remedies for gender-motivated crimes (in addition to the already existing criminal remedies that require a higher standard of evidence) further enhances women's legal position. On this, see Christina Hoff Sommers, *Who Stole Feminism: How Women Have Betrayed Women* (New York: Simon & Schuster, 1994), p. 223. See also Cathy Young's article on the 1998 Violence against Women Act, "VAWA II: A Feminist Boondoggle?" (forthcoming, 1998).

29. See Peter Monaghan, "A Sexual Harassment Case Tarnishes the Image of Canada's Simon Fraser U.," *Chronicle of Higher Education*, December 19,

1997, pp. A43–44. In this case, Rachel Marsden, a third-year student, charged that Liam Donnelly, the coach of the swimming team, had harassed her, had had an affair with her for over a year, and had raped her. The police, to whom she initially went, declined to investigate the case, citing lack of evidence, but this did not prevent a panel at Simon Fraser from finding her charges to be true. Donnelly was fired, and the university paid Marsden twelve thousand dollars in compensation. Donnelly then produced evidence that it was Marsden who had hounded him for eighteen months. As a result, he was reinstated, and the university's sexual harassment policy was overhauled.

The problem, as some critics have pointed out, is not only sexual harassment policy itself but also the persons who implement the policy. In the SFU case, the then-head of the Office of Harassment Policy befriended the complainant and, furthermore, handpicked the members of the panels appointed to overhear complaints. Something of the atmosphere created by sexual harassment vigilantism can be gauged by the detail that from 1990 through 1997, the SFU Office of Harassment Policy received approximately six hundred complaints, of which 97 percent were resolved without official proceedings. What should one conclude from this detail? That sexual harassment is rampant? Or that a great many ordinary behaviors are being reclassified as discriminatory?

30. Cornell's secret filing system came to light in the context of the case against Professor James Maas. For details on the Maas case, see the *Center for Individual Rights Docket Report*, special issue (August 1995). Available on the Internet at http://www.wdn.com/cir/mass.htm. Protests led to a revision of Cornell's procedures.

31. Dziech and Weiner, *The Lecherous Professor*, pp. 115–46.

32. Howard Lurie, e-mail message to asc-l@csulb.edu, March 30, 1998.

33. Susan Estrich and Stuart Taylor, Jr., "Did Clinton Harass Paula Jones?" exchange of views in *Slate*, November 1996.

34. Gloria Steinem, "Feminists and the Clinton Question," *New York Times*, March 22, 1998, p. 15.

35. Similarly, the National Organization for Women declined to enter into Paula Jones's appeal of Judge Susan Webber Wright's dismissal, in April 1998, of her suit. Wright had found that Jones was not emotionally afflicted or punished in the workplace as a result of President Clinton's alleged advances. Eugene Volokh, "Was Wright Wrong? Who Knows?," *Wall Street Journal*, April 3, 1998, notes that while Judge Wright concluded that Clinton's behavior toward Paula Jones was not "severe" enough to create a "hostile environment," other judges have found that a single epithet uttered by a supervisor to a subordinate could be harassment. Volokh argues that it makes little sense to use terms like "right" and "wrong" in relation to hostile-environment harassment decisions. "The law is so mushy that it really is a matter of which judge or jury you draw. . . . What exactly do 'severe,' 'hostile,' 'abusive' and 'offensive' mean? Nobody knows. Judge Wright's guess is as good as any." Volokh warns that such "vague, subjective law is a recipe for injustice."

36. A similar comment was made fifteen years earlier in an essay by H. F. Adams, "Work in the Interstices: Women in Academe," *Women's Studies International Forum* 6, no. 2 (1983): 135–41: "Thirteen years of teaching in universities has at last disclosed to me the secret that there is no second sex in academe. There is only one sex: male."

37. Claims such as Scollay and Bratt's seem not to change over the years. Caroline Ramazanoglu, "Sex and Academic Life, or You Can Keep a Good Woman Down," in *Women, Violence, and Social Control*, ed. Jalna Hanmer and Mary Maynard (Atlantic Highlands, NJ: Humanities Press, 1987), pp. 61–74, for example, first defines "violence" as anything that diminishes another human being (p. 64). Hence, sexual harassment is an issue of "male violence against women" (p. 65). Then she goes on to congratulate women on dropping out of the academic rat race, where "objectivity" is still the cornerstone (p. 69) and where women can succeed only by becoming "abnormal" (p. 71).

38. To the examples of the myth of "systemic sexism" that are most familiar to U.S. readers—"recovered" memories of childhood sexual abuse, sexual harassment charges run amok—one might also add (as a demonstration of the continental reach of feminist mythologies) an important Canadian example. The Canada Panel on Violence against Women in 1993 published a report (which took more than two years to produce at a cost of more than $10 million) stating that "Canadian women are all too familiar with inequality and violence which tether them to lives few in the world would choose to lead." No wonder Canadian feminist critic Donna Laframboise, in her book *The Princess at the Window: A New Gender Morality* (Toronto: Penguin Books, 1996), pp. 41–42, calls the report "a national embarrassment." She considers it evidence of the fact that the extremist thinking she criticizes is not confined to small groups of marginalized feminists.

39. The gross abuses I have observed within universities have had to do not with sexism but with personal likes and dislikes and their inordinate effect on personnel decisions that should be made on strictly professional grounds. Both men and women are subject to such unfair treatment.

40. Bronislaw Malinowski, *Myth in Primitive Psychology* (New York: Norton, 1926).

41. "Special Report of the Status of Women Council Concerning Vision 2000" (presented at the Faculty Senate, University of Massachusetts at Amherst, December 4, 1997, Sen. Doc. No. 98-015). Professor Ann Ferguson, director of women's studies, and Carol Wallace, director of the Everywoman's Center, cochaired the council that prepared the report. The Vision 2000 plan itself was written by the New England Council of Land-Grant University Women in February 1997.

42. New England Council of Land-Grant University Women, "Vision 2000" (February 1997).

43. New England Council of Land-Grant University Women, "Vision 2000" (February 1997).

44. New England Council of Land-Grant University Women, "Vision 2000" (February 1997).

45. When this comment was quoted in a column by John Leo in *U.S. News and World Report*, January 19, 1998, Professor Ferguson denied having made it. Records of the Faculty Senate meeting of December 4, 1997, reveal that she had in fact said, "We can't lose track of the wider goal in order to defend some narrow definition of academic freedom, which might amount to a right not to have to respond to new knowledges that are relevant to someone's own field of expertise." See letter by Professor Robert M. Costrell, *Daily Hampshire Gazette*, February 2, 1998. See also my critique of the Vision 2000 plan, "Why Not a Feminist Overhaul of Higher Education?" *Chronicle of Higher Education*, January 23, 1998, p. A56.

46. Jean Bethke Elshtain, conversation with author, April 1997.

47. MacKinnon, "Sexual Harassment: Its First Decade in Court," p. 104.

48. MacKinnon, "Sexual Harassment: Its First Decade in Court," p. 111.

49. Harsh K. Luthar, "The Neglect of Critical Issues in the Sexual Harassment Discussion: Implications for Organizational and Public Policies," *Journal of Individual Employment Rights* 4, no. 4 (1995–96): 261–76. Luthar told me that he had spent four years trying to find a journal that would accept his article for publication, quite unlike the typical experience of writers on sexual harassment, whose work has become a growth industry.

50. Equal Employment Opportunity Commission, "Sexual Harassment Charges FY 1991–FY 1997" (data compiled by the EEOC's Office of Research, Information and Planning from its Charge Data System–National Data Base).

51. Howard Gadlin, in his essay "Mediating Sexual Harassment," in *Sexual Harassment on Campus*, ed. Sandler and Shoop, p. 201, states that 85 to 90 percent of the sexual harassment cases that come to him as a university ombudsperson (at UCLA) involve allegations by women of harassment by men. Only a close study of the SHI's operations on university campuses would enable us to decide whether these figures chart serious misconduct or merely reflect women's ever-increasing training in taking offense at words or gestures containing a touch of sexual innuendo.

52. Cathy Young, *Ceasefire: Beyond the Gender Wars* (New York: Free Press, 1999), chapter 6, has an excellent analysis of the issue of false allegations of rape.

53. Luthar, "Neglect of Critical Issues in Sexual Harassment Discussion," pp. 265–66.

54. Katie Roiphe, *The Morning After: Sex, Fear, and Feminism on Campus* (Boston: Little, Brown, 1993).

Chapter 3

1. Bernice R. Sandler and Robert J. Shoop, eds., *Sexual Harassment on Campus: A Guide for Administrators, Faculty, and Students* (Boston: Allyn & Bacon, 1997). As in chapter 2 above, page references to this book are incorporated parenthetically into the text of this chapter.

2. And older. Newspaper accounts over the past few years include cases of women students over forty years of age filing sexual harassment charges

after consensual affairs (both heterosexual and homosexual) with professors went sour.

3. For a very different view of this issue, see Peg Tittle, "On Prohibiting
   Relationships between Professors and Students," and Barry M. Dank and
   Joseph S. Fulda, "Forbidden Love: Student–Professor Romance," both in
   Sexuality and Culture, vol. 1 (1997).

4. Decision of Arbitrator Thomas E. Angelo, *Arbitration between Ramdas Lamb
   and Board of Regents of the University of Hawaii*, Honolulu, Hawaii, July 10,
   1994, n.p.

5. Testimony of Susan Hippensteele, *Arbitration between Ramdas Lamb and
   Board of Regents of the University of Hawaii*, April 7, 1994 (last day of arbitration), vol. 5, pp. 721, 739.

6. Confidential e-mail message to the author, May 21 and 30, 1998.

7. Decision of Arbitrator Angelo.

8. *Campus Chronicle* (University of Massachusetts at Amherst), November 6,
   1987, p. 5.

9. Billie Wright Dziech and Linda Weiner, *The Lecherous Professor: Sexual Harassment on Campus*, 2d ed. (Urbana: University of Chicago Press, 1990),
   pp. 118–19. First published in 1984.

10. Deposition of Susan Hippensteele, *Gretzinger v. University of Hawaii and
    Ramdas Lamb*, U.S. District Court for the District of Hawaii, Civil No. 94-
    00684 ACK, February 28, 1995, vol. 1, p. 27.

11. Deposition of Hippensteele, *Lamb Arbitration*, April 7, 1994, vol. 5, p. 751.

Chapter 4

1. Jo Trigilio, Department of Philosophy, California State University, Chico,
   e-mail message to wmst-l@umdd.umd.edu, February 19, 1998.

2. See Cathy Young, *Ceasefire: Beyond the Gender Wars* (New York: Free Press,
   1999), chapter 6, for a far more realistic assessment of the problem of
   false allegations. Susan Sarnoff, whose early work was as a victim advocate
   and who is the author of *Paying for Crime: The Policies and Possibilities of
   Crime Victim Reimbursement* (Westport, CT: Praeger, 1996), wrote to me
   that when her dissertation demonstrated "that sexual assault victims receive 76% of the funds meant for all crime victims, I was shunned, black-
   listed and worse" (e-mail message to author, August 23, 1997). In a recent
   article, "Measuring the Iceberg," *Women's Freedom Network Newsletter* (Fall
   1997), Sarnoff explains why it is likely that false reports of rape have
   increased in recent years: "The myth of unreported rape, then, is the
   myth of the submerged part of the iceberg that victim advocates want us
   to believe is enormous and ever-growing." Sarnoff also notes that victim
   advocates "refuse to recognize the improvements they themselves have
   effected." She discusses the important negative consequences of the myth
   of unreported rape such as scaring women, deflecting attention and services from high-risk women, perpetuating the myth that "all men are potential rapists," and false accusations and convictions. She says, "While
   some researchers argue that false reports may make up more than 40%

of all rape reports, only the most fanatical ideologues insist that the number falls below 8%."

3. Testimony of Wanda Dicks, *Arbitration between Ramdas Lamb and Board of Regents of the University of Hawaii*, before Arbitrator Thomas E. Angelo, Honolulu, Hawaii, April 5, 1994, vol. 3, p. 383.

4. Testimony of Tim Tidwell, *Lamb Arbitration*, April 5, 1994, vol. 3, pp. 371–73. Many other students gave similar testimony. A contentious issue arose from the fact that Mie Watanabe, the investigating officer who went into action once sexual harassment charges had been filed, had made no effort to interview those students who supported Lamb. A few of them had taken the initiative and spoken to Watanabe; they later criticized her written summaries as misrepresentations of their views.

5. Alan M. Dershowitz, "Justice" at http://www.vix.com/pub/men/harass/dershowitz.html.

6. Closing argument of Clayton Ikei, *Gretzinger v. Ramdas Lamb*, United States District Court for the District of Hawaii, Civil No. 94-00864BMK, August 22, 1996, vol. 13, p. 137.

7. Closing argument of Ikei, p. 144.

8. "Grooming" is a particularly noxious term by which fear of niceness is being spread throughout the academy. It has been used for decades in the literature relating to sexual offenders and has evidently been borrowed, because of its nefarious associations, by the SHI.

9. George Tanabe, the chair of Lamb's department, in his testimony before Arbitrator Thomas E. Angelo, described a training session conducted by Hippensteele for the departmental faculty in the wake of the allegations against Lamb, in which it was made clear that "whether or not something proper or improper was taking place [was] totally in the minds and the understandings of the student. If they so perceived a problem, there was a problem." *Lamb Arbitration*, February 17, 1994, vol. 2, p. 223. Hippensteele also told faculty that they were right to feel "severely limited in what we could say and do without fear of being charged with harassment or discrimination," since the student's "perception would indicate the presence of a problem" (p. 224). She also explained "grooming" in such a way that, Tanabe testified, a woman student in the room "complained that we were discriminating against women, because we were being reluctant about being nice to female students. . . . And so either way, whether we're being nice or whether we were not being nice, we were discriminating against [them]" (p. 228). Tanabe also testified to the contradictory position in which he, as chair, found himself: "My problem is that any action I took assumed that the complaints were legitimate, and this is an assumption that I have to make prior to any investigation to determine whether or not the complaints are legitimate. And so I found myself in the difficult position of having to take some kind of action, and I cannot, and I still cannot, make the distinction between what might be called legitimate actions before an investigation is carried out and corrective or punitive or disciplinary action" (p. 221).

10. Deposition of Susan Hippensteele, *Gretzinger v. University of Hawaii Profes-*

sional Assembly and Ramdas Lamb, U.S. District Court for the District of
Hawaii, Civil No. 90-00684 ACK, May 3, 1995, vol. 3, p. 326.

11. See K. L. Billingsley's article on the case, "A Lamb to the Slaughter?"
Heterodoxy 5, no. 1 (January–February 1997): 1.

12. Ramdas Lamb, e-mail message to author, January 9, 1998.

13. See David E. Rovella, "When Free Speech and Sex Harassment Clash,"
National Law Journal, May 11, 1998, p. A21; *Gretzinger v. University of
Hawaii Professional Assembly and Ramdas Lamb*, U.S. District Court for the
District of Hawaii, No. 97-15123, D.C. No. CV-94-00684 BMK, May 6,
1998; Craig Gima, "UH Professor Wins Appeal By Accuser," *Honolulu
Star-Bulletin*, July 9, 1998, p. A4.

14. Ramdas Lamb, e-mail message to asc-1@csulb.edu, June 2, 1998.

15. Heinz-Joachim Klatt, "Sexual Harassment Policies as All-Purpose Tools
to Settle Conflicts," *Sexuality and Culture* 1 (1997): 45–69.

16. Ferrel M. Christensen, *Sexual Harassment Must Be Eliminated*, General Issues Education Foundation Occasional Papers Series, no. 3 (Alberta: General Issues Education Foundation, 1994), p. 27. Hans Bader writes, more
generally, that "[h]arassment law is on a collision course with the First
Amendment" because harassment claims are often based on speech—
jokes, political statements, religious proselytizing, or art on the topics of
race, religion, or sex—that is said to create a "hostile or offensive work
environment." "Free Speech Trumps Title VII Suits," *National Law Journal*, November 24, 1997. On page A19, Bader discusses several suits in
which First Amendment rights won out in the end.

17. Information on the Vega case comes from official documents sent to me
by Professor Vega.

18. Eddie Vega, e-mail message to author, May 27, 1998.

19. Eddie Vega, e-mail message to author, May 27, 1998.

20. See *About Women on Campus* 4, no. 4 (Fall 1995): 7.

21. Klatt, "Sexual Harassment Policies as All-Purpose Tools to Settle Conflicts," p. 62. In 1991, Klatt was himself charged with sexual harassment
by two students who took offense at his calling another student in his class
by the nickname "Lucky Lucy." What followed was, he writes, "worthy of
Kafka." Months later, he was called before a one-man tribunal, was not
allowed to hear the testimony of witnesses or to cross-examine them, and
was told a final judgment would be made without further input from him
and without the possibility of an appeal. Two years later, he was exoner-
ated (pp. 63–64).

22. Letter from C. S. Wallace to Linda L. Slakey, May 1, 1998 (copy provided
by Professor Palmer). Wallace was also, as noted in chapter 2 above, cochair of the committee promoting the Vision 2000 proposal.

23. Evidently some of the students felt that describing RU 486 as inducing
abortion was a prejudicial view of it, and thus an "opinion," not a "fact."
Yet a study by radical feminist scholar Janice G. Raymond (also on the
faculty at UMass-Amherst), coauthored with Renate Klein and Lynette
J. Dumble, *RU 486: Misconceptions, Myths, and Morals* (Cambridge, MA:
Institute on Women and Technology, 1991), states as its opening line,

"Initial euphoria greeted the arrival of RU 486, the new chemical aborti-facient" (p. 1). This work deplores the dangers RU 486 poses to women's health. One can easily envision a situation in which while some of Professor Palmer's students object to his antipathetic labeling of RU 486 as an abortifacient, others object to his failure to denounce the drug as a threat to women's health; both sides could then charge him with "hostile environment" harassment.

24. Letter from John Palmer to Robert Ackermann, Ombudsman, May 1, 1998.

25. Letter from Robert Ackermann to Christopher Woodcock, Chair, Biology Department, May 11, 1998.

26. One of these letters of support stated:

> I was saddened and upset to read that your style of teaching is coming under attack. I have found your straight-forward style [of] teaching very beneficial. It is my opinion that these students who have attacked you are far too sensitive and unwilling to hear anything that is not told to them exactly the way they want to hear it. I have found them to be obnoxious and disruptive in class, often addressing issues that are not relevant to the real message of the lecture.

Another student, identifying herself as "pro-choice," wrote that she "did not see the same things the other nine students did," and offered to gather up pro-Palmer forces to take to the Ombuds Office. Letters dated May 13, 1998 (copies provided to me by Professor Palmer).

27. Leroy Young, letter to author, August 2, 1995.

28. News release from Plymouth State College President Donald P. Wharton, March 28, 1994.

29. Jim Finnegan, " 'What Happened with Leroy?' " *Union Leader,* April 29, 1994.

30. Leroy Young, e-mail communication, July 25, 1997.

31. See Denise K. Magner, "College Reinstates Controversial Professor, Then Fires Him Once Again," *Chronicle of Higher Education,* February 9, 1996, p. A20.

32. Leroy Young, introducing himself to asc-l@csulb.edu, July 7, 1995.

33. Tatum Young, personal communication with author, March 16, 1998.

34. Denise Magner's article "College Reinstates Controversial Professor, Then Fires Him Once Again," quoted Tracy Schneider's lawyer, Susanna G. Robinson, as declaring that the university should have stepped in because "[t]his guy has a history of doing this," a statement Leroy Young says is an outright lie.

35. Leroy Young, e-mail message to author, March 1998.

36. Ted McDonough, "Sex in the Open," *Moscow Pullman (Washington),* June 14–15, 1997, p. 1A.

37. Memo from Peggy Chevalier, Chair, Faculty Status Committee, June 20, 1996 (regarding the petition of Dr. Valerie Jenness).

38. Eric Sorensen, "Dismissal Was Based on Sex, Ex-WSU Prof Says in Claim," *Spokane Spokesman-Review,* June 9, 1997, p. A5.

39. Marc Ethier, "Washington State U. Accused of a Double Standard on Indiscretions by Professors," *Chronicle of Higher Education*, June 27, 1997, p. A14.

40. Letter from Valerie Jenness to the State of Washington, Division of Risk Management, April 16, 1997 (copy provided by Valerie Jenness).

41. Peggy Chevalier, June 20, 1996, memo.

42. Sorensen, "Dismissal Was Based on Sex, Ex-WSU Prof Says," p. A6.

43. Valerie Jenness, review of *Feminist Accused of Sexual Harassment*, by Jane Gallop, forthcoming in *Sexuality and Culture*, vol. 2 (1998). My thanks to Professor Jenness for providing me with the typescript of her review.

44. Jenness has written to me that her gut feeling is that sexual harassment has lost its feminist frame as it has been increasingly redefined, appropriated, and used against women—especially against lesbians and women of color. E-mail correspondence, January 4, 1998.

45. Valerie Jenness, telephone conversation with author, June 14, 1998.

46. See Vicki Schultz, "Reconceptualizing Sexual Harassment," *Yale Law Journal* 107, no. 6 (April 1998): 1685–1805; and Jeffrey Rosen's critique of Schultz's argument in "In Defense of Gender-Blindness," *New Republic*, June 29, 1998, pp. 25–35.

47. Rosen, "In Defense of Gender-Blindness," p. 33.

48. For Canadian cases, see John Fekete's excellent work, *Moral Panic: Biopolitics Rising* (Montreal: Robert Davies, 1994).

49. Helen Garner, *The First Stone: Some Questions about Sex and Power* (1995; reprint, New York: Free Press, 1997), p. 111.

50. Janet Malcolm, review of *The First Stone: Some Questions about Sex and Power*, by Helen Garner, *New Yorker,* July 7, 1997, p. 75.

51. Garner, *The First Stone*, pp. 15–16 (italics in original).

52. Garner, *The First Stone*, p. 120.

53. Garner, *The First Stone*, p. 120 (italics in original).

54. Garner, *The First Stone*, p. 112.

55. Garner, *The First Stone*, p. 100.

56. Garner, *The First Stone*, p. 103.

57. Garner, *The First Stone*, pp. 112–13.

58. But the book also brought Garner hundreds of letters (about two-thirds of them from women, she says) expressing relief that someone was at last saying that daily life is not as horrible and destructive to women as feminist orthodoxy insists it is.

59. Malcolm, review of *The First Stone*, p. 75.

60. Garner, *The First Stone*, p. 140 (italics in original).

Chapter 5

1. Jane Gallop, *Around 1981: Academic Feminist Literary Theory* (New York: Routledge, 1992).

2. Jane Gallop, *Feminist Accused of Sexual Harassment* (Durham: Duke University Press, 1997).

3. Jane Gallop, "*The Lecherous Professor*: A Reading," review of *The Lecherous*

Professor: Sexual Harassment on Campus, by Billie Wright Dziech and Linda Weiner, *Differences* 7, no. 2 (1995): 1–15.

4. Gallop, *Feminist Accused,* p. 1.
5. Jane Gallop, letter to the editor, *Lesbian and Gay Studies Newsletter,* July 1993, p. 2.
6. Gallop, *Feminist Accused,* p. 6.
7. Gallop, *Feminist Accused,* pp. 85–86.
8. Gallop, *Feminist Accused,* p. 86.
9. Gallop, *Feminist Accused,* p. 86.
10. Gallop, *Feminist Accused,* pp. 7–9.
11. Jane Gallop, "Feminism and Harassment Policy," *Academe* 80, no. 5 (September–October 1994): 16.
12. Gallop, *Feminist Accused,* p. 10. Carolyn Grose, "Same-Sex Sexual Harassment: Subverting the Heterosexist Paradigm of Title VII," *Yale Journal of Law and Feminism* 7, no. 2 (1995): 375–98, makes a similar argument: Sexual harassment theory by definition relies on a heterosexual model of interaction (p. 382). Title VII does not prohibit discrimination on the basis of sexual orientation, and, argues Grose, until it does provide such protection, any attempt to use Title VII in cases of same-sex harassment will merely lead to intensified heterosexism and homophobia (pp. 377–78). My thanks to Valerie Jenness for calling this article to my attention.
13. Alice Echols, *Daring to Be Bad: Radical Feminism in America, 1967–1975* (Minneapolis: University of Minnesota Press, 1989), p. 181.
14. Gallop, *Feminist Accused,* p. 11.
15. Gallop, *Feminist Accused,* p. 76.
16. Deposition of Susan Hippensteele, *Gretzinger v. University of Hawaii and Ramdas Lamb,* U.S. District Court for the District of Hawaii, Civil No. 94–00684 ACK, February 28, 1995, vol. 1, pp. 18–19.
17. Gallop, *Feminist Accused,* p. 12.
18. Gallop, *Feminist Accused,* p. 13.
19. Gallop, *Feminist Accused,* p. 12.
20. Gallop, *Feminist Accused,* pp. 17–18.
21. Gallop, *Feminist Accused,* p. 20.
22. Gallop, *Feminist Accused,* p. 19.
23. Gallop, *Feminist Accused,* p. 20.
24. Gallop, *Feminist Accused,* p. 11.
25. Gallop, *Feminist Accused,* p. 24.
26. Gallop, *Feminist Accused,* p. 25.
27. Gallop, *Feminist Accused,* p. 25.
28. National Organization for Women, "Issue Report: Sexual Harassment" (NOW Web site: http://www.now.org, February 20, 1998).
29. Gallop, *Feminist Accused,* p. 25.
30. Gallop, *Feminist Accused,* p. 41. Bell Hooks offers a somewhat different defense of professor–student affairs in her essay "Passionate Pedagogy: Erotic Student/Faculty Relationships," *Z Magazine* 9, no. 3 (March 1996): 45–51. Hooks avoids defending these relationships on the grounds of freedom of association, attempting instead to justify them as of particular

intellectual value, thus leaving such relationships vulnerable to attack, by implication, if they fail to meet lofty intellectual aims.

31. Gallop, *Feminist Accused*, p. 42.
32. Gallop, *Feminist Accused*, p. 42.
33. Janet Malcolm, "It Happened in Milwaukee," review of *Feminist Accused of Sexual Harassment*, by Jane Gallop, *New York Review of Books*, October 23, 1997, p. 8 (italics in original).
34. Gallop, *Feminist Accused*, p. 49.
35. Gallop, *Feminist Accused*, p. 50.
36. Gallop, *Feminist Accused*, p. 51.
37. Gallop, *Feminist Accused*, p. 79.
38. Gallop, *Feminist Accused*, p. 28.
39. Robin Wilson, "A Professor's Personal Teaching Style Wins Him Praise and Costs Him His Job," *Chronicle of Higher Education*, November 14, 1997, p. A12. See also Ruth Shalit's detailed account of the case in "The Man Who Knew Too Much," *Lingua Franca*, February 1998, pp. 31–40.
40. See Daphne Patai and Noretta Koertge, *Professing Feminism: Cautionary Tales from the Strange World of Women's Studies* (New York: BasicBooks, 1994), especially chapters 4 and 7.
41. Jane Gallop, "Feminism and Harassment Policy," p. 18.
42. Linda Vaden Gratch, "Recognizing Sexual Harassment," in *Sexual Harassment on Campus: A Guide for Administrators, Faculty, and Students*, ed. Bernice R. Sandler and Robert J. Shoop (Boston: Allyn & Bacon, 1997), p. 286.
43. Andrea Dworkin, *Letters from a War Zone: Writings, 1976–1987* (New York: Dutton, 1988), p. 14.
44. Michael Mills, message to asc-l@csulb.edu, November 10, 1997 (italics in original).
45. Gallop, *Feminist Accused*, p. 55.
46. Helen Garner, *The First Stone: Some Questions about Sex and Power* (1995; reprint, New York: Free Press, 1997), p. 93.
47. Gallop, "Feminism and Harassment Policy," p. 21.
48. Nadine Strossen, chapter 8, "Defining Sexual Harassment: Sexuality Does Not Equal Sexism," in her *Defending Pornography: Free Speech, Sex, and the Fight for Women's Rights* (New York: Scribner, 1995), p. 119 (italics in original). Strossen considers this part of the "escalating war against sexual expression" (p. 140).
49. Gallop, "Feminism and Harassment Policy," p. 21.
50. Valerie Jenness, review of *Feminist Accused of Sexual Harassment*, by Jane Gallop, forthcoming in *Sexuality and Culture*, vol. 2 (1998). My thanks to Professor Jenness for making the typescript available to me in advance of publication.
51. Jenness, review of *Feminist Accused*, typescript, p. 2.
52. An analysis rooted in "patriarchy's" detrimental effects on women would, of course, have no difficulty explaining away the apparent contradiction.
53. Jenness, review of *Feminist Accused*, typescript, p. 6.
54. Gallop, *Feminist Accused*, pp. 37–38.
55. Jenness, review of *Feminist Accused*, typescript, p. 10.

56. "Synopsis of Facts in Support of the Appeals of Professors Carl Pope, Stan Stojkovic, and Rickie Lovell to the University and Faculty Rights and Responsibilities Committees of the University of Wisconsin-Milwaukee" (prepared by Anne Shindell, the respondents' attorney).

57. Scott Kerr, "Accused Say UWM Overzealous," *Milwaukee Shepherd Express*, November 18–25, 1993, pp. 4–5.

58. Stan Stojkovic, written statement, May 1998 (italics in original).

59. Audrey Cohan et al., *Sexual Harassment and Sexual Abuse: A Handbook for Teachers and Administrators* (Thousand Oaks, CA: Corwin Press, 1996), p. 34.

60. Gallop, *Feminist Accused*, p. 27 (italics in original).

Chapter 6

1. Ian Craib, "Social Constructionism as a Social Psychosis," *Sociology* 31, no. 1 (February 1997): 1–15.

2. Karen DeCrow, interview by Jack Kammer, in his *Good Will toward Men: Women Talk Candidly about the Balance of Power between the Sexes* (New York: St. Martin's Press, 1994), p. 58. Kammer's book contains interviews with prominent women who criticize the excesses of feminism. Collectively, the contributions serve as a memorable exposé of the current antagonism toward men. In a similar vein, Katie Roiphe, in *The Morning After: Sex, Fear, and Feminism on Campus* (Boston: Little, Brown, 1993), p. 136, wryly comments, "The original sin is being born a man. Embracing an ideology with 'phallocentric' as one of its gravest aspersions must be hard on those who happen to have a phallus attached to their own body." Emily White, discussing Judith Levine's book *My Enemy, My Love: Man-Hating and Ambivalence in Women's Lives*, comments, "If woman is patriarchy's darkness, man is often feminism's. He is perceived as impenetrable, inescapable, when actually he's rife with frailties and failings." "Et Tu, Brute," *Village Voice*, April 14, 1992, p. 69.

3. For an overview of the role of lesbian separatism in the development of the critique of heterosexuality, see Rosemarie Tong, *Feminist Thought: A Comprehensive Introduction* (Boulder: Westview Press, 1989), especially chapter 4, "Radical Feminism on Gender and Sexuality."

Lillian Faderman, in *Odd Girls and Twilight Lovers: A History of Lesbian Life in Twentieth-Century America* (New York: Penguin Books, 1991), p. 212, describes the 1970s: "Because a general disenchantment with and suspicion of all males was central to lesbian-feminist doctrine, the gay man was naturally seen as being no less an enemy than any other human with a penis, and lesbian-feminists could make no lasting coalition with gay men in a gay revolution." Faderman also reminds us that despite the disapproval of NOW founder Betty Friedan, who called lesbians the "lavender menace,"

[i]n a 1971 resolution, NOW identified lesbians as the frontline troops of the women's movement and accepted the lesbian-feminist

analysis that the reason lesbians had been so harassed by society was that they were a significant threat to the system that subjugated women—the very system that heterosexual women were trying to challenge and destroy by their feminism. The 1971 resolution acknowledged the inherent feminism of lesbianism and the anti-feminism of lesbian persecution.

Faderman writes: "Lesbianism even came to be regarded as the quintessence of feminism" (p. 206), and concludes: "There were probably more lesbians in America during the 1970s than any other time in history, because radical feminism had helped redefine lesbianism to make it almost a categorical imperative for all women truly interested in the welfare and progress of other women" (p. 207).

Arlene Stein, in *Sex and Sensibility: Stories of a Lesbian Generation* (Berkeley: University of California Press, 1997), discusses the high percentage of former separatists who later "turned straight." One woman she interviewed commented that the women who were the " 'biggest manhaters, the women who would have nothing to do with men for years—those were the women who went straight' " (p. 161). "Other women agreed," she says, "that many of the women who had been the most adamant ideologues were now with men" (p. 162).

4. Sheila Jeffreys, *Anticlimax: A Feminist Perspective on the Sexual Revolution* (London: Women's Press, 1990), p. 299. Jeffreys has continued to write in the same vein. See, for example, her essay "How Orgasm Politics Has Hijacked the Women's Movement," *On the Issues* (Spring 1996), in which she insists on the inseparability of sex and sexual violence and laments that "an unreflective politics of orgasm seems to have won out" among feminists.

5. Jeffreys, *Anticlimax*, pp. 300–301.

6. For women, such "sameness" seems to lead to diminished sexual activity. As Elaine Creith notes in *Undressing Lesbian Sex: Popular Images, Private Acts, and Public Consequences* (London and New York: Cassell, 1996), p. 108: "Since the 1980s, this low or absent desire seems to be the most documented aspect of lesbian sexuality, to the extent that any commentary ignoring what is colloquially known as 'bed death', would appear woefully inadequate." Celia Kitzinger argues for the need to resist such analyses. "The Psychologisation of Lesbian Relationships: The Case against 'Merger,' " in *An Intimacy of Equals: Lesbian Feminist Ethics*, ed. Lilian Mohin (New York: Harrington Park Press, 1996), pp. 106–17.

7. I have examined about twenty such codes, from colleges and universities around the country, public and private, large and small. The language of "power" and the denunciation of "power differentials" seems universal.

8. Robert L. Carothers and Jayne E. Richmond, "The Role of the President in Sexual Harassment Prevention," in *Sexual Harassment on Campus: A Guide for Administrators, Faculty, and Students*, ed. Bernice R. Sandler and Robert J. Shoop (Boston: Allyn & Bacon, 1997), p. 320.

9. Catharine MacKinnon, of course, does not argue for such a separation of

sex and power. Rather, she seems to believe that sex itself as practiced by men *is* power and, hence, that it would be wrong to say that sexual harassment is "about power" and not "about sex."

10. See Francine D. Blau, "Trends in the Well-Being of American Women, 1970–1995," *Journal of Economic Literature* 36 (March 1998): 112–65. Blau describes the "substantial progress toward gender equality" over the past twenty-five years and notes that these "relative gains appear to be matched by progress for women overall in an absolute sense. Women's real wages increased substantially over the 1969–1994 period, while men's stagnated" (pp. 160–61). My thanks to Robert Costrell for bringing Blau's work to my attention.

11. Mary Crawford, "Identity, 'Passing,' and Subversion," in *Heterosexuality: A Feminism and Psychology Reader*, ed. Sue Wilkinson and Celia Kitzinger (London: Sage, 1993), p. 44.

12. Sandra Lee Bartky, "Hypatia Unbound: A Confession," in *Heterosexuality*, ed. Wilkinson and Kitzinger, p. 41. Bartky goes on to explain how she laboriously undertook to sacrifice being passionately erotic (toward men she judged inappropriate because they were "father" figures to her), in order to become, instead, passionately political (p. 42).

13. Sandra Lipsitz Bem, "On the Inadequacy of Our Sexual Categories: A Personal Perspective," in *Heterosexuality*, ed. Wilkinson and Kitzinger, p. 51.

14. Shulamit Reinharz, "How My Heterosexuality Contributes to My Feminism and Vice Versa," in *Heterosexuality*, ed. Wilkinson and Kitzinger, p. 66.

15. To be sure, some lesbian scholars have criticized the intolerance within lesbian feminism. See, for example, Shane Phelan, *Identity Politics: Lesbian Feminism and the Limits of Community* (Philadelphia: Temple University Press, 1989). Elizabeth Kennedy, in a review of Phelan's book in the *NWSA Journal* 2, no. 3 (Summer 1990): 495–97, praises Phelan for "courageously" showing the limitations of lesbian feminism as a movement by exploring "how it fell apart over the issues of pornography and sadomasochism." Phelan argues that the radical feminist "defense of community has congealed to such a point that it allows for no disagreement and cannot deal with the complexity of human experience, while the advocates of sadomasochism rely too completely on subjective experience" (Kennedy, p. 496).

16. Adrienne Rich, "Compulsory Heterosexuality and Lesbian Existence," *Signs: Journal of Women in Culture and Society* 5, no. 4 (Summer 1980): 631–60. Rich's essay is a key document that has had an enormous impact over the past two decades. It has been widely anthologized and is regularly taught in women's studies courses. In her recent work, Judith Butler refers to the presumably indisputable reality of compulsory heterosexuality without even citing Rich, so well known has the phrase become. See Butler's "Melancholy Gender/Refused Identification," in *Constructing Masculinity*, ed. Maurice Berger, Brian Wallis, and Simon Watson (New York: Routledge, 1995), pp. 21–36. Rich has been criticized by other fem-

inists for her concept of a "lesbian continuum" that deemphasizes genital sex. See Ann Ferguson, Jacquelyn N. Zita, and Kathryn Pyne Addelson, "On 'Compulsory Heterosexuality and Lesbian Existence': Defining the Issues," in *Feminist Theory: A Critique of Ideology*, ed. Nannerl O. Keohane, Michelle Z. Rosaldo, and Barbara C. Gelpi (Chicago: University of Chicago Press, 1982), pp. 147–88.

17. Wilma Mankiller et al., eds., *Reader's Companion to U.S. Women's History* (Boston: Houghton Mifflin, 1998), p. 255.

18. Daphne Patai and Noretta Koertge, *Professing Feminism: Cautionary Tales from the Strange World of Women's Studies* (New York: BasicBooks, 1994), p. 44.

19. Prominent among those who have made similar criticisms of second-wave feminist orthodoxies is Lynne Segal. In *Straight Sex: Rethinking the Politics of Pleasure* (Berkeley: University of California Press, 1994), Segal argues for a sexual liberation that includes heterosexual relations, is rooted in desire, and is capable of subverting both the dominant sexual discourse of heterosexuality and the feminist critiques of heterosexuality. Cultivation of heterosexual guilt and the denial of women as sexual agents, Segal states, merely replace "sexual freedom with the most pernicious form of moral authoritarianism" (p. 266)—even if done in the name of feminism. As against such a stance, she celebrates the contributions of lesbian feminists, such as Joan Nestle, who fight sexual repression on all fronts.

20. Catharine A. MacKinnon, "Liberalism and the Death of Feminism," in *The Sexual Liberals and the Attack on Feminism*, ed. Dorchen Leidholdt and Janice G. Raymond (New York: Pergamon Press, 1987), p. 3.

21. E-mail messages to femisa@csf.colorado.edu, April 1995.

22. Valerie Solanas, *SCUM Manifesto* (New York: Olympia Press, 1968), p. 3, reprinted in part in Valerie Solanis [*sic*], "Excerpts from the SCUM (Society for Cutting Up Men) Manifesto," in *Sisterhood Is Powerful*, ed. Robin Morgan (New York: Random House, 1970).

23. Solanas, *SCUM Manifesto*, p. 41.

24. Solanas, *SCUM Manifesto*, p. 43.

25. Solanas, *SCUM Manifesto*, p. 43.

26. Solanas, *SCUM Manifesto*, p. 43. Compare this with Otto Weininger's hierarchy, discussed later in this chapter, in which women are the lowest of the low.

27. Victor Bockris, *The Life and Death of Andy Warhol* (New York: Bantam, 1989), p. 236. Atkinson in 1974 characterized Solanas's *SCUM Manifesto* as "the most important feminist statement written to date in the English language." Quoted by Alice Echols, *Daring to Be Bad: Radical Feminism in America, 1967–1975* (Minneapolis: University of Minnesota Press, 1989), p. 174. On Betty Friedan and NOW's critique of Atkinson and Solanas, see Echols, *Daring to Be Bad*, pp. 168–69.

28. See, for example, Janet Maslin, review of *I Shot Andy Warhol* (movie), *New York Times*, April 5, 1996.

29. Vivian Gornick, introduction to *SCUM Manifesto*, by Valerie Solanas (New York: Olympia Press, 1970), pp. xv, xxxv.

30. Sally Miller Gearhart, "The Future—If There Is One—Is Female," in *Reweaving the Web of Life: Feminism and Nonviolence*, ed. Pam McAllister (Philadelphia: New Society Publishers, 1982), pp. 267–84.

31. Gearhart, "The Future—If There Is One—Is Female," p. 274.

32. Gearhart, "The Future—If There Is One—Is Female," p. 270.

33. Gearhart, "The Future—If There Is One—Is Female," p. 274.

34. Rachel Bedard, "Re-entering Complexity," in *Reweaving the Web of Life*, ed. McAllister, p. 401.

35. Bedard, "Re-entering Complexity," p. 402. In a chapter entitled "Sleeping with the Enemy? Ex-Lesbians and the Reconstruction of Identity," p. 154–83, in *Sex and Sensibility*, Arlene Stein describes the downplaying of sexual desire among some lesbian feminists in the 1970s for the sake of political identity and unity, which resulted in the subsequent return of some women to heterosexuality in the 1980s. Stein astutely analyzes the interplay of "internal" and "external" selves, and of desire and social context, in the permutations of sexual identity (p. 180), noting that prohibitions against moving in and out of the lesbian category are imposed by both heterosexuals and homosexuals (p. 181).

36. Bedard, "Re-entering Complexity," p. 403.

37. Mary Daly, *Gyn/Ecology: The Metaethics of Radical Feminism* (Boston: Beacon Press, 1978), p. 59.

38. Joyce Trebilcot, "Taking Responsibility for Sexuality," in *Philosophy and Sex*, ed. Robert Baker and Frederick Elliston, rev. ed. (Buffalo, New York: Prometheus Books, 1984), p. 421.

39. Trebilcot, "Taking Responsibility for Sexuality," pp. 422–24.

40. Trebilcot, "Taking Responsibility for Sexuality," pp. 426–27.

41. Doris C. DeHardt, "Feminist Therapy with Heterosexual Couples: The Ultimate Issue Is Domination," in *Heterosexuality*, ed. Wilkinson and Kitzinger, p. 253.

42. Marilyn Frye, "Critique," in *Philosophy and Sex*, ed. Baker and Elliston, p. 454.

43. Marilyn Frye, "Willful Virgin, or Do You Have to Be a Lesbian to Be a Feminist?" in *Willful Virgin: Essays in Feminism, 1976–1992* (Freedom, CA: Crossing Press, 1992), p. 129. Originally given as a speech in 1990 at the National Women's Studies Association Conference.

44. Frye, *Willful Virgin*, p. 130.

45. Frye, *Willful Virgin*, p. 136.

46. Frye, *Willful Virgin*, p. 132.

47. Rich, "Compulsory Heterosexuality."

48. Frye, *Willful Virgin*, p. 132. See also Frye's depiction of how lesbians challenge the PUD (patriarchal universe of discourse), in her response, in *Off Our Backs*, July 1993, p. 20, to some lifelong lesbian critics of her use of the word "virgin." Frye states that the PUD's vocabulary "creates and enforces a reality that is unacceptable, unendurable."

49. Alice Echols, *Daring to Be Bad: Radical Feminism in America, 1967–1975*, pp. 362–63. Echols is speaking here explicitly of Andrea Dworkin and Catharine MacKinnon, both of whom, she says, have ostensibly repudiated essentialism.

50. Ian Craib, "Social Constructionism," points to a similar paradox in the widespread use by sociologists of the idea of "social constructionism." He treats the idea, only somewhat tongue in cheek, as if it were a patient walking in and declaring, "I am a social construct." Affirming that he has never met such a person, Craib observes that in his academic work he has come across many people who, in effect, say, "The people around me are social constructs" (p. 5), a view, Craib notes, that denies subjective agency to others but not to oneself as a knowing subject.

51. Alison M. Thomas, "The Heterosexual Feminist: A Paradoxical Identity?" in *Hetereosexuality*, ed. Wilkinson and Kitzinger, pp. 83–85.

52. See Judith Butler, *Gender Trouble: Feminism and the Subversion of Identity* (New York: Routledge, 1990). Butler criticizes Foucault for accepting the body as a given, that is, as something that exists "prior to its cultural inscription" (p. 130). By contrast, she extends social constructionism from gender to sexual identity (and, of course, heterosexuality) itself. For her, gender is always a *doing*, and "the substantive effect of gender is performatively produced and compelled by the regulatory practices of gender coherence" (pp. 24–25). She also writes, "Gender is the repeated stylization of the body, a set of repeated acts within a highly rigid regulatory frame that congeal over time to produce the appearance of substance, of a natural sort of being" (p. 33). For a succinct critique of Butler, see Barbara Epstein, "Postmodernism and the Left," *New Politics*, n.s., 6, no. 2 (Winter 1997): 130–44, who writes: "[Butler's] assertion that sexual difference is socially constructed strains belief. It is true that there are some people whose biological sex is ambiguous, but this is not the case of the vast majority of people. Biological difference has vast implications, social and psychological; the fact that we do not yet fully understand these does not mean that they do not exist" (pp. 137–38).

53. See Anne Fausto-Sterling, *Myths of Gender: Biological Theories about Men and Women* (New York: Basic Books, 1985); and Anne Fausto-Sterling, "How Many Sexes Are There?" *New York Times*, March 12, 1993, p. A29 (L).

54. This is not an inaccurate reading of Fausto-Sterling. See, for example, her sarcastic essay "How to Build a Man," in *Constructing Masculinity*, ed. Berger, Wallis, and Watson, pp. 127–34, the whole point of which is to dismantle as mere "narrative" male scientists' linking of biology with gender.

55. Deborah C. Stearns, "Gendered Sexuality: The Privileging of Sex and Gender in Sexual Orientation" *NWSA [National Women's Studies Association] Journal* 7, no. 1 (Spring 1995): 8–29.

56. Elizabeth A. Smith, "Butch, Femmes, and Feminists: The Politics of Lesbian Sexuality," *NWSA Journal* 3, no. 1 (Spring 1989): 398–421, admits that the assertion that sexuality is a social construct is not a "comfortable" place for lesbian historians (p. 398).

57. John Colapinto, "The True Story of John/Joan," *Rolling Stone*, December 11, 1997, p. 55. See also Milton Diamond, "Sexual Identity and Sexual Orientation in Children with Traumatized or Ambiguous Genitalia," *Jour-

nal of Sex Research 43, no. 2 (1997): 199–211; Milton Diamond and H. Keith Sigmundson, "Sex Reassignment at Birth: Long-Term Review and Clinical Implications," *Archives of Pediatrics and Adolescent Medicine* 151 (March 1997): 298–304; and William Reiner, editorial comment, *Archives of Pediatrics and Adolescent Medicine* 151 (March 1997): 224–25.

58. Catharine A. MacKinnon, *Sexual Harassment of Working Women* (New Haven: Yale University Press, 1979), p. 153.
59. My statement to John Leo, cited in his column "Boy, Girl, Boy Again," *U.S. News and World Report*, March 17, 1997, p. 17.
60. Leonore Tiefer, "The Medicalization of Impotence: Normalizing Phallocentrism," *Gender and Society* 8, no. 3 (September 1994): 363. My thanks to Cathy Young for this example.
61. Laurie Ingraham, interview by Jack Kammer, in his *Good Will toward Men*, p. 46.
62. Ingraham, interview, p. 50.
63. John Stoltenberg, *The End of Manhood: A Book for Men of Conscience* (New York: Dutton, 1993), p. xiv.
64. Stoltenberg, *End of Manhood*, p. 211.
65. Stoltenberg, *End of Manhood*, p. 211.
66. Elisabeth Badinter, *XY: On Masculine Identity*, trans. Lydia Davis (New York: Columbia University Press, 1995), p. 123.
67. John Stoltenberg, *Refusing to Be a Man: Essays on Sex and Justice* (1989; reprint, New York: Meridian, 1990), p. 28, quoting from Andrea Dworkin, *Woman Hating* (New York: Dutton, 1974), p. 183 (italics in original).
68. Badinter, *XY: On Masculine Identity*, p. 124.
69. Stoltenberg, *Refusing to Be a Man*, p. 88, quoted by Badinter, *XY: On Masculine Identity*, p. 124.
70. Andrea Dworkin, *Our Blood: Prophecies and Discourses on Sexual Politics* (New York: Harper & Row, 1976), p. 13. My thanks to Cathy Young for calling this passage to my attention.
71. Stoltenberg, *End of Manhood*, pp. 7–8.
72. Stoltenberg, *End of Manhood*, p. 34.
73. Robert Jensen, "Patriarchal Sex," *Feminism and Men* 17, nos. 1–2 (1997): 91.
74. Jensen, "Patriarchal Sex," pp. 94–96.
75. Robert Jensen, "Getting It Up for Politics: Gay Male Sexuality and Radical Lesbian Feminism," in *Opposite Sex*, ed. Sara Miles and Eric Rofes (New York: New York University Press, forthcoming).
76. Jensen, "Patriarchal Sex," p. 96.
77. Carol Queen, *Real Live Nude Girl: Chronicles of Sex-Positive Culture* (Pittsburgh and San Francisco: Cleis Press, 1997).
78. Jensen, "Patriarchal Sex," p. 97, quoting Andrea Dworkin, *Intercourse* (New York: Free Press, 1987), p. 63.
79. Badinter, *XY: On Masculine Identity*, p. 124.
80. Jensen, "Patriarchal Sex," p. 98.
81. Daphne Patai and Angela Ingram, "Fantasy and Identity: The Double Life of a Victorian Sexual Radical," in *Rediscovering Forgotten Radicals:*

British Women Writers, 1889–1939, ed. Angela Ingram and Daphne Patai (Chapel Hill: University of North Carolina Press, 1993), pp. 265–302.

82. Irene Clyde [Thomas Baty], *Eve's Sour Apples* (London, 1934), p. 12.

83. Clyde, *Eve's Sour Apples*, p. 20.

84. Clyde, *Eve's Sour Apples*, p. 28.

85. Clyde, *Eve's Sour Apples*, p. 30.

86. Clyde, *Eve's Sour Apples*, p. 28.

87. Naomi Mitchison, *The Home and a Changing Civilisation* (London: John Lane, 1934), pp. 146–47 (italics in original).

88. Carol Queen, "On Being a Female Submissive (and Doing What You Damn Well Please)," in *Real Live Nude Girl*, p. 175 (italics in original).

89. Jensen, "Patriarchal Sex," p. 99.

90. Allan Hunter, "Same Door, Different Closet: A Heterosexual Sissy's Coming-Out Party," in *Heterosexuality*, ed. Wilkinson and Kitzinger, pp. 150–68.

91. Otto Weininger, *Sex and Character* (London: William Heinemann, 1906 [1903]), p. 302.

92. Weininger, *Sex and Character*, p. 286.

93. Weininger, *Sex and Character*, p. 335.

94. Solanas, *SCUM Manifesto*, p. 8.

95. Queen, "Pornography and the Sensitive New Age Guy," in *Real Live Nude Girl*, p. 147.

96. Jensen, "Patriarchal Sex," p. 107–8.

97. In this, too, Jensen is indebted to antisex feminism. He cites the argument put forth by A Southern Women's Writing Collective, "Sex Resistance in Heterosexual Arrangements," in *The Sexual Liberals and the Attack on Feminism*, ed. Leidholdt and Raymond, pp. 140–47, who write that for male supremacy to be defeated, sex has to stop: "*If it doesn't subordinate women, it's not sex*" (p. 143, italics in original).

98. Sharon Olds, *The Gold Cell* (New York: Alfred A. Knopf, 1987), p. 16. First published in Ann Snitow, Christine Stansell, and Sharon Thompson, eds., *Powers of Desire* (New York: Monthly Review Press, 1983), p. 300, where it appears with a slight variation: "Gold straw fills the air."

99. E-mail messages to wmst-1@umdd.umd.edu, May 1996.

100. Robin Morgan, *The Anatomy of Freedom: Feminism, Physics, and Global Politics* (Garden City, NY: Anchor Press/Doubleday, 1982). Morgan warns that heterophobia is no antidote to homophobia. Both, she writes, "are, simply, sexual-fundamentalist reductions of curiosity and desire" (p. 154). Though apparently arguing against "sexual fundamentalism," Morgan in fact reveals her own heterophobia throughout her book. She denounces those lesbians who "degrade their own love by settling for butch/femme roles that pathetically imitate the worst of patriarchal heterosexuality" (p. 106). She also denounces feminists such as Deirdre English and Ellen Willis merely for objecting to censorship. (Morgan calls their objections "defending pornography" [p. 115] and pretends to be shocked that these women dare call themselves feminists.)

101. See, for example, Sue L. Cataldi, "Reflections on 'Male Bashing,'" *NWSA*

Journal 7, no. 2 (Summer 1995): 76–85. Against the massive evidence to the contrary, this feeble essay characterizes as "false, generally," the charges that "feminists are critical of men simply for being men" and that feminism promotes the idea that "all men are bad." The target of feminist critique is sexism in a male-dominated society, Cataldi asserts (p. 78). Then there is the feminist paragon, Kay Leigh Hagan, whose essay "A Good Man Is Hard to Bash: Confessions of an Ex-Man-Hater," in *Feminism and Men: Reconstructing Gender Relations*, ed. Steven P. Schacht and Doris W. Ewing (New York: New York University Press, 1998), pp. 161–71, recounts how she overcame her justified hatred of men by associating herself with a few Good Men. The stupefying inanity and arrogance of this paradigmatic morality tale is hard to convey in a few lines. Hagan describes her passage from rage to recognition as she moves beyond her oppression as a woman and a lesbian, comes to deplore her own privilege as a white, middle-class, and physically able person, and begins to use this insight as the key to an understanding of even the most obnoxious men. This generosity, in turn, enables her to identify and seek out Good Men (who listen, reflect, look to women for guidance, ask permission before touching, and generally reject their male prerogatives) and enlist them as allies in the struggle toward a new "culture of partnership" in preparing which feminists act as a "transition team." My thanks to Steven P. Schacht for making a typescript of this essay available to me prior to publication.

By contrast with these two articles (which are the sorts of texts beloved in women's studies courses), see Susan H. Williams and David C. Williams, "A Feminist Theory of Malebashing," *Michigan Journal of Gender and Law* 4, no. 1 (1996): 35–128, a careful and detailed consideration of "male-bashing" as a rhetorical strategy in academic dialogue.

102. Tama Starr has compiled two humorous volumes of what she calls "inter-gender hostility, from yuks to real acrimony." The first, devoted to men's misogynistic comments, is titled *The "Natural Inferiority" of Women: Outrageous Pronouncements by Misguided Males* (New York: Poseidon Press, 1991), and the second, *Eve's Revenge: Saints, Sinners, and Stand-Up Sisters on the Ultimate Extinction of Men* (New York: Harcourt Brace, 1994). Starr says, "When I started the second book I thought it would be roughly parallel with the first, the other side of the same coin. But it wasn't. The material was so different, with its weird skreeky music, that it demanded different treatment." The two volumes, Starr notes, induce laughter (if they do) in completely different ways. Comparing the two attitudes, she says, "makes persuasive Kipling's stereotype: 'The female of the species is deadlier than the male.' " E-mail message to author, April 18, 1998.

103. See, for example, Martha C. Nussbaum's "Rage and Reason," an extremely respectful review of *Life and Death: Unapologetic Writings on the Continuing War against Women*, by Andrea Dworkin (New York: Free Press, 1997), in *New Republic*, August 11–18, 1997, pp. 36–42. Nussbaum treats Dworkin variously as a philosopher and as a prophet and ends up endorsing Dworkin's view that "you cannot separate the so-called abuses of women from the so-called normal uses of women"—about which Nuss-

baum comments, "This sentence certainly does not say that all acts of intercourse are abuses" (p. 39). Nussbaum does confess to some "general worries" about Dworkin's projects, but even these are articulated with great solicitude.

Chapter 7

1. A key work in popularizing the phrase is Arlyn Diamond and Lee R. Edwards, eds., *The Authority of Experience: Essays in Feminist Criticism* (Amherst: University of Massachusetts Press, 1977).

2. Adrienne Rich, *Of Women Born* (London: Virago, 1977), p. 10. From a 1975 essay.

3. Catharine A. MacKinnon, "Sexual Harassment," in *The Reader's Companion to U.S. Women's History*, ed. Wilma Mankiller et al. (Boston: Houghton Mifflin, 1998), p. 534. Note the concept-stretching in MacKinnon's phrasing—the seamless shift from "sexual harassment" to "sexual abuse."

4. *Ellison v. Brady*, 924 F.2d 872 (9th Cir. 1991).

5. Sigrid MacDonald made this point in personal e-mail correspondence to me, August 1997.

6. See Judith Grant, *Fundamental Feminism: Contesting the Core Concepts of Feminist Theory* (New York: Routledge, 1993), for an illuminating discussion of the development of "experience" as a conceptual tool for feminists. Grant writes, "Oppression included anything that women *experienced* as oppressive" (p. 30, italics in original). And again:

   > Once one assumed that women were oppressed as women and that women's experiences were the proof of their oppression, it followed that female political oppression had to be charted where women experienced it: in their daily lives. Therefore, "the personal is political" combined with the categories "men" and "women" to facilitate the idea that a system of domination was entrenched at the level of every woman's most intimate relation with every man and that those relationships were, moreover, political. (p. 37)

7. Barbara A. Gutek and Maureen O'Connor, "The Empirical Basis for the Reasonable Woman Standard," *Journal of Social Issues* 51, no. 1 (1995): 151–66.

8. Linda LeMoncheck, "Taunted and Tormented or Savvy and Seductive," in *Sexual Harassment: A Debate*, by Linda LeMoncheck and Mane Hajdin (Lanham, MD: Rowman & Littlefield, 1997), pp. 66–68.

9. See John Fonte, "The Tragedy of Civil Rights," *Society* 34, no. 5 (July–August 1997): 67. As noted in chapter 1 above, "intent" was later modified to "intent or effect"—the language found in sexual harassment law as well.

10. Jan Salisbury and Fredda Jaffe, "Individual Training of Sexual Harassers," in *Sexual Harassment on College Campuses: Abusing the Ivory Power*, ed. Michele Paludi (Albany: State University of New York Press, 1996), pp. 142–52. This volume is an updated version of Paludi's 1990 collection

Ivory Power: Sexual Harassment on Campus. The success of her earlier work apparently allowed Paludi to leave her academic position and set up her own consulting firm devoted to sexual harassment issues.

11. Salisbury and Jaffe, "Individual Training of Sexual Harassers," p. 147.

12. Salisbury and Jaffe, "Individual Training of Sexual Harassers," p. 148 (italics in original).

13. Salisbury and Jaffe, "Individual Training of Sexual Harassers," p. 148.

14. Salisbury and Jaffe, "Individual Training of Sexual Harassers," pp. 149–50.

15. See Joan W. Scott, "Experience," in *Feminists Theorize the Political*, ed. Judith Butler and Joan W. Scott (New York: Routledge, 1992), pp. 22–40. "What counts as experience is neither self-evident nor straightforward; it is always contested, always therefore political" (p. 37).

16. Celia Kitzinger, "Experiential Authority and Heterosexuality," in *Changing Our Lives*, ed. Gabriele Griffin (London: Pluto Press, 1994), p. 142.

17. Kitzinger, "Experiential Authority," p. 142.

18. Kitzinger, "Experiential Authority," p. 143.

19. Kitzinger, "Experiential Authority," p. 143 (italics in original).

20. Judith Grant, *Fundamental Feminism*, p. 78. My thanks to Jeffrey Rosen for suggesting to me the connections outlined in the remainder of this paragraph.

21. Carol Mitchell, "Hostility and Aggression toward Males in Female Joke Telling," *Frontiers* 3, no. 3 (Fall 1978): 22.

22. Robin West, "A Comment on Consent, Sex, and Rape," *Legal Theory* 2, no. 3 (September 1996): 248.

23. West, "Consent, Sex, and Rape," p. 248.

24. Robin West, "The Difference in Women's Hedonic Lives: A Phenomenological Critique of Feminist Legal Theory," *Wisconsin Women's Law Journal* 3 (1987): 81.

25. West, "Women's Hedonic Lives," p. 82.

26. Robin West, "The Harms of Consensual Sex," *APA [American Philosophical Association] Newsletter on Feminism and Philosophy, and Philosophy and Law* 94, no. 2 (Spring 1995): 53.

27. West, "Harms of Consensual Sex," p. 53.

28. West, "Harms of Consensual Sex," p. 54.

29. West, "Harms of Consensual Sex," p. 54.

30. West, "Consent, Sex, and Rape," p. 248.

31. Dee L. R. Graham, with Edna I. Rawlings and Robert K. Rigsby, *Loving to Survive: Sexual Terror, Men's Violence, and Women's Lives* (New York: New York University Press, 1994).

32. Graham, *Loving to Survive*, p. 244.

33. Graham, *Loving to Survive*, p. xv.

34. Graham, *Loving to Survive*, p. 232.

35. Such ideas already existed twenty years ago. See Susan Rae Peterson, "Coercion and Rape: The State as a Male Protection Racket," in *Feminism and Philosophy*, ed. Mary Vetterlin-Braggin, Frederick A. Elliston, and Jane English (Totowa, NJ: Littlefield, Adams, 1977), pp. 360–71, which is a clear predecessor of Graham's recent work.

36. Graham, *Loving to Survive*, p. 71.
37. Graham, *Loving to Survive*, p. 72.
38. Graham, *Loving to Survive*, p. 69.
39. Robin Briggs, *Witches and Neighbors: The Social and Cultural Context of European Witchcraft* (New York: Viking, 1996), p. 260. Briggs also notes the important role women played in accusing others of witchcraft (p. 265).
40. Graham, *Loving to Survive*, p. 70. See Cathy Young, *Ceasefire: Beyond the Gender Wars* (New York: Free Press, 1999), chapter 4, on violence against women. Young points out that mass murderers do not in fact target women more than men.

On domestic abuse of men by women, see Philip W. Cook's thorough survey of the literature, *Abused Men: The Hidden Side of Domestic Violence* (Westport, CT: Praeger, 1997), which notes that a comprehensive National Family Violence Survey covering fifteen years concluded that approximately two million men a year are "seriously assaulted by their mates, as are 1.8 million women" (p. 12). Wives had 20 percent greater likelihood than husbands of being killed by a spouse (p. 20); looking at the nature of injuries, there is evidence that females do equal or greater harm to males than males do to females; that is, Cook explains, males "may suffer serious injury more often, whereas females likely suffer a greater number of total injuries ranging from minor to serious" (p. 18). As for violence toward children by parents: "[W]omen kill their children more often than fathers do (55 percent versus 45 percent)," Cook states (p. 20), citing U.S. Department of Justice, Office of Justice Programs, *Murder in Families*, Bureau of Justice Statistics Special Report NCJ-143498 (Washington, DC: GPO, July 1984), Cook's notes 51 and 53, p. 174. Cook refers to Murray Straus's work "Physical Assaults by Wives: A Major Social Problem," in *Current Controversies on Family Violence*, ed. R. J. Gelles and D. R. Loseke (Newbury Park, CA: Sage, 1993), which points to the "selective inattention" given to the data about abused men by the media (pp. 172–73, note 21, in Cook). Cook also includes a chapter called "Resistance and Acceptance" that provides data on abused men, detailing the hostility with which feminists have responded to Straus and other scholars (such as Richard Gelles and Suzanne Steinmetz) whose research on family violence includes violence directed by women toward men.

Of particular interest is the work of David Thomas, *Not Guilty: The Case in Defense of Men* (New York: William Morrow, 1993). Thomas interviewed Erin Pizzey, who wrote the first book on domestic violence, *Scream Quietly, or the Neighbors Will Hear* (1974) and is recognized as the founder of the movement against domestic violence. In 1971 she started the first shelter for battered women, Chiswick Women's Refuge, in London. In discussing her five years in the United States, Pizzey comments that she believes there "are as many violent women as men." Why, then, does the women's movement ignore this problem? Pizzey says:

> [T]here's a lot of money in hating men, particularly in the United States—millions of dollars. It isn't a politically good idea to threaten

the huge budgets for women's refuges by saying that some of the women who go into them aren't total victims. Anyway, the activists aren't there to help women come to terms with what's happening in their lives. They're there to fund their budgets, their conferences, their traveling abroad, and their statements against men. (p. 186–87)

In 1982, when Pizzey's book (coauthored with Jeff Shapiro) *Prone to Violence* (London: Hamlyn Paperbacks, 1982), about women's role in domestic violence, came out, it encountered enormous feminist hostility and Pizzey's life was even threatened, she told Thomas (pp. 188–89).

On the controversial subject of lesbian battering, see Claire M. Renzetti, *Violent Betrayal: Partner Abuse in Lesbian Relationships* (New York: Sage Publications, 1992), which concludes that "violence in lesbian relationships occurs at about the same frequency as violence in heterosexual relationships" (p. 115), but carries a double stigma (p. 130) both because of friends' disbelief (excusing or denying the battering, or assuming that "mutual battering" was occurring), and the lack of available social services and options for help. By contrast, Ruthann Robson, an attorney on the faculty of CUNY Law School, in her book *Lesbian (Out)law: Survival under the Rule of Law* (Ithaca, NY: Firebrand Books, 1992), has a chapter, "The Violence among Us," that is focused not on its purported theme but on the supposed political consequences of addressing the issue of violence in lesbian relationships. She argues that discussing the subject of violence among lesbians "domesticates" both lesbians and the feminist critique of male violence. It is especially "suspect," she writes, when done by nonlesbians (p. 162). But even lesbians need to be wary of availing themselves of the "rule of law," and its labels of "perpetrator" and "victim" (p. 163). Robson is worried that "lesbians have replaced battered husbands as the category that disenables any critique of male violence" (p. 163). She does not discuss the statistics and research that demonstrate that the incidence of partner abuse is similar for lesbians and heterosexuals. Lesbian identity politics seems to make it impossible for her to recognize the commonality of what is patently a human problem, not just a male problem.

41. Graham, *Loving to Survive*, p. xiii.
42. Lest readers think Graham, too, belongs to an obscure lunatic fringe, it should be noted that she is a consultant with the Cincinnati police department on matters of domestic violence. My thanks to Cathy Young for bringing Graham and her work to my attention.
43. Wendy Patton and Mary Mannison, "Beyond Learning to Endure: Women's Acknowledgement of Coercive Sexuality," *Women's Studies International Forum* 21, no. 1 (1998): 31.
44. See Leslie Francis, ed., *Date Rape: Feminism, Philosophy, and the Law* (University Park: Pennsylvania State University Press, 1996). This volume includes Lois Pineau's essay, "Date Rape: A Feminist Analysis" (pp. 1–26), which won the 1992 Berger Memorial Prize of the American Philosophi-

cal Association, for the best recent essay in the philosophy of law. It also includes critics' responses to the essay, Pineau's counterresponse, and a dialogue with one of her critics.

45. See, for example, Peggy La Cerra, "Gender-Specific Differences in Evolved Mating 'Strategies': The Revolutionary Basis of Sexual Conflict," *Sexuality and Culture* 1 (1997): 151–73, and Joseph S. Fulda, "The Complexities of Sexual Harassment: A Sociobiological Perspective," *Lincoln Review* 11, no. 1 (Winter–Spring 1993): 13–17. See also note 52, chapter 6, above.

46. Pineau, "Date Rape," p. 116.

47. Pineau, "Date Rape," p. 119. Interestingly, feminists do not usually wonder what are the legitimate grievances men harbor against women that might explain the high rates of male violence against women, so often cited by feminists.

48. Pineau, "Date Rape," p. 128.

49. Pineau, "Date Rape," p. 129.

50. Pineau, "Date Rape," p. 131.

51. Pineau, "Date Rape," p. 128.

52. Matthew R. Silliman, "The Antioch Policy: A Community Experiment in Communicative Sexuality," in *Date Rape: Feminism, Philosophy, and the Law*, ed. Francis, pp. 172–73.

53. Montana Katz and Veronica Vieland, *Get Smart! What You Should Know (but Won't Learn in Class) about Sexual Harassment and Sex Discrimination*, 2d ed. (New York: Feminist Press, 1993), pp. 117, 120.

54. Katz and Vieland, *Get Smart!*, pp. 118–20.

55. Catherine A. MacKinnon, *Only Words* (Cambridge: Harvard University Press, 1993). See David Crystal, *The Cambridge Encyclopedia of Language* (Cambridge: Cambridge University Press, 1987), p. 121; Mary Louise Pratt, *Toward a Speech Act Theory of Literary Discourse* (Bloomington: Indiana University Press, 1977); and J. L. Austin, *How to Do Things with Words*, ed. J. O. Urmson (Oxford: Clarendon Press, 1962).

56. Pratt, *Toward a Speech Act Theory of Literary Discourse*, p. 81.

57. See Carlin Romano, "Between the Motion and the Act," *Nation*, November 15, 1993, pp. 563–70. In their angry responses to Romano's fantasy of raping MacKinnon (his way of criticizing her book *Only Words*), Lindsay Waters et al., of Harvard University Press, objected to Romano's "use of rape as a tool for the conduct of criticism." *Nation*, December 27, 1993, p. 786. Evidently MacKinnon's tendency to erase any distinction between words and deeds is catching.

58. Joel Best, *Threatened Children: Rhetoric and Concern about Child-Victims* (Chicago: University of Chicago Press, 1990), pp. 80, 65. The tendency for harassment to stretch to encompass ever new dimensions is evident in recent publications. See Jerome J. Holzbauer and Norman L. Berven, "Disability Harassment: A New Term for a Long-Standing Problem," *Journal of Counseling & Development* 74, no. 5 (May/June 1996): 478–83, who use the literature on sexual harassment for a model of the harmful psychological effects that can be attributed to any form of harassment; Carol

Brooks Gardner, *Passing By: Gender and Public Harassment* (Berkeley: University of California Press, 1995), who shows how easily new definitions of harassment can be fitted into the existing heterophobic framework: "Public harassment . . . can be an emblem of the harasser's ratification and support of the existing hierarchy of heterosexual preference and the existing romantic basis for attraction, centered on appearance-based evaluation" (p. 159); and Ann Harsenpflug, "Visually Hostile Environments as Sexual Harassment," *Initiatives* 57, no. 3 (1996): 11–18.

59. On MacKinnon's use of speech-act theory, see Judith Butler's illuminating recent book, *Excitable Speech: A Politics of the Performative* (New York: Routledge, 1997), which concludes, "The word that wounds becomes an instrument of resistance in the redeployment that destroys the prior territory of its operation. . . . Insurrectionary speech becomes the necessary response to injurious language, a risk taken in response to being put at risk, a repetition in language that forces change" (p. 163).

60. MacKinnon, *Only Words*, p. 46.

61. John Searle, *Speech Acts: An Essay in the Philosophy of Language* (London: Cambridge University Press, 1969), p. 12.

62. Pratt, *Toward a Speech Act Theory of Literary Discourse*, pp. 80–81. See also John R. Searle and Daniel Vanderveken, *Foundations of Illocutionary Logic* (Cambridge, England: Cambridge University Press, 1985).

63. Judith Grant, p. 36 (quoting Ti-Grace Atkinson).

64. Nadine Strossen, *Defending Pornography* (New York: Scribner, 1995), p. 169.

65. Janice Raymond, *A Passion for Friends: Toward a Philosophy of Female Affection* (London: Women's Press, 1986), p. 167.

66. Raymond, *Passion for Friends*, pp. 169–70.

67. Raymond, *Passion for Friends*, p. 59. Raymond, a professor of women's studies at the University of Massachusetts at Amherst, argues for the "lack of emotional and sexual fulfillment of women in heterosexual relations," which she considers evidence of the "fact that there is nothing 'natural' about the whole gamut of hetero-relations." Raymond views "penis-vagina relations" as "rationalized," that is, spuriously presented as a necessity for the preservation of the species. "Reproduction can be accomplished in several ways, however," she notes, "without ordaining heterosexuality as normative, natural, and not to be deviated from, and without orchestrating hetero-relations as the inevitable accompaniment to this supposed biological fact" (p. 57). Raymond defines "hetero-reality" as "the world view that woman exists always in relation to man" (p. 3).

68. Mitchell, "Female Joke Telling," p. 21.

69. For a positive and in no sense antifeminist view of sexuality as a source of pleasure and intimacy, and a strong critique of MacKinnon's and Dworkin's ideas on this subject, see *With Pleasure: Thoughts on the Nature of Human Sexuality*, Paul R. Abramson and Steven D. Pinkerton (New York: Oxford University Press, 1995). My thanks to Angela Pattatucci for bringing this important book to my attention.

Chapter 8

1. For a thorough and sensitive exploration of this problem, see George Kateb, *Utopia and Its Enemies* (New York: Free Press of Glencoe, 1963), to which the present book owes much. While recognizing the potential threat to individual variation represented by the pursuit of equality, Kateb also warns against celebrating the sheer messiness of life for its own sake. What is needed, he argues, is balance: awareness of when the effort is not worth the candle, because its consequences will be worse than the original problem. Kateb is impressive in another respect as well: his appropriate sense of sadness that utopian aims cannot easily be fulfilled (p. 229). To translate his comments into the context of this book: One should not gloat over feminist excesses and failures; one should lament them.

2. [Bertha Thomas], "A Vision of Communism: A Grotesque," *Cornhill's Magazine* 28 (September 1873): 300–310.

3. Jerome K. Jerome, "The New Utopia," in *Diary of a Pilgrimage (and Six Essays)* (Bristol: J. W. Arrowsmith, 1891), pp. 261–79.

4. Kurt Vonnegut, Jr., "Harrison Bergeron," in *Welcome to the Monkey House* (New York: Dell Publishing, 1970), pp. 7–27.

5. University of Massachusetts at Amherst, "Proposed Harassment Policy" (distributed on October 20, 1995). The cover letter, dated September 20, 1995) (1) stated that the University and the Graduate Employee Organization, which together had worked out the policy, were "unanimous in [their] support of [its] basic elements"; (2) invited discussion of it by the entire university community, to help "in the resolution of our remaining differences"; and (3) affirmed the administration's desire "to have a policy in place early in the spring 1996 semester." Because of both the content of the proposed policy and the summary way in which it was presented to the university, a process apparently designed to discourage genuine discussion, about half a dozen faculty members, including myself, publicly protested it. As of the time of writing (January 1998), the proposed policy is in limbo, but UMass chancellor David K. Scott has expressed his determination to pursue what he prefers to characterize as a "harassment" policy rather than a "speech" code. See also notes 6–7, below.

6. The proposed policy also stated:

> Verbal conduct may include, but is not limited to, epithets, slurs, negative stereotyping, threatening language, or written or graphic material that serves to harass an individual or group of individuals.
> . . .
> This policy . . . shall apply to all members of the campus community: undergraduate and graduate students, faculty members, professional and classified staff members, administrators, and graduate student employees.
> This policy . . . shall apply to all activities from which a potentially aggrieved individual or group cannot readily absent themselves; this includes but is not limited to University housing and

meal facilities, work areas, classrooms for courses in which the griev-
ant is a student or a paid or volunteer instructor.

Visitors invited to the University to express their own opinions
in public forums shall not be subject to this policy; however, individuals or groups of individuals whose visitors violate this policy in
some other arena of the University (e.g., in lecture hall or University housing) shall be responsible for the actions of said visitors.

Contradictorily, it included a "saving" paragraph:

Nothing in this policy shall be taken to preclude the introduction, in a course or other academic setting, [of] any material which
the instructor deems relevant to his or her instruction, even if such
material might be considered offensive to some who are exposed to
it; and nothing in this policy shall be construed to allow the restriction of a faculty member's academic freedom.

Proposed implementation of the policy involved setting up a "harassment board" on which student representatives would be the single largest
category and on which professional staff, classified employees, and faculty would also serve. Thus, faculty members could find themselves subject to proceedings at which nonfaculty individuals, in contravention of
AAUP (American Association of University Professors) guidelines, would
adjudicate charges that might result in the termination of a faculty member's employment.

7. See letters criticizing the policy, by Professors Roland Chilton, Robert
Costrell, Herbert Gintis, Paul Hollander, and Daphne Patai, in *Campus
Chronicle* (University of Massachusetts at Amherst), November 10, 1995.
In his response (*Campus Chronicle*, November 17, 1995), Chancellor Scott
compounded the problem by repeatedly couching his defense of the pro-
posed policy in terms of the "feelings" of offended individuals. See also
Kevin Cullen, "Codified Tolerance Criticized at UMass," *Boston Globe*, No-
vember 4, 1995, and my letter of response, dated November 7, 1995;
Fred Contrada, "Proposal Finds Few Supporters," *Springfield (Massachusetts) Union-News*, November 10, 1995; article and editorial in *Daily Hampshire Gazette*, November 20, 1995, and November 17, 1995, respectively;
Laurie Loisel, "UMass Harassment Policy Brings Storm of Criticism," *Am-
herst Bulletin*, November 24, 1995, and my letter in response, printed on
December 1, 1995; Sean Glennon, "Speaking of the First
Amendment . . .," *Valley Advocate*, December 14, 1995, and, in the same
issue, Frank Njubl, "Speech Codes Backfire"; Christopher Shea, "A
Sweeping Speech Code," *Chronicle of Higher Education*, November 17,
1995; and Tim Cornwell, "Amherst Verbal Code Starts War of Words,"
Times Higher Education Supplement (London), November 24, 1995.

Anthony Lewis, in a highly critical *New York Times* article titled "Living
in a Cocoon," November 27, 1995, cited Chancellor Scott to the effect
that a code is required by federal Department of Education regulations.
This evoked a response by Norma V. Cantu, assistant secretary for civil

rights, Department of Education, who, in a letter to the *New York Times*, December 8, 1995, clearly stated that Department of Education regulations do not endorse or prescribe speech codes. Tovia Smith also reported on the proposed code on National Public Radio, *Morning Edition*, December 5, 1995.

Grateful thanks to Harvey A. Silverglate, of the Boston law firm Silverglate & Good, for his memorandum to me, dated November 24, 1995, with a detailed critique of the proposed UMass policy; to Jonathan Knight, associate secretary of the AAUP, for his letter of November 28, 1995 (addressed to Professor Robert Costrell), explaining why the UMass policy, "if enacted as currently written, would pose a serious threat to the freedom to teach and the freedom to learn at the University of Massachusetts, Amherst"; and to both Harvey Silverglate and Professor Eugene Volokh, of the UCLA Law School, for consultations via e-mail.

8. Meeting of December 21, 1995. Critics of the policy in attendance with me were Robert Costrell, professor of economics, and Roland Chilton and Gordon Sutton, professors of sociology.

9. This "double standard" approach was explicitly articulated by the University of Massachusetts at Amherst's associate chancellor, Susan Pearson, on a Boston radio talk show (*Connections* on WBUR) hosted by Christopher Leyden, December 5, 1995. It is based on the work of critical race theorists Mari Matsuda, Charles R. Lawrence III, and Richard Delgado, whose articles Pearson distributed to us at the December 21, 1995, meeting. At that meeting, in response to my direct question as to whether he endorsed such a "double standard," the chancellor, with some circumlocution, affirmed that this was what he had in mind. After all, he said, minority students were suffering as a result of the unpleasant things said to them. For an illuminating discussion of these issues, see Lawrence Douglas, "The Force of Words: Fish, Matsuda, MacKinnon, and the Theory of Discursive Violence," *Law and Society Review* 29, no. 1 (1995): 169–91.

10. Annette Kolodny, *Failing the Future: A Dean Looks at Higher Education in the Twenty-first Century* (Durham: Duke University Press, 1998).

11. Kolodny, *Failing the Future*, p. 105 (italics in original).

12. Kolodny, *Failing the Future*, pp. 105–6.

13. Kolodny, *Failing the Future*, p. 103.

14. Kolodny, *Failing the Future*, p. 104 (italics in original).

15. Kolodny, *Failing the Future*, p. 106.

16. Linda Greenhouse, "High Court Ruling Says Harassment Includes Same Sex," *New York Times*, March 5, 1998, p. A1.

17. Jeffrey Rosen, "Men Behaving Badly," *New Republic*, December 29, 1997, p. 19.

18. Kristin Downey Grimsley, "For Employers, a Blunt Warning," *Washington Post*, June 27, 1998, p. A10.

19. Aldous Huxley, *Brave New World* (New York: Harper & Row, 1969), p. 243.

20. Edmund Cooper, *Who Needs Men?* (London: Hodder and Stoughton, 1972).

21. Pamela Kettle, *The Day of the Women* (London: Leslie Frewin, 1969).
22. See, for example, Wayne Washington, "No Eyeful, So City Gets an Earful," *Star-Tribune Newspaper of the Twin Cities*, August 5, 1995, p. 1A.
23. Joan I. McEwen, "Report in Respect of the Political Science Department of the University of British Columbia" (prepared for the deans of the Faculty of Arts and Graduate Studies, University of British Columbia, Vancouver, Canada, June 15, 1995).
24. Eventually, the worm turned and the report itself came under scrutiny. For an insightful analysis, see M. Patricia Marchak, *Racism, Sexism, and the University: The Political Science Affair at the University of British Columbia* (Montreal: McGill-Queen's University Press, 1996).
25. John Fekete, *Moral Panic: Biopolitics Rising* (Montreal: Robert Davies, 1994). Fekete's book is a rich source of information on feminist excesses in Canada, where things are arguably more far gone than in the United States.
26. Daphne Patai and Noretta Koertge, *Professing Feminism: Cautionary Tales from the Strange World of Women's Studies* (New York: BasicBooks, 1994), p. 80.
27. John J. Furedy, "Academic Freedom versus the Velvet Totalitarian Culture of Comfort on Current Canadian Campuses: Some Fundamental Terms and Distinctions," *Interchange* 28 (1997): 331–50. Furedy provides examples of all these practices in Canadian universities, but their parallels are easy to find in the United States.
28. Equally pertinent is the detail that the burning of books in Germany in May 1933 was not, as hitherto believed, orchestrated by Goebbels, Hitler's propaganda minister, but was initiated by the German Students Association, a non-Nazi organization founded in 1919 to represent German university students at the national level. The GSA in April 1933 organized a propaganda campaign called "Against the Un-German Spirit." This campaign included an anti-Semitic poster and a script for ceremonial book-burning and, indeed, culminated, in early May 1933, in book-burnings in German universities. See Ehrhard Bahr, "Nazi Cultural Politics: Intentionalism vs. Functionalism," in *National Socialist Cultural Policy*, ed. Glenn R. Cuomo (New York: St. Martin's Press, 1995), pp. 5–22. Bahr, drawing on the work of Geoffrey J. Giles, *Students and National Socialism in Germany* (Princeton, NJ: Princeton University Press, 1985), notes that "non-Nazi organizations, such as the German Students' Association, were eager to preempt the policies of rival Nazi organizations" (*National Socialist Cultural Policy*, p. 12).
29. Anchee Min, *Red Azalea* (New York: Pantheon, 1994), p. 38.
30. Huxley, *Brave New World*, p. 15 (italics in original).
31. Charlotte Beradt, *The Third Reich of Dreams: The Nightmares of a Nation, 1933–1939*, trans. Adriana Gottwald (Northamptonshire, G.B.: Aquarian Press, 1985), p. 21.
32. Eugene Zamiatin, *We*, trans. Gregory Zilboorg (New York: E. P. Dutton, 1924), p. 22.
33. George Orwell, *Nineteen Eighty-Four* (New York: Harcourt Brace Jovanovich, 1949).

34. For a critical, yet generous, review of the feminist collapse of the public/ private dichotomy, see Judith Wagner DeCew, "The Feminist Critique of Privacy," chapter 5 in *In Pursuit of Privacy: Law, Ethics, and the Rise of Technology* (Ithaca: Cornell University Press, 1997).

35. Ray Bradbury, *Fahrenheit 451* (1953; reprint, New York: Ballantine Books, 1991), p. 83.

36. Bradbury, *Fahrenheit 451*, p. 87.

37. Bradbury, *Fahrenheit 451*, pp. 59–62.

38. Fyodor Dostoyevsky, *The Brothers Karamazov*, trans. David Magarshack (Harmondsworth, Middlesex: Penguin Books, 1958), pp. 289–311.

39. Kate Zhou, e-mail message to femisa@csf.colorado.edu May 5, 1995. My thanks to Professor Zhou for allowing me to cite her words. I have made a few slight corrections to her English.

40. On the failure to speak out while one still can, see Yang Jiang, *A Cadre School Life: Six Chapters*, trans. Geremie Barmé with the assistance of Bennett Lee (Hong Kong: Joint Publishing Co., 1982). The author describes her experiences during the Cultural Revolution of 1966–69.

41. Katharine Burdekin [Murray Constantine], *Proud Man* (New York: Feminist Press, 1993); reprint of 1934 edition, with foreword and afterword by Daphne Patai.

Acknowledgments

My first debt is to Jean Bethke Elshtain, who called me one day and expressed interest in my initial work on heterophobia, asking me if I had more to say on the collapse of "cross-gender trust." As it turned out, I did. To Jean and to Wilfred McClay and Ted McAllister, her co-editors in this series on American Intellectual Culture, my thanks for their initial enthusiasm for this project and their patience while my ideas about it clarified, until I understood how sexual harassment related to the larger picture feminism has been drawing.

Stephen Wrinn, my editor at Rowman & Littlefield, was of great help in his careful reading and excellent suggestions regarding the manuscript, and above all in his unfailing support for the project.

The lively exchanges on Barry Dank's Academic Sexual Correctness E-Mail List (asc-l@csulb.edu) helped focus my thinking about the subject of sexual harassment and relationships in academe. I am especially grateful to the dozen or so "regulars" I got to know on the list and with whom I have corresponded privately. Barry Dank first urged me to write about the issue of sexual harassment several years ago, and has always been available for bibliographic and other kinds of assistance.

Vera Klinkowsky, someone else I got to know through e-mail, proved to be an enterprising and able research assistant, ferreting out information and references for me; I am fortunate to have been able to count on her excellent research skills.

Several friends and acquaintances have talked with me over the past few years about the issues addressed in this book. I owe special thanks to Paulann Hosler Sheets, one of my oldest friends, whose legal training was an important resource to me at several crucial junctures. Cathy Young has been a wonderful and reliable e-mail correspondent, even while she was hard at work on her own book at the same time. Charley

Shults, Hugh Potter, and Robert Costrell made helpful comments on an early draft of the manuscript, as did Eugene Volokh, who read the manuscript at a later stage. Several readers sent valuable comments about the manuscript to my editor. To all these people, my warm thanks and appreciation. Needless to say, I alone am responsible for any errors that appear in the book.

Finally, my sister, Jennifer Schneider, has been a steadfast friend through the hardships of the past few years, and my husband, Gerald Strauss, has been there, discussing the book with me as it took shape. Many years ago, under the influence of radical feminist ideas, I announced to him one day, "Men hate women." He responded, "If men hate women, then I hate you. That can't be right." How unright it is, I have had plenty of opportunity to discover.

*   *   *

Grateful acknowledgment is made to several publications, where earlier versions of some chapters appeared: "Galloping Contradictions: Sexual Harassment in Academe," *Gender Issues* 16, nos. 1–2 (Spring 1998), published by Transaction Periodicals Consortium; "Reasonable Women: Harassment and the Redefinition of Heterosexuality," in *Rethinking Sexual Harassment*, Women's Freedom Network Working Paper 3, ed. Cathy Young (Washington, DC: Women's Freedom Network, 1998); "The Making of a Social Problem: Sexual Harassment on Campus," *Sexuality and Culture* 1 (1997), published by Transaction Periodicals Consortium; "Heterophobia: The Feminist Turn against Men," *Partisan Review* 4 (1996); "There Ought to Be a Law," *William Mitchell Law Review* 22, no. 2 (1996); and "What's Wrong with Women's Studies," *Academe* 81, no. 4 (July–August 1995).

I am also grateful for permission to reprint the following material: From Bernice R. Sandler and Robert J. Shoop, *Sexual Harassment on Campus: A Guide for Administrators, Faculty, and Students.* Copyright © 1997 by Allyn & Bacon. Reprinted and adapted by permission. From Sharon Olds, "Outside the Operating Room of the Sex-Change Doctor," from *The Gold Cell* by Sharon Olds, copyright © 1987 by Sharon Olds. Reprinted by permission of Alfred A. Knopf Inc.

Index

double standards, 54, 120, 121
fables, 69
ideology, in English-speaking world, 99
leveling impulse, 188
marriage, 142
mistrust of authority, 34
pedagogy, 70, 111, 115, 205
    practiced by men, 114–15
rewriting of experience, 168
rhetoric, xiii, 120
teaching style, 115
theorizing about men, 144
vision of future, 138, 139
Feminist Accused of Sexual Harassment, 106–21, 125
feminist extremists, 143, 145, 182
    agenda of, 130
    antagonism toward men, 171
    attitudes of, 159
    continuity of, 143
    as exempt from own rules, 145
    failure to draw distinctions, 152
    political power of, 12
    prominence of, 158, 160
    redefinition of heterosexuality by, 171, 175
    rhetoric, 136
    and sexual harassment law, 11
feminist men, 141, 149
feminist theory, 102, 167–68
Feminists, The (group), 109
feminists accused of sexual harassment, 56, 90, 98, 105–21
FEMISA (e-mail list), 136, 137, 205, 206
Ferguson, Ann, 59, 189, 224n45
"fighting words," 187
Firing Line, 183
First Amendment, 57, 86, 87, 89, 187, 196, 227n16
First Stone, 99
first-wave feminism, 131–32
Fitzgerald, Edward, 3
flattery, as sexual harassment, 76
flirting, 41, 102
Foucault, Michel, 199, 237n52
Fourteenth Amendment, 22, 89
Fox-Genovese, Elizabeth, 98, 106
free speech, 57, 58, 102, 120, 202, 205, 206
    assault on, 161
    curtailment of, 123
    on FEMISA, 205
    movement, 197, 206
    and patriarchy, 158
    professors' rights to, 87
    restrictions on, 187

rights, violated by sexual harassment law, 87, 227n16
freedom
    of association, 111, 161, 202, 205, 206
    as burden, 200–07
    of conscience, 204
    curtailment of, 207
    imperiled by sexual harassment industry, 212
    taken for granted, 203, 196–97
    as threat to women, 205
Freud, Sigmund, 169
Friedan, Betty, 232n3
Frontiers, 169
Fundamental Feminism, 169
Furedy, John, 197
future
    feminist visions of, 138, 139, 144–45, 159, 183, 185, 207, 211–12
    heterophobes' view of, 160
    men's roles in, 138, 140
    satires of, 192
    sex in, 154
Frye, Marilyn, 129, 142, 170
    on heterosexuality, 129

Gadlin, Howard, 224n51
Gallop, Jane, 14, 30, 56, 105–21, 122, 181
    accused of sexual harassment, 106
    charges against, 107–8
    on consensual relations, 107, 109
    defense of feminist pedagogy, 115
    defense of sex, 113–14
    on erotic pedagogy, 109, 110
    flamboyance of, 105
    rhetoric of, 107
    seduction of professors by, 112
    on sexuality, 108, 119
    on sexualizing the classroom, 110
    teaching style of, 106, 107, 111
Gardner, Carol Brooks, 245n58
Garner, Helen, 99–103, 119
    on flirting, 102
    on male power, 101–2
    on punitiveness of feminism, 100
gay activism, as zero-sum game, 147
gay and lesbian bashing, 159
Gay and Lesbian Conference, First Annual Graduate Student, 108
gay men, 6, 149, 181, 232n3
gay sex, as patriarchal, 152
gays, 71, 134, 149
Gearhart, Sally Miller, 139–41, 143
gender
    as basis for discrimination, 169
    and biology, 148
    equity, accountability for, 59

About the Author

❧

DAPHNE PATAI was born in Jerusalem and came to this country as a child. She received a B.A. from Indiana University and a Ph.D. from the University of Wisconsin. Currently a professor of Brazilian literature at the University of Massachusetts at Amherst, she spent ten years with a joint appointment in Women's Studies before returning full-time to the Department of Spanish and Portuguese. She is the author of numerous articles in the fields of women's studies, oral history, Brazilian literature, and utopian studies, and she has written and/or edited nine books, including *The Orwell Mystique: A Study in Male Ideology, Brazilian Women Speak: Contemporary Life Stories,* and, most recently (with Noretta Koertge), *Professing Feminism: Cautionary Tales from the Strange World of Women's Studies.* She is the recipient of fellowships from the Guggenheim Foundation, the National Endowment for the Humanities, and the National Humanities Center.

American Intellectual Culture

Series Editors: Jean Bethke Elshtain, University of Chicago, Ted V. McAllister, Hillsdale College, Wilfred M. McClay, Tulane University

The books in the American Intellectual Culture series examine the place, identity, and public role of intellectuals and cultural elites in the United States, past, present, and future. Written by prominent historians, philosophers, and political theorists, these books will examine the influence of intellectuals on American political, social, and cultural life, paying particular attention to the characteristic forms, and evolving possibilities, of democratic intellect. The books will place special, but not exclusive, emphasis on the relationship between intellectuals and American public life. Because the books are intended to shape and contribute to scholarly and public debates about their respective topics, they will be concise, accessible, and provocative.

When All the Gods Trembled: Darwinism, Scopes, and American Intellectuals
   by Paul K. Conkin, Vanderbilt University
Heterophobia: Sexual Harassment and the Future of Feminism
   by Daphne Patai, University of Massachusetts at Amherst

Forthcoming Titles

Modern Inconvenience: The Social Origins of Antifamily Thought
   by Elisabeth Lasch-Quinn, Syracuse University
Academic Politics: The Colonial Colleges and the Shaping of American Intellectual Culture
   by J. David Hoeveler, University of Wisconsin, Milwaukee
History and Public Memory in America
   by Wilfred M. McClay, Tulane University
Integrating the World: Cold War Intellectuals and the Politics of Identity
   by Christopher Shannon, the George Eastman House
A Pragmatist's Progress? Richard Rorty and American Intellectual History
   by John Pettegrew, Lehigh University
Ralph Waldo Emerson and the Problem of Democracy
   by Peter S. Field, Tennessee Technological University
The Murder of Joy: Paul Goodman and the American Battle over Maturity
   by Robert Oliver, University of Wisconsin, Madison
The Public and Protagonist: Tocqueville and American Intellectuals, 1835–2000
   by Matthew Mancini, Southwest Missouri State University